D1511284

PSYCHODYNAMIC STUDIES ON AGING:

Creativity, Reminiscing, and Dying

PSYCHODYNAMIC STUDIES ON AGING:

Creativity, Reminiscing, and Dying

The Boston Society for Gerontologic Psychiatry, Inc.

Edited by

SIDNEY LEVIN, M.D.
and
RALPH J. KAHANA, M.D.

INTERNATIONAL UNIVERSITIES PRESS, INC.
New York

Contributors

SAMUEL ATKIN, M.D.
Training Analyst, New York Psychoanalytic Institute
Attending Psychiatrist, Hillside Hospital
Associate Clinical Professor, Albert Einstein Medical
School

MARTIN A. BEREZIN, M.D.
Training Analyst, Boston Psychoanalytic Society and In-
stitute
Visiting Psychiatrist, Beth Israel Hospital, Boston, and
Attending Psychiatrist, McLean Hospital
President, The Boston Society for Gerontologic Psychia-
try, Inc.

DAVID A. BROWNE, M.D.
Senior Psychiatrist in charge of the Geriatric Service,
Boston State Hospital
Clinical Instructor in Psychiatry, Tufts and Boston Uni-
versity Schools of Medicine

ROBERT N. BUTLER, M.D.
Research Psychiatrist and Gerontologist, The Study Cen-
ter, The Washington School of Psychiatry
Faculty, The Washington Psychoanalytic Institute
Assistant Clinical Professor of Psychiatry, George Wash-
ington University Medical School

[3]

STANLEY H. CATH, M.D.
Member, Boston Psychoanalytic Society and Institute
Staff, Bedford V.A., Boston State, and New England Center Hospitals
Assistant Clinical Professor of Psychiatry, Tufts University School of Medicine

THOMAS P. HACKETT, M.D.
Associate Psychiatrist, Massachusetts General Hospital
Instructor in Psychiatry, Faculty of Medicine, Harvard University
Lecturer in Psychology, Simmons College

RALPH J. KAHANA, M.D.
Member, Boston Psychoanalytic Society and Institute
Associate Visiting Psychiatrist, Beth Israel Hospital, Boston
Clinical Associate in Psychiatry, Faculty of Medicine, Harvard University

ROBERT J. KASTENBAUM, PH.D.
Director of Psychological Research, Cushing Hospital, Framingham, Massachusetts
Lecturer in Psychology, Clark University

ELIOT LANDSMAN, M.D.
Member, Boston Psychoanalytic Society and Institute
Psychiatrist, Hebrew Rehabilitation Center for the Aged, Boston
Staff, Beth Israel Hospital, Medfield State Hospital, Faulkner Hospital

[4]

SIDNEY LEVIN, M.D.
Associate Training Analyst, Boston Psychoanalytic Society and Institute
Visiting Psychiatrist, Beth Israel Hospital, Boston, and Attending Psychiatrist, McLean Hospital
Clinical Associate in Psychiatry, Faculty of Medicine, Harvard University

ARTHUR W. McMAHON, JR., M.D.
Staff Psychiatrist, Boston Dispensary Out-patient Psychiatric Clinic
Courtesy Staff Psychiatrist, Tufts-New England Medical Center Hospitals
Assistant Professor of Psychiatry, Tufts University School of Medicine

ROBERT E. MOSS, M.D.
Member, Boston Psychoanalytic Society and Institute
Associate in Psychiatry, Boston University School of Medicine

JOEL ORDAZ, M.D.
Member, Boston Psychoanalytic Society and Institute
Staff, Rhode Island Hospital and Butler Hospital, Providence, Rhode Island

EDMUND C. PAYNE, JR., M.D.
Member, Boston Psychoanalytic Society and Institute
Associate Visiting Psychiatrist, Beth Israel Hospital
Assistant Clinical Professor of Psychiatry, Tufts University School of Medicine

[5]

NORVELL L. PETERSON, M.D.
> Lecturer, Gordon Divinity School, Wenham, Massachusetts
>
> Member of Clinic Committee, Mental Health Association of the North Shore, Salem, Massachusetts
>
> Advisory Board Member, Spring Lake Ranch, Cuttingsville, Vermont

PAUL J. RHUDICK, PH.D.
> Director Psychological Research, North Shore Guidance Center, Salem, Massachusetts
>
> Senior Research Associate, The Age Center of New England
>
> Lecturer in Psychology, Emmanuel College, Boston

SIDNEY TARACHOW, M.D.
> Deceased. Formerly President of the Psychoanalytic Association of New York
>
> Associate Director and Clinical Associate Professor of Psychiatry, Division of Psychoanalytic Education, Department of Psychiatry, Downstate Medical Center, New York

EARL M. WEDROW, M.D.
> Private Practice, Specializing in Geriatric Psychiatry, Boston, Massachusetts
>
> Consultant, Boston State Hospital

AVERY D. WEISMAN, M.D.
> Training Analyst, Boston Psychoanalytic Society and Institute
>
> Psychiatrist, Massachusetts General Hospital
>
> Assistant Clinical Professor of Psychiatry, Faculty of Medicine, Harvard University

Donald Wexler, M.D.
    Physician in Charge, Psychiatry Clinic, Boston City Hospital
    Staff, Mount Auburn Hospital and McLean Hospital
    Clinical Associate in Psychiatry, Faculty of Medicine, Harvard University

Edward L. Zarsky, M.D.
    Assistant Attending Psychiatrist, McLean Hospital
    Consultant, Massachusetts Mental Health Center
    Assistant in Psychiatry, Faculty of Medicine, Harvard University

Acknowledgments

The preparation of this book, under the auspices of the Boston Society for Gerontologic Psychiatry, Inc., was made possible only through the generous and dedicated cooperation of a number of people, to whom we wish to extend our thanks: members of the Program Committee (Drs. Stanley H. Cath, Martin A. Berezin, Arthur R. Kravitz, and Norman E. Zinberg) who made the initial arrangements for the symposium which is being reported; contributors who wrote and carefully edited their papers, discussions, and abstracts; and last, but not least, the editorial assistant, Miss Edith L. Annin, whose thoroughness and skill in organizing and correcting the manuscripts was as invaluable in the preparation of this volume as it was in the preparation of earlier publications of the Boston Society for Gerontologic Psychiatry, Inc.

SIDNEY LEVIN, M.D.
RALPH J. KAHANA, M.D.

Contents

PART I: Creativity, Reminiscing, and Dying   11

Introduction   13
SIDNEY LEVIN, M.D. and RALPH J. KAHANA, M.D.

*The Destiny of Creativity in Later Life: Studies of
    Creative People and the Creative Process*   20
ROBERT N. BUTLER, M.D.

Reminiscing in the Aged: An Adaptational Response   64
ARTHUR W. McMAHON, JR., M.D. and
PAUL J. RHUDICK, PH.D.

Denial as a Social Act   79
AVERY D. WEISMAN, M.D. and
THOMAS P. HACKETT, M.D.

The Physician and His Patient Who Is Dying   111
EDMUND C. PAYNE, JR., M.D.

PART II: Discussion   165

[9]

Discussants 167
   Samuel Atkin, M.D., Martin A. Berezin, M.D.,
   Robert N. Butler, M.D., Stanley H. Cath, M.D.,
   Arthur W. McMahon, Jr., M.D., Edmund C.
   Payne, Jr., M.D., Sidney Tarachow, M.D., Avery
   D. Weisman, M.D.

Part III: Aging—A Survey of the Psychiatric
   Literature 1961-1964 219

Foreword 221
   Robert E. Moss, M.D.

Aging—A Survey of the Psychiatric Literature 1961-1964 222

References 321

Index 337

PART I: CREATIVITY, REMINISCING, AND DYING

Introduction

Sidney Levin, M.D. and Ralph J. Kahana, M.D.

This book is a report of the 1964 symposium of the Boston Society for Gerontologic Psychiatry on *Vicissitudes of the Terminal Phase of Life*. Like the two previous volumes of this society, it explores the intrapsychic life of the aged person, dealing with healthy as well as pathological aspects. In the first volume, *The Normal Psychology of the Aging Process* (edited by Zinberg and Kaufman, 1963), a survey of relevant factors was made, including physical changes, personality changes, personal relationships, and social, economic, and cultural influences. Particular attention was paid to ego structure, regression, libidinal shifts and maintenance of self-esteem, and various meanings of independence. The second volume, *Geriatric Psychiatry: Grief, Loss, and Emotional Disorders in the Aging Process* (edited by Berezin and Cath, 1965), dealt largely with the most typical adaptive responses in old age. The multiple stresses depleting older persons were examined. Special emphasis was given to formal interdisciplinary studies, to theoretical consideration of the capacity to bear anxiety and depression in later life, and to the clinical application of psychoanalytic psychotherapy in the case of an

[13]

elderly woman with an hysterical disorder. A selective review of the recent literature in the field of geriatric psychiatry was included.

This volume presents four papers, with discussions, followed by an extension of the survey of the literature. The first two contributions, "The Destiny of Creativity in Later Life: Studies of Creative People and the Creative Process," by Robert N. Butler, and "Reminiscing in the Aged: An Adaptational Response," by Arthur W. McMahon, Jr. and Paul J. Rhudick, highlight issues pertaining to the maintenance of psychic health in the aging. The third and fourth contributions, "Denial as a Social Act," by Avery D. Weisman and Thomas P. Hackett, and "The Physician and His Patient Who Is Dying," by Edmund C. Payne, Jr., focus upon reactions to life-threatening or terminal illness. The material presented in these four articles reflects different ways of studying aging, including a multidimensional program of collecting historical and personal data (Butler), an account of a specific, naturalistic investigation of psychological phenomena (McMahon and Rhudick), and the evaluation of clinical experience and formulation of pertinent psychological theory (Weisman and Hackett, Payne). The authors pursue a wide range of topics and questions relevant to later life, among them, the effect of aging on creative style; the function of "living in the past"; the effect of depression on reminiscing; the significance of the mechanism of "denial"; and the physician's role with the terminal patient.

Dr. Butler's paper is very much in keeping with the present-day concern of understanding human existence in depth. He challenges the notions that creative people are unable to explain themselves or their works and that creativity invariably declines with age. In his project, which is already under way, creative people are being studied in relation to the life cycle and to the conditions that facilitate or interfere with their productive originality. Some of the data will be obtained in specially structured, recorded interviews and kept in an archive of live memoirs. The findings of this research can illuminate problems concerning personal identity and may ultimately influence social planning. Dr. Butler postulates that normal adaptation to aging may take the form of a "life review," which may find its resolution through creativity. And he suggests as one type of creative person the "autodidact," who starts from scratch, questioning everything, recreating whatever he deals with in his own image. The potential value of Dr. Butler's research will be apparent, especially to all who struggle with the limitations of conventional historical evidence.

The report of Drs. McMahon and Rhudick grew out of an incidental observation made during a multidisciplinary study of Spanish-American War veterans who apparently were aging successfully. It was noted that these men, who were mostly in their 80's, had a strong tendency to reminisce. Instead of dismissing this tendency as a commonplace, the authors set out to study its significance. They conclude that reminiscing serves adaptation and that the aged reminisce less in states of depression. They compare reminiscing with the process of working through personal losses by mourning. By analysis of the content of interviews, it was possible to classify the elderly men according to the way in which they reconstitute the past.

In their study of "Denial as a Social Act," Drs. Weisman and Hackett re-examine the basic psychological concept of "defense mechanism." They believe that this powerful explanatory concept, which has illuminated behavior and provided a key for psychotherapeutic efforts, may be regarded too mechanistically, as though a defense were a kind of automatic response activated mainly from within. Such a view neglects the wider context, which includes the social purpose of the defense. The authors base their inquiry upon observations of patients who have responded to life-threatening and terminal illness by rejecting and turning away from the distressing reality. These patients appear "unaware" of their predicament, often impeding rational and possibly life-saving treatment. Yet, in their efforts to contend with danger, their acts of denial not only *negate* certain events but also *affirm* a less threatening, alternative version of reality. Much of the motivation for denial is related to the need to preserve essential personal relationships. When patients feel threatened by abandonment, the fear of death tends to be most pronounced. If, out of their own anxiety, physicians and others who care for the patient treat only the organic dimension of illness, or if they indiscriminately limit their responses to "strengthening denial" without recognizing its social meaning, then the patient's worst dread of being isolated may come true. This paper illustrates how thoughtful clinicians can make effective use of psychological theory and, at the same time, use their experience to enrich that theory.

Dr. Payne's presentation is based upon his experience with terminally ill patients, their doctors, and their families, in a tumor clinic of a general hospital. He indicates how an understanding of impulses and defenses, personality development, and adaptation can augment the effectiveness of those who seek to sustain life and to relieve suffering. Recognizing the psychological enigma of death itself, he questions the nature of the universal fear of this "undiscover'd country." His inquiry follows two lines: he traces the history of the fear of death throughout life and studies its manifestations during fatal illness. He notes how the child's concept of death is affected by emotional conflicts as well as by the development of rational thinking. Starting at about age three, the child gives objective evidence that he is aware of death; he then recognizes that he may die; and, finally, he experiences anxiety about dying. Regardless of one's theoretical orientation, one cannot but conclude that there is something instinctive in man which is directed toward self-preservation and which gives rise to fear in the face of death. Under the stress of illness, childhood ideas connected with death may become revived in adult life. Then, for example, a realistic danger to life may be experienced mainly as a threat of being abandoned or of being attacked and punished.

When a person first encounters the fatal nature of his illness, the mobilization of an intense fear of death tends to bring out conspicuous psychological defenses. As he accommodates to his condition, the defenses tend to become less prominent. One's capacity either to acknowledge a threat of death or to block it out is not always directly correlated with psychological maturity and often varies during the course of the disease. These variations make demands upon the doctor for a flexible therapeutic approach. Dr. Payne completes his observations by considering the patient's family—the strain they undergo, their need for support, their ambivalence and guilt, and, from the physician's standpoint, some of the problems of management that they present.

The discussion of these papers moves from general consideration of the relationship between creativity, reminiscing, and dying to the evaluation of research methods and the sharing of clinical observations. In the terminal phase of life, physical decline leads to a struggle for basic biological survival, and the dying person experiences increasing anxiety and constriction of his activities. Creative efforts tend to resolve conflict and relieve feelings of isolation. It is believed that the dying patient may often be helped to operate on a creative level of voluntary responsible behavior. Thus, life can retain a more positive meaning for him. Further study of creativity and adaptation in later life is welcomed, and a number of suggestions are made for refining and improving such study. It is recommended that Dr. Butler's research should include clearer definitions of basic terms and that research like that of Drs. McMahon and Rhudick should attempt to distinguish depression from other maladaptive states such as apathy and paranoia. Normal reminiscence is differentiated from some of the psychopathological forms of reminiscence, for example, the confabulation in Korsakoff's psychosis. It is felt that the conditions under which normal reminiscence occurs need to be specified carefully. Which older person has the energy for it or is likely to find it gratifying and useful? Who listens?

The discussants agree as to the value of seeking to understand the terminal phase of life in the perspective of lifelong development. Examples are cited illustrating the continuity of the individual's attitudes toward dying from early childhood on. Renunciation of personal ties, possessions, attributes, achievements, aspirations, illusions, and so forth begins in infancy and continues throughout life, to become accelerated in old age and completed at death. Likewise, each individual has his own personal style of coming to terms with death. Although reliance upon the many forms and shades of denial is often prominent, this defense is only one of an ensemble of adaptive methods. Furthermore, although a fear of death is said to be more prevalent in our culture than in some others, it is often conspicuously absent. Deep, irrational convictions of our own invulnerability often appear to sustain us to the end. The fate of the aggressive drives, too, has an important impact upon the terminal phase of life. An individual with limited ability to neutralize aggression is less tolerant of separations and losses—crucial problems in the dying patient. The normal role of aggression in preserving life is often noted by the clinician, who may welcome the continuing appearance of "fight" in his critically ill patient and, conversely, may dread the apathy that presages death. In order for the physician and the patient's family to be most helpful, sublimation of their own aggressive and sadistic impulses is necessary. The dying person needs consideration and understanding to maintain the integrity of his personality. The possibility of his making constructive use of his remaining time or of fulfilling final wishes often hinges upon the empathic and nonrejecting response of his environment.

The Destiny of Creativity in Later Life:
Studies of Creative People and the
Creative Process

ROBERT N. BUTLER, M.D.

Among the curious notions about creative people is the belief that they can explain neither themselves nor their works. This idea does not derive from comprehensive study; it may be a stereotype when broadly applied, although applicable in individual cases. There is, after all, little reason to believe that creative people have less self-awareness and self-knowledge than most people; indeed, there is reason to suppose that the opposite is true.

Another notion is that creativity declines with chronological aging. In this case, supporting studies do exist, and their results are regarded as valid by many students of human behavior (Lehman, 1953; Berelson and Steiner, 1964). Nevertheless, the universal validity of the presumed relation between aging and loss of creativity has been questioned (Bjorksten, 1946; Dennis, 1956), and innumerable instances of persistent creativity into late life contradict this widely held belief.

It may not be surprising that contemporary knowledge is vague and confused concerning the obscure and seemingly

[20]

inscrutable processes of aging and of creativity. We stand in awe of both, fearing and respecting each, wishing we could defeat the one and enhance the other. The one is seen as darkness; the other, as light. Human interest in the relationships between aging and creativity is understandable and inevitable, but we are at a disadvantage because we do not know the fundamental nature of either. Do creativity and aging interact? Do they proceed independently? Are other factors involved? Are there relationships between phases of the life cycle and creative activity? The specific purpose of this presentation is to report on studies, which are in progress at the Study Center of the Washington School of Psychiatry, entitled "Studies of Creative People and the Creative Process After Middle Life."

After a description of goals and methods, as well as of the nature and sources of the subjects, we shall turn to the background of these studies. Because the project is young and the size of the sample small, only limited observations and reflections based upon data from direct interviews are available. To preserve confidentiality, no names will be given.

THE PROJECT

Goals

1. This project is intended to stimulate programs for the acquisition and preservation of tape-recorded interview memoirs, obtained after middle life, of persons who have made contributions which have enriched our national life. Toward that end, the principles and methodological issues in obtaining such personal documents are to be clarified, drawing upon the contributions of historiography, biography, psychoanalysis, and other relevant disciplines. In short, a model

interview procedure is to be constructed. According to the individual stipulations of the memoirists, memoir and associated materials are to be made available in repositories to scholars, historians, biographers, psychologists, psychiatrists, sociologists, linguists, journalists, and other accredited individuals for a variety of scholarly, scientific, and informational purposes. Specifically, the development of an archive of memoirs (memoirium) in the Study Center of the Washington School of Psychiatry for a variety of studies, especially those concerned with the advancement of knowledge of human behavior, is intended.

2. It is planned to investigate, through the medium of the tape-recorded interview, the nature of creative people and of the conditions that are conducive to or impede creativity. The relations between creative activity and phases of the life cycle are to be studied. Specifically, this investigation is to consist of: (a) exploration of the elements that contribute to the vicissitudes of creativity after middle age and into advanced age. An attempt will be made to examine what are the personal and external factors that account for the new development, the persistence, the decline, or the extinction of creative activity in older people. The interrelationships between creativity and personality, life experience, health, cultural conditions, and socioeconomic circumstances are also to be examined. (b) Cultural and personal (countertransference) factors in the response to and support or disavowal of creative persons and activities are to be studied.

Methods

1. It is planned to develop an extended, intensive, *collaborative* relationship with selected creative individuals and to tape-record interviews with them. Although there will be

neither a fixed duration nor a termination date for the studies, the investigator will make every effort to obtain comparable data from subject to subject. There will be occasion for short-term studies to test specific hypotheses or to focus inquiry on specific topics.

2. The perspectives of the psychoanalyst, biographer, and historian will be utilized. Undue structuring of interviews will be avoided in favor of following the lead of the person being interviewed. However, hypotheses (drawn from other students of creativity and of the life cycle or developed by the investigator) will be pursued, and checklist questionnaires will be developed and used to insure comparability of data.

The general strategy will approximate the use of the psychoanalytic relationship as a *mode of investigation*.[1] This may be defined as a one-to-one relationship in which information comes predominantly from the subject to the investigator, who assumes a more or less neutral and reflective position of inquiry whereby the subject's memories, reflections, and associations (content of thought and feelings) are the *primary data*. This strategy is adopted to reduce the introduction of the investigator's biases or theoretical preconceptions. It is also assumed that this strategy will help to facilitate the broadening of the subject's self-knowledge, recall, and insight into his life experience, character, and achievement. Transference and countertransference phenomena will be examined as they arise.[2] The evolution of a successful collaboration over a sufficient period of time, including the time

[1] Freud often described psychoanalysis as "a procedure for the investigation of mental processes which are almost inaccessible in any other way" (see, for example, Freud, 1923b, p. 235).

[2] The actualities of a distinction in process between psychoanalysis as a method of investigation and as a method of therapy may be questioned by some, but a distinct difference in conscious purpose is beyond question.

needed for revision and reinterpretation, should provide a reasonably comprehensive picture of the many elements which may be relevant to advancing our understanding of the vicissitudes of creativity: biologic, cultural, familial, psychological (motivational), and experiential.

3. There will be extensive critical evaluation of the literature of creativity (including that relevant to age), as well as of autobiographies, biographies, cultural history, and encyclopedias (materials on arts and sciences).

4. Psychological tests, social inventories, and medical examinations may be introduced to broaden the investigations, as well as collaboration with specialists of particular fields (literature, musicology, and others).

Nature and Sources of Subjects

1. Caution will be exercised in the use of the designation "creative." At the outset, subjects will be invited to participate on the basis of their general recognition as distinguished contributors to literature, the sciences, the performing and creative arts, government, politics, the military, the development of institutions, and other fields.

2. Other sources of data will include previous studies of aging (National Institute of Mental Health; Chestnut Lodge) and collected observations on the nature and conduct of scientific research.

Methodological Notes

1. *Distinctive quality of "live" memoirs.* Ordinarily, autobiographies are private written documents and are therefore revised and composed; they are not spontaneous. Taped, or live, memoirs are interpersonal, spoken, and spontaneous.

Revisions in thinking occur in the course of taped conversations, but all versions are available. Interviewing on tape a person who has already published an autobiography will permit the study of differences.

2. *Confidentiality* (Butler, 1963c). The *fact* of being studied will be held confidential if the memoirist wishes. The material belongs to the memoirist, and the interviewer is its custodian. Any variation from this general agreement is the privilege of the memoirist. Ultimately, the material is to be made available, partially or *in toto,* during life or at some specified time after death, to the public, to recognized scholars for specific and useful purposes, or to both. The memoirist may wish to arrange for publication of parts or all of the transcriptions.

3. *Personal attitudes.* Historically, the personal attitudes of biographers, ranging from admiration to envy, have been open to limited scrutiny (*cf.,* Boswell and Johnson). Taped biographies would open this issue (countertransference) to outside scrutiny.

4. *What is creativity?* A definition of creativity will not be presumed, but developed. Early foreclosure in definition can inhibit research. Persons selected for study will vary as to generally accepted conceptions of creativity.

5. *Psychoanalysis as history.* Relationships between the methods and tasks of the psychoanalyst and the historian have been recognized (Meyerhoff, 1962).

6. *Prerequisite research.* Research by the interviewer on (a) the individual subject and (b) the subject matter is necessary.

Background

In our culture and in our medical-psychological literature, the prevailing view of the aging emphasizes decline in mental as well as physical abilities. In his careful monograph, *Age and Achievement,* Harvey C. Lehman (1953) concludes, "Superior creativity rises relatively rapidly to a maximum which occurs usually in the thirties and then falls off slowly." There are innumerable exceptions to this generalization (including those cited by Lehman), however, and the conditions conducive either to the persistence or the decline of creativity are not well understood. The author of this paper wishes to explore this question.

In addition, the author has developed certain views concerning the positive, constructive, and expansive aspects of middle and later life through multidisciplinary and psychiatric investigations of human aging in medically healthy, community-resident elderly (Birren, Butler, Greenhouse, Sokoloff, and Yarrow, 1963; Butler, 1963a) and through clinical studies of the mentally disturbed elderly (Butler, 1960; 1961b; 1963b). In the studies of human aging made at the National Institute of Mental Health (NIMH), Bethesda, Maryland (1955-1962), the extent to which factors other than chronological aging affect the experience and characteristics of aging was noted: among these factors are personality, disease, socioeconomic conditions, and cultural attitudes. Furthermore, the elderly who are in good health and in favorable socioeconomic circumstances tend to remain in good mental health and continue to engage in constructive activities.

Indeed, the sample of the National Institute of Mental Health, selected for medical health and social competence, was quite different from other samples of the aged reported upon previously in the literature. The belief, for example, that cerebral blood flow and oxygen consumption necessarily decrease as the consequence of chronological aging per se was not confirmed; rather it was found that when such changes did occur, they were the probable result of arterio-sclerosis. Although some changes in EEG occurred, particu-larly a slowing in peak frequency, they were minimal, and again became marked largely in the presence of arteriosclerot-ic disease. Cognitive performance in this sample was superior to that of the young normal controls who were also tested and to that of previously tested samples of the aged, though the investigators did find evidence of some slowing in speed which they attributed to aging. It is interesting that psychometric tests appeared to be unusually sensitive to the presence of minimal states of disease, including arteriosclerosis. Whether alteration in speed is an intrinsic process associated with aging and whether it is a centrally occurring process are questions that require further definition. Environmental deficits, health status, arterial blood pressure, and depression (and indirectly audition) are major factors that influence both mean reac-tion time and a general speed factor—conclusions which were extracted from the psychometric data by means of a prin-cipal-component analysis. Social, personality, and health vari-ables therefore would appear to be of considerable impor-tance in explaining the manifestations of aging. Indeed, it is striking that in a population purposely biased in its selection for medical health and community residence, the powerful influence of these factors should be revealed.

A broad conclusion may be stated as follows: As a conse-quence of an intensive and extensive multidisciplinary study, the investigators found evidence to suggest that many mani-festations heretofore associated with aging per se reflect in-stead medical illness, personality variables, and sociocultural effects. This result would not surprise such observers as Zeman (1957), who has written of "the tendency in the past to blame many obscure conditions on old age."

[27]

In clinical studies (made at Chestnut Lodge and in private practice from 1958 on), as well as in the NIMH studies, the author has explored the nature of the psychology of experiencing the process of aging, of approaching death, of dying, and of the concomitant personal and social experiences of the later chapter of life. The postulate of a process, termed the "life review" (Butler, 1961a; 1963b), in which constructive outcomes can occur, appears useful in evaluating the psychological status of the older person.

The life review is visualized as a normative, universal process triggered by the sense of approaching dissolution and death, precipitated and reinforced by current isolating experiences, and mediating various observable effects—creative, adaptive, pathological, or more than one of these elements. The life review is seen as an intervening process between the sense of impending death and personality change and as preparatory to dying; the nature of its inception, course, and outcome is affected primarily by the lifelong unfolding of character.

The life review has protean manifestations. It may be social, as shown by the garrulous reminiscence of some elderly people, or it may be silent and only recognized after careful inquiry. This will not surprise psychoanalysts, who are accustomed to demonstrating phenomena during the successful analysis of defenses. Table 1 categorizes some aspects of the life review. Note the creative outcome involved in the writing of an autobiography or a book summarizing a life's work.

To recapitulate briefly: finding many people in middle and later life to be continually creative, impressed by the occurrence of a life review, and affected by the tendency toward cultural devaluation of the later periods of life, the author

TABLE 1
SOME ASPECTS OF THE LIFE REVIEW

I. *Reminiscence*
   Nostalgia; regret; pleasure in idealization of the past
II. *Complications of Reminiscence*
   Pain; guilt; obsessive rumination over the past; despair; depression; dread of future; suicide
III. *The Concomitants and Results of Resolution of the Above*
   Constructive reorganization; creativity; wisdom; atonement; philanthropy; serenity; contentment; summarization of one's life work in memoirs, treatises, history, or biography; maturity; autonomy; honesty; judgment; philosophical development; living in the present

wished to encourage the development of archives of memoirs of persons whose achievement, knowledge, experience should be preserved. Further, he wished to capitalize upon such autobiographical material (as well as to make it available to others) for explorations of the nature and vicissitudes of creativity. Various questions could be put to such data, if it were carefully and systematically collected.

A search for previous and contemporary work embodied in taped memoirs led to the realization that recordings made by people of achievement form an active and growing, if limited, field. Foremost is historiography. Allan Nevins (1938) proposed in 1938 the program now known as the Oral History Collection of Columbia University. (It was actually begun in 1948.) Scientists, artists, businessmen, governmental figures, and others have been interviewed. The volume *Felix Frankfurter Reminisces* (1960) resulted from this program. Special projects, including a "Popular Arts Project" and an "Aviation Project," have been developed. Catalogues are available (Columbia University, 1960; 1962).

Unfortunately Columbia's tapes usually are destroyed,[3] and rarely do they cover the entire life history. Often, specific

[3] These excerpts now are preserved.

segments or topics are covered; for example, Dean Acheson describes "the role of the press in international affairs" in 39 pages. Comparability of data is unlikely.

There is some material germane to creativity in this collection; for example, the painter Jack Levine discusses creativity. There is an important special project on Nobel laureates on scientific research. But there appears to be nothing specifically related either to creativity or aging (or the life cycle). There is no reason, of course, why historians should be interested in these specific questions, but, on the other hand, systematic, comprehensive materials might have lent themselves to the analysis of a variety of questions not anticipated at the time of interviewing.

It is unfortunate that the Oral History Collection has not been conducted with a more comprehensive approach, one that incorporated the skills of other disciplines and provided material for other fields besides history and biography. To paraphrase Clemenceau, history is too important to be left to historians. These objections pale, however, before the extraordinary contribution of oral history in giving to history the voices of its significant participants.[4]

[4] Professor Nevins does not take credit for the idea of oral history, the origin of which goes back at least to Hubert Howe Bancroft (1832-1918), American historian and publisher. He hired reporters to take down personal narratives from pioneers and early settlers and incorporated the material into his massive collections, such as *West American Historical Series,* 39 vols., 1875-1890 (personal communication from Mrs. John T. Mason of Columbia's Oral History Research Office). The author also learned recently (personal communication from Dr. Louis M. Starr) of the work of Dr. Bluma Swerdloff in collaboration with the Oral History Research Office. Her interest lies in applying theories of psychiatric social work and techniques of interviewing to oral history and in making a pilot study of pioneers in the psychoanalytic movement. Heinz Hartmann, Sandor Rado, Abram Kardiner, and Rudolph Loewenstein have participated in her project.

Still earlier than the Oral History Collection is the work of folklorist Alan Lomax, who recorded on acetate discs the jazz pioneer Jelly Roll Morton in 1938. He not only obtained reminiscences but recorded Morton playing his compositions on the piano. This is the earliest recorded memoir (Lomax, 1950) that the author has been able to locate. These recordings have been preserved (there was also a limited edition for the public).

After this lengthy description of the background, goals, and methods of the project, consideration of some specific topics follows.

OBSERVATIONS AND REFLECTIONS

Creativity and Decline with Chronological Aging

At the outset, this paper expressed doubt about the contemporary belief that creativity decreases as a function of chronological age. What are some of the specific objections (see especially Stein and Heinze, 1960) that have been raised, primarily to Lehman's work?

1. *Decrease in availability of time.* Bjorksten (1946) found in a small (and unsatisfactory) study of a group of successful chemists that the curve of time available for creative work paralleled Lehman's curve on age versus output.

2. *Not uniform but differential decline in abilities.* Brozek (1951) suggested that "abilities exercised during our adult years (such as vocabulary, the capacity to understand and use different words) do not decline with adult age and may even increase" (p. 359). He also observed that differences within groups classified according to age were greater than differences between such groups. He further noted that for many, creative works occur in the later years.

3. *Decline occurs later than Lehman's conclusions.* Clague (1951) concludes that "the data on the earnings of American Men of Science suggest, however, that by and large it is not before the sixties that professional ability and productive capacity began to decline among highly trained scientists."

4. *Objections to methodology.* Dennis (1956) contests Lehman's procedure of combining the data for men of different degrees of longevity, a procedure which results in "higher average productivity in the early decades." He also contends that there were errors in sampling and in the selection of age intervals. He objects to the criterion of "significant" contribution employed by Lehman. Lehman (1956) has responded to Dennis' critique.

So much for the controversy in the literature. Although it is tempting to make a straw man of Lehman, he does not in fact deny the persistence of creativity into old age or its new development; nor can anyone deny that decline often occurs. The issue arose because Lehman was understood to conclude that creativity declined as a function of chronological aging. In his reply to Dennis, he indicates that it is not age but the factors that accompany age that are critical. Nevertheless, some damage has been done because, however unwittingly, Lehman has contributed to the prevailing stereotype that with chronological aging comes creative decline. It is my belief that this notion is a stereotype; at the very least, the topic is still open to study.

Let us consider two hypotheses which may account for the vicissitudes of creativity after middle life and into late life. These hypotheses derive from the NIMH studies, from clinical work, and from the theoretical conceptions of psychoanalysis (including the work of Benedek, 1950, and Erikson, 1959). (1) *The multiplex theory:* Influences in addition to or other

[32]

than chronological aging per se facilitate or inhibit creativity. Among such influences are physical diseases, personal losses, sociocultural conditions, and personality structure. (2) *The characteristic mode-life cycle theory:* Qualitative and quantitative changes in the creative process, in both content and form, vary with phases of the life cycle. Phase here refers not only to chronological age but to the complex of normative personal, physical, and social concomitants of the era. One might consider the multiplex theory as included within this broad generalization.

The previous concentration of students of aging on measuring decline encourages by contrast the study and documentation of instances of persistent and new creativity in old age. Table 2 offers illustrations of persistent creativity in later life: Sophocles, Michelangelo, Titian, Tintoretto, Cervantes, Hals, Voltaire, Goethe, Tennyson, Humboldt, Franck, Hugo, Verdi, Tolstoy, Shaw, and Freud are a few famous examples.

TABLE 2
ILLUSTRATIVE LATE MASTERPIECES

		Date	Age
Titian	*The Battle of Lepanto*	1575	98
Tintoretto	*Fall of the Mahha*	1594	76
Cervantes	*Don Quixote de la Mancha*	1605-15	58-68
Hals	*The Governors of the Almshouse*	1664	84
Humboldt	*Kosmos*	1845-62	76-91
Franck	*Symphony in D Minor*	1886-88	64-66
Verdi	*Falstaff*	1893	80
Tolstoy	*What Is Art?*	1896	88
Freud	*The Ego and the Id*	1923	67
Shaw	*Saint Joan*	1924	68

It is not necessary, however, to turn to distant history. In our own time we have witnessed the important contributions of a great many elderly men, including one telling example of enlightened personnel policy in an industrial concern:

[33]

Dr. Benjamin M. Duggar, who was arbitrarily retired from his university professorship, was hired by a pharmacological firm where he discovered aureomycin, certainly repaying the company in full measure for its confidence.

In the professions, sciences, arts, theater, politics, one could mention many other older people who continue to be creative and productive. To illustrate newly developing creativity are the often cited Grandma Moses and the less frequently cited William F. DeMorgan (1839-1917). DeMorgan was an English novelist, artist, and inventor and a friend of the Pre-Raphaelites. In his early life he designed glass and tiles and rediscovered a process for making colored lusters. With the decline of his pottery business in Chelsea and in poor health, he retired in 1905 at 65. At this age he wrote his first and instantly successful novel, *Joseph Vance,* which was published in 1906. In the remaining 11 years of his life, he wrote approximately a novel a year. Other instances of willingness to "try something new" may be cited: Santayana, the philosopher, wrote his first novel, *The Last Puritan,* at 72, in 1936; Sandburg, the poet, wrote his first novel, *Remembrance Rock,* at 70, in 1948. Sherrington, the physiologist, turned to philosophy in *Man on His Nature* in his old age.

Citing instances of persistent or new creativity, however, does not prove or disprove a relationship between aging and creativity. Lehman understood that internal and external conditions are so important that his findings ultimately may be explained as a consequence of them; and it is these conditions that warrant further study.

Further Remarks on Characteristic Mode-Life Cycle Theory

Evidence for a theory of characteristic intellectual modes with respect to the various phases of the life span may be found in Lehman's (1953) *Age and Achievement*. In Chapter 14 of this work, "Older Thinkers and Great Achievements," Lehman presents "ample evidence that any stereotyped conception of later maturity is quite untenable . . . . This chapter sets forth brief biographical notes regarding an appreciable number of individuals who did notable creative work late in life—in some instances their most important work." In direct connection with a "characteristic mode" theory, moreover, he provides a list which "suggests that the contributions of later maturity are likely to differ from the contributions of early youth in that the elderly are more likely to do . . . work" of a particular kind (pp. 220-221). To develop the point further, following Lehman, one may categorize the contributions of late life thus:

1. *Comprehensive reconstructions of a lifetime of scholarship, study, and reflection.* Ulisse Aldrovandi's (1522?-1605?) magnum opus, *Natural History*, consists of 13 volumes, the first six of which were completed between the ages of 77 and 83. Galileo Gallilei's (1564-1642) *Dialoghi delle nuave scienze,* in which he recapitulated the results of his early experiments and mature meditations on the principles of mechanics, was published in 1636 at age 72. Jean B. Lamarck's (1744-1829) *Histoire naturelle des animaux sans vertebrae,* 1815-1822, was written at ages 71-78.

2. *Revision, reconsideration, and retraction.* St. Augustine; Tolstoy; Toynbee.

3. *Continuing development of material.* The Spanish musician, Casals, then 73, is quoted as having said in 1950 at an orchestral rehearsal, "Now we shall improvise. All my life I am working for the right expression of this piece. It is sixty years now, and I have not found it. Perhaps we can find it together." The melodies which are the bases of Elgar's *Wand*

of Youth Suites were composed when the composer was 12. When almost 72, 60 years later, he discovered the pieces among his juvenilia and reworked them. He died at 77 (1857-1934).

4. *Cosmology.* The first two volumes of Alexander Humboldt's (1769-1859) *Kosmos,* 1845-1847, were published at ages 76-78; the third and fourth volumes, 1856-1858, at ages 87-89; the fifth volume, posthumously, 1862. He sought to formulate the known facts about the universe into a uniform conception of nature. This work is regarded as one of the world's greatest scientific achievements. Pierre Simon Laplace (1749-1827) wrote *Mecanique Celeste,* 1799-1828, at ages 50-79.

5. *Lexicography.* Maximilian Paul Émile Littre (1801-1881) completed his *Dictionnaire de la langue Française,* 1863, at age 62 (though he had begun it 20 years earlier).

6. *History.* George Bancroft (1800-1891), in his late life revisions, "sought to correct the mistakes of earlier editions, to profit by newly acquired information, and to reduce the floridity of much of his earlier writing." Bernal Diaz del Castillo (c. 1492-1581), Spanish soldier under Cortez in the conquest of Mexico, wrote one of the epic chronicles of all time, *True History of the Conquest of New Spain,* in his old age.

7. *Life cycle.* Of course it is not only the aged who are concerned with the understanding of the processes of life, growth, development, and transmission of traits, but it may be that such processes are of particular concern to them. Pierre Joseph Van Benden (1809-1894) at 74 began the study of the early history of the animal egg. He reported reduction of the chromosome number in the egg cells to half that in the body cells and held that chromosomes have a genetic continuity throughout the life cycle. William Harvey (1578-1657), in his *Exercitationes de Generatione Animalium*

[36]

(1651), showed that the embryo developed from the egg by the process of "epigenesis."

8. *Psychology.* Franz Brentano (1838-1917), wrote *Sinnes-psychologie,* 1907, at age 69. Sigmund Freud (1851-1939) continued to contribute new ideas and observations, summarize, and revise until his death *(vide infra).*

9. *Geriatrics.* Pierre Brisseau (1631-1717), in 1705, at age 74, was the first to demonstrate by dissection the clouded lens in cataract. Sir John Floyer (1649-1734) wrote the first treatise of the diseases of old age, *Medicina Gerocomica,* 1724, at age 75. Benjamin Franklin (1706-1790), in 1784, at age 78, when he needed two pairs of spectacles, one for far sight and one for near, invented bifocal eyeglasses. Friedrich Hoffman (1660-1742) described senility as a disease in 1731, at age 71.

10. *Memoirs.* François René Chateaubriand (1768-1848), wrote *Mémoires d'outre-tombe* (Memoirs from Beyond the Tomb), at ages 65-80. (*Vide infra* concerning autobiographical materials composed in later life.)

11. *Maintenance of life, rejuvenation.* Giovanni Colle (1558-1630) gave the first definite description of blood transfusion in 1628, at age 70. Charles E. Brown-Séquard (1817-1894) wrote on rejuvenation.

Lehman, then, was not unaware of the difficulties of his task; he tried to take into account quality as well as quantity. If his conclusions were generally valid that maximal creativity occurs during youth, it would still remain uncertain how this "finding" is to be regarded. This is not to denigrate Lehman's work, but rather to point out that it is also important to recognize the *qualitatively* different tasks of later life as a field for investigation. As Lehman himself says, "The old usually possess greater wisdom and erudition." He also shows a general awareness of the less favorable conditions for creativity in later life, ranging from social to medical factors. How time or chronological aging relates to creativity remains unsettled.

The following points summarize the foregoing discussion: (1) The relationship of creativity and aging has not been satisfactorily studied. (2) Medical, personal, social, and other factors that are not age-specific affect creativity. In the presence of health and in the absence of personal and social adversity, creativity is more apt to persist into late life. (3) Qualitative changes in the creative products may occur; that is to say, their content and form may vary as a function of characteristics of the phase of later life. Certain creations can

TABLE 3

SOME CAPACITIES AND POTENTIAL FUNCTIONS IN SOCIETY
ASSOCIATED WITH MIDDLE AND LATER LIFE

Middle and Later Life Capacities

    Accumulated knowledge
    Accumulated skills
    Judgment, sagacity, deliberation
    Wisdom, understanding, prudence, perspective
    Serenity, contentment, calm
    Philosophical development
    Independence; autonomy; freedom
    Candor; honesty
    Interpersonal understanding; sympathy; empathy
    Maturity; dependability
    Authority; prestige

Middle and Later Life Functions

    Instruction, teaching
    Consultation, advice, troubleshooting
    Listening, reflecting
    Counseling
    Observation over time (historian; biographer)
    Editing
    Administration
    Monitoring

only occur in full measure in later life (or after a great deal of "living"): comprehensive reconstructions of a lifetime of scholarship, study, and reflection; comprehensive historical works; memoirs. Certain interests are more marked in later life: interest in the life cycle, interest in geriatric problems. (4) The absence of so-called new ideas or new forms is not a test of creativity per se, because one's mode of being, one's past interests, training, skills, experience, may be creatively elaborated and extended. Although first and highly significant creative works are likely to be produced in early years (20-35), the fact that other "new directions" do not occur is not equivalent to declining creativity. (5) Direct, intensive and comprehensive study of creative people in the course of the life cycle is necessary.

Decline and Extinction of Creativity in Old Age

Among many who may be cited as revealing decline in creativity in old age are Edwin Arlington Robinson (after 59), Emerson (after 63), and Kant (after 74). Sibelius, along with E. M. Forster, seemed to exhibit a "stoppage" (a word of uncertain meaning) in creativity relatively early in life. Forster aged 85 in 1964, has not published a novel in 40 years (since 1924). Yet, even in 1964, some would regard him, as Alan Pryce-Jones states, as the "chief living novelist in English." He has written six novels (one is unpublished), one volume of short stories, two biographies, some criticism, some essays, a remarkable guidebook, the text for Benjamin Britten's opera *Billy Budd,* and some talks for broadcasting. As Pryce-Jones puts it, "Having stated his case, he writes no more fiction." However, he has continued to write. Clearly, one would have to investigate seeming instances of "stoppage" in the creative process before drawing conclusions relative to aging.

[39]

Creativity and the Life Cycle

It is not at present possible to do more than sketch a picture of creativity in relation to stages in the life cycle.[5] When such a sketch can be developed into an organized body of knowledge, it should have many practical applications to pedagogy, social organization, employment practices, and other fields. For instance, at the beginning of the life cycle, it may be that adolescence[6] is a time for a kind of creative experience different from what our culture currently provides—one more in keeping with the intense social and sexual impact of the period. At the other end of the life cycle, greater tailoring of the gifts of experience to the needs of society may occur someday. It is a logistical problem of relating creative expression to opportunity and to the particular phases of the life cycle. Table 4 tabulates certain capacities and functions after middle life.

TABLE 4

SOME MAJOR SOURCES OF IDEAS AND DATA CONCERNING
CREATIVE PEOPLE AND CREATIVE ACTIVITY

1. *Analysis of Creative Products,* i.e., writings, music, art
   Disciplines: literary criticism; musicology; art history; psychoanalysis
   Notes, manuscripts, juvenilia, notebooks: Faraday, Camus' *Juvenilia;* the Brontes; Elgar
2. *Biographies and Histories,* by writers with personal or remote relationship to subject

---

[5] Efforts toward a new discipline, or at least a special frame of reference, are increasing, but there is no word for the study of the entire life cycle and its stages. Developmental psychology, on the one hand, and gerontology, on the other, are too limited. It would be helpful if someone, perhaps a scholar of classical languages, could offer or construct a term meaning "life-cycle-ology."

[6] Leo A. Spiegel (1951), speaking of adolescence, writes, "Creativity receives a massive stimulus and daydreams occupy a greater area in mental activity."

3. *Autobiographical Material*
   Autobiographies, memoirs, journals, diaries, letters—early through late life: Stravinsky; Berlioz; Arnold Bennett; Jane Austen.
   Fictionalized autobiography: Joyce's *Portrait of the Artist as a Young Man*
4. *Philosophical Writings about Creativity and Aesthetics*
   Bergson; Nietzsche; Croce; Langer.
5. *Observations and Writings by Artists and Writers about Their Creativity*
   Tolstoy; Thomas Hart Benton.
6. *Direct Study*
   a. Conversations: Eckerman and Goethe; Boswell and Johnson; Lomax and Morton; Phillips and Frankfurter; Craft and Stravinsky; the *Paris Review* interviews
   b. In course of therapy: unselected, accidental opportunity to study creative persons
   c. Taped memoirs: (e.g., Frankfurter)
   d. Direct study of child development: Piaget; Terman's gifted children
   e. Interpretive narrative based on direct observation
7. *Special Testing*
   Psychological testing: perceptual, cognitive, and other functions; personality testing, including projective devices
   Physiological tests: medical, genetic, age-relevant
8. *Ancillary, Corroborative*
   Observers of creative people: school teachers, school files, etc.

We know something of the intense curiosity of the child—his elaborated theories of his origin, of sexuality, even of the universe. We know a little of the increased administrative and other extracreative requirements of middle life. We know something of the qualities associated with later life. But we do not yet know how to use this information.

Longevity and Creativity

Lehman observed that "with some dramatic exceptions, our greatest creative thinkers have been rather long-lived." Can it be that great people who attain great age are members of a biological elite? Are great age and creativity associated? Albert Schweitzer showed astonishing capacities for both physical and mental labor all his life and into his old age. Two possibilities would seem worth studying: (1) that longevity and creativity are associated and (2) that certain great men, particularly great teachers, are subject to higher rate of homicide than most people. If this is true (Socrates, Archimedes, Jesus, Caesar, Lincoln, Ghandi), the reason may be the envy of greatness noted earlier.

Creativity and the Personal Significance of Death

Aspirations toward immortality have often been ascribed to great men. A powerful sense of the rapid pressure of time, of the transience of life, may be a motivating factor in creative activity. A number of writers have speculated upon this question, including the psychoanalyst Rickman (1940).

In his work so far, the author has been impressed with the significance of the interior experiences of time and death in creativity. If, as it appears, the desire to make one's personality imperishable is an element in the impulse to create, it may be linked with the issue of personal identity. A further advantage in studying old people to increase our understanding of creativity derives from the opportunity to study the lifelong vicissitudes of identity and the meanings of time and death, put into relief by proximity to death. Other advantages include the opportunity to review the entire life experience and obtain a perspective upon it. With old age, moreover, there appears to be greater freedom for personal revelation (Birren *et al.*, 1963).

Freud and Old Age

No one practicing psychoanalysis and subspecializing in old age can avoid considering three aspects of Freud and his work: (1) Freud's pessimism about the treatability and the "mental elasticity" of people after middle age, (2) Freud himself after his own middle age, and (3) Freud's "Thanatos" and other thanatologies. Here, we may consider these topics briefly.

The history of psychoanalytic attitudes and views begins with Freud. Freud was pessimistic in general about old age, and, in particular, about the applicability of psychoanalysis as a therapy in old age. Furthermore, psychiatry as a whole has been pessimistic about the treatability of old people— neither Freud nor psychoanalysis is solely responsible for this point of view, which approaches therapeutic nihilism.

Freud stated in *On Psychotherapy* (1904), when he was 48: "The elasticity of the mental processes, on which the treatment depends is as a rule lacking—old people are no longer educable." It is instructive to study Freud himself in relation to his own mid-life and old age and to his concern with death. In Freud's own remarks, in Jones' (1957) biography (especially Volume III, *The Last Phase, 1919-1939*), and in other sources, we may examine Freud's personal experiences of growing old as well as his views, theories, and observations about aging and death. One is immediately impressed by the fact that Freud's own major contributions came in middle and later life. Jones (1957) admiringly observes that among the features of the last phase of Freud's life, "One was the truly astonishing fresh outburst of original ideas he produced in those years, just when it was thought he had rounded off his life's work. These ideas effected a revolution in both the theory and the practice of psychoanalysis, and they furnished stimuli which are still bringing about fruitful results" (p. xi).

[43]

Freud was born in 1856. He was nearly 40 when he described the dynamics of resistance, transference, repression, and defense in his (and Breuer's) *Studies in Hysteria* in 1895. Freud analyzed the first middle-aged man—himself. Note the Irma Dream and Erikson's (1954) "The Dream Specimen of Psychoanalysis." Erikson writes, "The Irma Dream places the dreamer squarely into a crisis of middle age. It deals most of all with matters of Generativity, although it extends into the neighboring problems of Intimacy and of Integrity." The setting of the dream was a birthday party.

Freud was 44 when his magnum opus, *The Interpretation of Dreams,* was published in 1900. He was to live nearly as long again, another 39 years. His classical and basic papers on technique were written between 1910-1915, that is to say, when he was between 54 and 59 years of age. *Beyond the Pleasure Principle,* formulating the death instinct, came in 1920, at age 64. The structural hypothesis was still to come with the appearance of *The Ego and the Id* in 1923, when Freud was 67. Ultimately, we note that at age 81, in 1937, his remarkable *Analysis Terminable and Interminable* appeared. Despite profoundly felt losses of loved ones and severe physical suffering (cancer of the mouth plagued him for the last 16 years of his life, requiring 33 operative procedures), he remained productive—creative—until his life ended at age 83. Thus, we have in Freud, himself a pessimist on the matter, an excellent case of the persistence of creativity after middle life into old age.

It is noteworthy that Freud, as aforesaid, was deeply troubled by death. He predicted his premature death, and selected successively his age at death as 42, as 61 or 62, and then as 81½. He was profoundly affected by his father's death and was shaken by the human destruction of World War I.

Eissler (1955), however, in *The Psychiatrist and the Dying Patient,* doubts that personal biases on Freud's part determined the conception of the death instinct.

The "Live Memoir"—The Nature of Biography and Autobiography

For reasons already given, the direct study of creativity after middle life is a major purpose of this study. Direct study of creative persons has been comparatively rare. Neither Lehman's work nor traditional psychoanalytic pathography has involved direct study.

At the very least, a result of this project should be the accumulation of significant life histories. But even this is an impossibly large project for one person. The studies described here can only attempt to build a model procedure, aimed at integrating the psychoanalytic and the gerontological (or life cycle) approach into the collaborative historical study of an individual life.

There is an increasing number of collections of oral history evolving in universities and elsewhere. Let us hope that there will be progress toward the collection of more comparable and comprehensive data. We may expect, moreover, that both the technique of the interview and the conceptual advances of modern behavioral and social sciences, as well as the theories of psychoanalysis, will influence the approach to oral history. The experience of the present project may be of some value in the course of such developments.

In the limited experience thus far, it is apparent that therapeutic overtones arise; much contact occurs, but good things require time. It is exciting, but it is time-consuming. The investigator must study and prepare; he must be available; he must invent questions.

[45]

Earlier some of the distinctive qualities of the taped, or spoken, interview memoir were mentioned. These in themselves suggest a study. Personal documents, such as autobiographies, journals, diaries, letters, and juvenilia, deserve critical and scientific study in terms of both substance and methodology (see Table 4). What are the motives and the problems of biographers and autobiographers? How are resulting documents to be made objective? What contributions do they make to the transmission of culture and to historiography? Students of literature and of history and Ph.D. candidates in search of theses might be encouraged to study such personal documents, and might work in collaboration with psychiatrists and other behavioral scientists. Relationships between history and psychoanalysis, the psychiatric anamnesis, transference and countertransference—these are among the topics whose study would be in pursuit of the notion that "the proper study of mankind is man."

Some studies of autobiography have been made, but to the psychiatrist they leave much to be investigated. Misch (1951), Burr (1909), Shumaker (1954), and Lillard (1956) have written about autobiography. Plank (1953) has considered certain aspects in articles appearing in *The Psychoanalytic Study of the Child*. Allport (1942) has considered the broader subject of personal documents in a small. monograph. Psychoanalysts have drawn conclusions from autobiographical material (Schreber, 1903; Freud, 1911).

TABLE 5
AUTOBIOGRAPHICAL MATERIALS OF LATE LIFE

		Date	Age
Saint Augustine	*Confessions*	400	46
Benevenuto Cellini	*Autobiography*	1558	57-62
Geronimo Cardano	*De propria vita*	1575	74

Louis De Rouvroy, Saint-Simon	*Memoirs*	1739-51	64-76
Jean Jacques Rousseau	*Confessions*	1781;1788	after 53
Johann W. Van Goethe and Eckermann	*Truth and Poetry* *Conversations with Goethe*	1811	after 60
Lorenzo Da Ponte	*Memoirs*	1823	74
Giovanni Jacopo Casanova	*Memoires*	1826-38	65-73
René de Chateaubriand	*Mémoires d'outre-tombe*	1849-50	after 70
Cardinal Newman	*Apologia pro Vita sua*	1864	63
Benjamin Franklin	*Autobiography*	1868	65-82
John Stuart Mill	*Autobiography*	1873	62-67
Leo Tolstoy	*Confession*	1879-81	51-53
	Last Diary	1910	82
Ulysses S. Grant	*Personal Memoirs*	1885-86	62
John Ruskin	*Praeterita*	1885-89	after 59
Thomas Carlyle	*Reminiscences*	1886	71
Mary Baker Eddy	*Retrospection and Introspection*	1891	70
Charles Robert Darwin	*Recollections of the Development of My Mind and Character*	1892	67
Otto Von Bismarck	*Gedanken und Erinnerungen*	1898	after 75
Daniel Paul Schreber	*Memoirs of a Nerve Patient*	1903	58-60
Henry B. Adams	*The Education of Henry Adams*	1906	68
Carl F. G. Spitteler	*My Earliest Experiences*	1920	68
Selma Lagerlöf	*Marbacka*	1922	64
Frank Harris	*My Life and Loves*	1923-27	67-71
Sigmund Freud	*Autobiography*	1924	68
	Postscript	1935	79
Louis Sullivan	*Autobiography of an Idea*	1924	c. 65
Lincoln Steffens	*Autobiography*	1931	65
William Henry Hudson	*Far Away and Long Ago*	1918	70
Somerset Maugham	*The Summing Up*	1938	64
H. G. Wells	*Experiment in Autobiography*	1934	68
Victor George Heiser	*An American Doctor's Odyssey*	1936	67
Edgar Lee Masters	*Across Spoon River*	1936	67

[47]

Mary Austin	*Earth Horizon*	1932	64
Havelock Ellis	*My Life*	1939	80
Igor Stravinsky	*An Autobiography*	1935	53
and Robert Craft	*Conversations*	1959	76
	Memories and Conversations	1960	78
	Expositions & Developments	1962	80
Nikolai Berdyaev	*Dream and Reality*	1937	63
Jelly Roll Morton	*Jelly Roll Morton*	1938	53
and Alan Lomax			
Sean O'Casey	*Inishfallen, Fare Thee Well*	1949	65
George Bernard Shaw	in *Selected Prose*	1952	70
Bernard Berenson	*Rumor and Reflection*	1952	80-82
	Sunset and Twilight	1963	82-93
Felix Frankfurter	*Reminiscences*	1960	73
Gerald Brenan	*A Life of One's Own*	1963	69
Lewis L. Strauss	*Men and Decisions*	1962	64
Edward Steichen	*A Life in Photography*	1963	84
Phyllis Bottome	*The Goal*	1963	79
Carl G. Jung	*Memories, Dreams, Reflections*	1963	82
Maurice Samuel	*Little Did I Know*	1963	70
Colette	*The Blue Lantern*	1963	73-75
Dwight D. Eisenhower	*Mandate for A Change 1953-56*	1963	73
Morris Ernst	*Untitled: The Diary of My 72nd Year*	1963	72

By comparing the naturally occurring autobiographical process (Shumaker, 1954; Lillard, 1956), one is helped in constructing the format and questionnaire of the live memoir (see Table 5). For instance, autobiographies tend to include little on early life. Anna R. Burr (1909) found references to the first three years of life, for example, in only 39 of approximately 300 autobiographies which she studied. Autobiographies also tend to emphasize crucial or exciting incidents and conflicts, but not periods of relative calm, as Allport indicates.

[48]

One could not use currently available autobiographical material with any assurance of comparability of data; indeed, many autobiographies are fragments or topical pieces. Even the definition of an autobiography is difficult (Shumaker, 1954). It may be that the taped memoir *as experiment* would help the literary scholar in his quest for a definition of autobiographical forms.

Autobiographies have a universal appeal, and certainly they have a professional appeal to the psychoanalyst, the gerontologist, and the student of creativity—not to mention the historian. Autobiographies tend to be composed in later life, and some contain descriptions of the personal experience of growing old. Some of these accounts are extremely valuable. *The World As Seen at Eighty,* by the great Spanish neurohistologist Ramon y Cajal, is an excellent example. Other valuable works are Bernard Berenson's *Sunset and Twilight* and the Rev. John La Farge's *Reflections on Growing Old.* Sean O'Casey, Goethe, and Somerset Maugham, among others, are important sources of data concerning the subjective experience of aging. Perhaps most remarkable of all is the *Last Diary* of Leo Tolstoy.

The exploitation of autobiographies to further our understanding of a particular phase of the life cycle is not novel. Norman Kiell (1963) has studied autobiographies, diaries, and letters relevant to adolescence. He has also used fiction, which can contribute to our knowledge of old age (Butler, 1961a; 1963e).

Therapeutic Aspects of Memoirs

Salutary effects come from the process of reviewing one's life. Requesting a memoir for posterity is in itself an affirmation. It is not surprising that in the process of this study, "therapeutic digressions" have occurred. Of course, that is a poor description. The unfolding, while not a unity, is not compartmentalized either. It is a flux—the review proceeds where it may. It does not *interfere* with the research. Research and therapy are not necessarily opposites. Socrates, who enjoined "Know thyself," said something more: "The unexamined life is not worth living." This is a very strong statement, but it defines an attitude. In its converse, it is a basis of therapy; the examined life is worth-while.

Di Lampedusa, the author of *The Leopard*, was urged to write by his wife, a psychoanalyst, and to draw on his recollections. The implied necessity of dealing with death is vividly emphasized in Tolstoy's *Last Diaries*. Tolstoy understood what Erikson was later to call identity. The following is an entry of January 15, 1910 (p. 43):

> I remembered very vividly that I am conscious of myself in exactly the same way now, at eighty-one, as I was conscious of myself, my "I", at five or six years of age. Consciousness is immovable. Due to this alone there is the movement which we call "time." If *time moves on*, then there must be something that stands still, the consciousness of my "I" stands still.

Undertaking one's memoirs is not always therapeutic, of course. Some people may become disturbed (compare patients who become transiently upset during psychotherapy), and others may refuse to give their memoirs. Some older people do not want to make their wills, select grave sites, write memoirs; there is too great a note of finality.

The Autodidact

There is a quality of character in many creative people which may be described as the autodidactic position and process. The autodidact is literally a self-teacher. The central focus is upon the self—an essential belief in the self, an exploitation of it, and the exhaustion of all its possibilities. The autodidact tries to learn everything for himself; he teaches himself what he already knows and what others have already found out, and in the process uncovers or creates what only he can teach.

Although confidential materials from the present study must be left aside, we find vivid historical examples of autodidacts in several fields: Charles Darwin in science, Nicholai Berdyaev in philosophy, George Bernard Shaw in literature, Henri Rousseau in art. There is still much to be learned about the autodidactic process, but let us try to formulate the conception.

According to the *Oxford English Dictionary*, the word autodidact (it is a Greek word literally meaning "self-taught") was first used by Sir Thomas More in 1534. The notion is thus not new, but so far as the author is aware neither description nor psychodynamics have been presented.

The autodidact is not a self-learner; the etymology must be taken quite literally. He is a self, teaching himself. It is an adventure of the self; at times this quality accounts for the imperious "handsome is as handsome does" attitude of some creative persons. The autodidact, though longing for the absolute, finds nothing self-evident—except for the luminously self-evident idea that literally nothing is luminously self-evident except one's self. In the course of time, the autodidact constructs for himself aspects of reality sifted through himself, absorbed, and remolded. Then he may make or seem to make all kinds of assumptions, and he may appear credulous or dogmatic, stubborn or certain; but he is never really certain, or at least never for long.

Solipsism is not intended here, for there is no such system in itself that is self-evident to the autodidact. Even if one accused him of solipsism, he would honestly and correctly deny it. For the autodidact (in the extreme, to place the matter in striking relief) could never *quite* adopt a system that had been previously developed. Indeed, the autodidact is apt to deny that he is an autodidact, but if we approach him about underlying processes, we may confirm his autodidacticism. He will admit, even idolize, the influences of his teachers upon him, but, in fact, he has changed these influences, altered the meanings, and amplified the substances of such experiences *after his own image*. He may name enthusiastically *his* idols, *his* major influences. But one must study the process of his idolization. He remains as always at the heart of the matter; it is *his* idol. He is not the parrot, of which there are many, but the autodidact, of which there are few. The parrot does not create his idol; the idol creates him; without the idol—the book, the teacher, the parent—the parrot does not exist.

If the autodidact has a mistress, he is not *her* lover; she is *his* creation (compare Pygmalion). Her existence is *his* production. Two autodidacts could not be in love with each other, if love means mutuality of the idealized conception; two autodidacts love the self in the other. This is not to be confused with narcissism. It is not a question of a mirror; it is a matter of creation, not reflection.

As long as the autodidact continually recovers and recreates the self in equilibrium with the (*his*) milieu, affects are positive; as long as there is disequilibrium, affects are negative. He generally tends toward disequilibrium and negative affectivity. He is almost invariably suffering.

We may observe intermittent (and paradoxical) states—both courage and cowardice, certainty and doubt, furor and calm, clarity and confusion. The demon of the autodidact is constant self-appraisal.

The autodidact is privy to the process that defines him. Always the realist, he cannot possibly deny *his* reality, however he may describe and name it. He knows himself, his powers *and also his limits*; he is learned about his self.

Can an autodidact be a psychoanalyst and can a psychoanalyst analyze an autodidact? The answer is yes to both questions. To begin with, the first psychoanalyst was an autodidact; he analyzed himself. Psychoanalysis is an autodidactic manifestation, but few psychoanalysts are autodidacts, and, of course, few autodidacts are psychoanalysts.

The autodidact often needs and occasionally seeks psychoanalysis, because he is often symptomatic—symptomatic because he must struggle with the problem of being an autodidact. For being an autodidact, it must now be clear, can be a dreadful state. When the autodidact is unsuccessful, when for whatever reason he cannot be himself, he is in torment. He may prefer to destroy himself.

George Berkeley (1685-1753), the British philosopher, affirmed that the external world exists only as perceptions in the mind; perhaps this is the classical theory of autodidactism, but it is not a theory of process. In the autodidactic process, the external world is recreated through the perceptual and integrative processes of the self. The external world is not abjured; it is only that the contemporary descriptions and explanations of it are considered incomplete. Having processed the external world, the autodidact will compare his results with others' and accept those that agree with *his,* at least tentatively, although he will continue to test—the more so when *his* findings are at variance with those of others. He is, it will be noted, as distrustful of his own findings as he is of others'. He is only momentarily reassured when the findings of others concur, for this merely interrupts the painful internal process and provides a brief relief (equilibrium).

The autodidact, then, *treats as hypothesis what most persons treat as fact.* We may, for the moment, share with Sherrington (1951) his interest in Jean Fernel, a Renaissance physician who questioned the four elements and thus, in effect, the medicine of his era, not to mention its geodesy and cosmology. Fernel wrote (as cited by Sherrington, p. 27): "Not that I suggest there is nothing in the theory of the four elements..." (which is exactly what he was doing, but playing the wary autodidact). "These elements seem established by all likelihood of reason" (indeed, that is his point: by reason, not by demonstration). "What I want to be clear about is that those, who make the four elements the cause of all which is, are greatly led away by their own arguments. The causes of many happenings belong elsewhere." (Thus, he states his direct opposition.) As Sherrington puts it (p. 27), Fernel insists that "a long-sanctioned dogma, not demonstrable by observation, is hypothesis."

One might ask whether independence of mind does not describe the phenomenon referred to here as autodidacticism. Independence of mind does not go far enough, however; it does not emphasize the central focus upon the self and the teaching of the self. It is not simply that the autodidact doubts and distrusts, but that he assumes that whatever has been said, or is thought to be understood, is *incomplete.* There is something more—if only one searches further, studies more, and reflects more comprehensively. One must start from scratch, at the ground, and blaze one's own trail to the unattainable summit; not destructively per se, not only through doubt, but also through personal optimism about the possibility of a solution, always, however, cast in terms of an ultimate and personal despair because nothing can be whole or complete. *This appears to be the incisive issue, that the self is not complete; the*

[54]

autodidact, studying himself, finds he is not whole. And this sense of incompleteness is a sense and fear of alienation.

The autodidact may be unable to report his findings because they are "incomplete." He may delay publication, as did Darwin (obsessiveness is not a sufficient explanation). An autodidact, Darwin started at the ground and learned everything for himself—even what had been learned before. Had it not been for the graciousness of Alfred Russel Wallace, Darwin might not have had priority for his discoveries. Himmelfarb's (1959) biography is perhaps more revealing than Darwin's (1876) autobiography of the autodidactic quality of the great nineteenth-century biologist.

Himmelfarb points out that "the image of the passionless, painstaking scientist following his data blindly, and provoked to a new theory only when the facts can no longer accommodate the old, turns out to be, in the case of Darwin as of others, largely mythical" (p. 163). "There is no doubt that Darwin's own point of departure was an examination of 'absolute origins and absolute finalities,' the ultimate 'why.' Nor is it by accident that this was so. Darwin was able to give ultimate answers because he asked ultimate questions" (p. 156).

Berdyaev, too, may be classified as an autodidact. As he describes in his unique autobiography, *Dream and Reality* (1950), he meant his book to be "a philosophic autobiography or a history of the spirit and self-knowledge." "This book is frankly and openly egocentric," he wrote. "But egocentricity, repulsive though it is, may be redeemed by the fact that I call my self and my life to question and make them the object of critical inquiry" (pp. vii-viii). Berdyaev is frank about his alienation and his wish to cope with it. To Berdyaev, he, Berdyaev, is perishable, and so *his* life is dedicated to his existence alone; he can only believe, truly believe, in himself.

[55]

No one else is trustworthy (this is not paranoia). Only he can lead himself to understanding. He helps us to understand what is meant by consecration to one's art, of one's devotion. It is not an external matter; it is not art for art's sake or science for science's sake; it is not pure art or pure science, but pure self, and the individual human instrumentality is the pure expression.

This is why, failing actual immortality, there is a search for historical imperishability (continuity of self if not completeness). One may live on through one's works, one's own manifestations. The epiphany of the autodidact, his ultimate apotheosis, is his recognition, especially his enduring recognition.

The autodidact may succeed in achieving an *institutionalization* of his (the) self; thus, we refer to systems as Aristotelian, Newtonian, Darwinian, Freudian,[7] Shavian, and so on.

Henri Rousseau taught himself to paint. Although the fact of self-education (without formal education) does not define an autodidact, they may go together, perhaps more frequently than otherwise. The French composer Chabrier, largely self-taught, Grandma Moses, Edward Gibbon, and others who were largely self-educated were probably autodidacts.

Shaw spoofed his autodidacticism in the same way he spoofed so many other things. He more than institutionalized himself; he erected a myth, and, as with myths, the origins of his creation are nearly forgotten. As Erikson (1956) writes, "Shaw must always exempt himself from any universal law."

[7] Sullivan is one of several psychiatrists who have achieved institutionalization (Sullivanian). He could not read Freud; he had to rediscover and name differently much that Freud had discovered, and, in the process, he discovered new knowledge which he could impart.

[56]

Shaw (1921) wrote, "I cannot learn anything that does not interest me . . . . I am firmly persuaded that every unnatural activity of the brain is as mischievous as any unnatural activity of the body" (p. 50). "Whether it be that I was born mad or a little too sane, my kingdom was not of this world" (p. 65).

This sketch has not meant to imply that autodidacticism explains creativity or that it is a necessary or sufficient condition. It may be an important characteristic or ingredient; it may help to delineate the obscure processes of discovery and creativity (perhaps these are distinctly different) in *some* people. It may help to clarify the nature of influence (a continuum of autogenesis versus plagiarism or, more politely, derivation). It may provide insights into the autobiographical process. It may delineate the creative aspects of ego autonomy as conceptualized in psychoanalytic theory.

The Transmission of Culture

Man has described himself as wise and has distinguished himself from other animals by emphasizing his capacities for forethought, language and symbolic thinking, and the transmission of culture. Yet, in many important instances, man has failed to create and maintain the conditions which bring these capacities to their fulfillment, especially in our culture. One striking instance of this failure to realize the potentialities of man has been the frequent disuse or misuse of those qualities which are more greatly associated with middle and later life, such as experience, accumulated skills, knowledge, judgment, wisdom, serenity, and philosophical development. To what extent are the potential contributions of the elderly neglected or utilized, or both, in diverse cultures—for example, in the role of grandparents, in consultation and teaching, in the transmission of culture? If our culture could find ways to utilize better its reservoir of contributory elderly, there is reason to believe that there would be a reduction of psychiatric problems in later life (Butler, 1961c).

Proposal for a National Archive of Memoirs

The writing of memoirs is essentially fortuitous. The National Archives contain documents and records of national interest, but the life histories of those responsible for such documents and records are not collected. Why not introduce a federal program for obtaining the private memoirs of persons who have made significant contributions to our national life? When to release such material would be the decision of the memoirist, a control which might reduce the defensiveness or self-justifying tendencies of autobiographical material published during an author's lifetime. Consider, for example, how political figures might write about one another if they were writing for posterity rather than for immediate publication. Avoidance of gigantism in memoirs would require consideration of the problems of selection, scope, and so on. One might ask, as Henry Steele Commager (1947) did:

> Do not enough public men, out of vanity or self-justification or for whatever reason, compose their autobiographies? Yet if we turn to the first great crisis of our history—the Revolution and the founding of the Republic—we are struck at once with the paucity of formal personal material . . . . None of the great figures of this era, except John Adams, compiled memoirs—neither Washington nor Hamilton nor Jefferson nor Sam Adams nor Henry nor Marshall. Franklin, to be sure, left us a precious fragment of autobiography, but it tells us nothing of the Revolution or of the critical period. Nor were the generals more articulate; Greene, Gates, Wayne, Marion and

the others followed Washington's example of silence. . . .
The most interesting histories have been those penned
by participants. Yet, for all their color and character they
are, inevitably, suspect. The memoir is, after all, a personal record; it tends to be narrow, partisan, individual-
istic, a paean of triumph or an apology. Memory is
a treacherous thing, and the most personal records
are stained with the color of personality.

His statements give all the more reason for the interview
memoir, which can provide checks and revisions, and for the
contribution of the psychoanalytic perspective. Also, of course,
multiple autobiographies offer cross-checks.

A collection of the personal memoirs of our outstanding
citizenry need not and in fact should not be nationally cen-
tralized. The government could participate as financial sup-
porter of a national program (through the National Archives,
presumably) for the tape-recording of governmental figures.
Beyond that, the government could act as catalyst in encouraging local programs in universities, societies (for example,
the Vocarium of the American Psychiatric Association),
libraries, and other institutions through matching plans. Details would have to be spelled out later, but the establishment
of a U.S. Commission on Oral History would be useful in
these respects.

Who should staff archival memoir programs? What disciplines should be represented? By background and training
the historian is the central figure, but there are substantial
reasons why psychoanalytic conceptions and interview techniques should be integrated into the approach.

Commager (1963), again, speaking of presidential memoirs,[8] remarks:

[8] Several of the presidential libraries (Truman's, Eisenhower's, and Kennedy's) include some oral history.

[59]

A number of our Presidents have left detailed accounts of their Presidency—diaries by John and John Quincy Adams, an autobiography from Van Buren, a detailed Presidential diary from James K. Polk, memoirs by Hoover and Truman, voluminous correspondence of Washington, Jefferson, Madison, Theodore Roosevelt, Wilson, and Franklin Roosevelt—and now these substantial volumes from President Eisenhower. We cannot, therefore, complain of paucity of material. But we can, perhaps, complain about the persistent failure of Presidents to speculate, to reflect, to interpret, their experience with the great office.

It would be useful to focus also, as Commager proposes, on the "influences and considerations that go into decision making." Arthur Schlesinger, Jr., on his retirement as Special Assistant to the President, was quoted by the *Washington Star* as remarking on the complexity of presidential decisions and referring to the "glib tidiness" he himself had used in describing decisions of the Roosevelt era in his own books.

Pathography has been utilized in the explanation of decision making. Literary critics, journalists, and political scientists sometimes use psychiatric theory, as in Arnold A. Rogow's study of James Forrestal (1963) and Gene Smith's (1964) study of Wilson (especially the last years, which are of interest to gerontologists).

There is no doubt that history, and the public, should be apprised of the mental and physical health of its leaders—King Ludwig, Adolf Hitler, Woodrow Wilson, Franklin Delano Roosevelt, James Forrestal, and John G. Winant, for example. Harold Lasswell long ago (1930) stressed the relations of psychopathology and politics. It is not intended, however, that the National Archives become a mental health

[60]

station nor a vehicle for character assassination. Rather, an important derivative of an archival program would be a growing reservoir of data pertaining to the elements in decision making, including psychological and psychopathological factors.

Memoirs from the living participants would be relevant to studying theories of history; for example, the Marxist view of historical determination versus personalities. Emerson once said, "There is properly no history: only biography." Memoirs composed in a favorable setting, moreover, would supplement the vast field of reportage, which is the great modern source of raw data for history.

Should government be in the business of history? One hundred and seventy-three years ago Thomas Jefferson appealed to the nation to preserve its historic documents. The government in many ways is in the process of preserving as well as making history. Heckscher (1963) clarified the extent to which in many "hidden" ways the government supports the arts; for instance, in the design of money and stamps. Similarly, the government already supports historiography.

Scholars have urged Congress to provide more financial support for history. In June 1963, Congress was requested to vote $500,000 to edit and publish state papers. The National Historical Publications Commission proposed, with President Kennedy's backing, an appropriation to finish work on the papers of John Adams, John Quincy Adams, Benjamin Franklin, Alexander Hamilton, James Madison, and Thomas Jefferson.

Without the efforts of Forrest C. Pogue (1963) to record the recollections of George C. Marshall, there would be no personal document from Marshall, who had refused an offer of a million dollars for his autobiography. Fortunately, in

1956, three years before his death, he agreed to be interviewed, if his biography were not published during his lifetime. He gave 52 hours of interviewing to a nonprofit foundation created solely for the purpose of documenting his career. If a National Archive of Memoirs existed, we should not have to rely on such fortunate chances.

Concluding Remarks

Psychoanalysis has long considered the question of creativity (Kris, 1952; Phillips, 1963), and with the advances of ego psychology, there is much that psychoanalysis can be expected to contribute to our understanding of creativity and the life cycle. Psychoanalysis, which has insisted that the patient speak for himself, can help the creative person to speak for himself.

A strong word must be said, however, for the right not to speak. In this era of the tape recorder and the camera, of exhaustive documentation, the rights of silence and privileged communication must be preserved. It would be most unfortunate if memoirs were granted under social pressure.

This paper has reported on studies which are in progress at the Study Center of the Washington School of Psychiatry. It has presented general considerations on the destiny of creativity. Patterns or vicissitudes of creativity occur in later life; there is no uniform pattern of decline. Persistent and new creativity may occur as well as decline and extinction. There are two hypotheses which may explain these patterns: one theory gives a multicausal explanation; the other proposes a qualitative variation of creativity in relation to phases of the life cycle.

We have seen that Freud was an unusually excellent example of a person whose creative activity extended into old age. Ironically, Freud was personally pessimistic about mental functioning and treatability in later life.

We have noted briefly the contrasts and similarities between taped interview memoirs and traditional autobiographies. Memoirs have both scientific and therapeutic value.

It is hoped that the study of the lives of creative persons would offer insights into the creative process. Some persons are autodidacts, and it may be that autodidacticism is related to creativity or discovery, or both.

Uncontrolled length or proliferation of memoirs would be pointless, but the organized selection and depositing of the comprehensive personal histories and reflections of noteworthy contributors to our national life would help to fulfill the notion that "the proper study of mankind is man." We should do well to collect life histories as avidly as we collect relics to place in our nation's attic.

Reminiscing in the Aged:
An Adaptational Response

ARTHUR W. MCMAHON, JR., M.D.
AND PAUL J. RHUDICK, Ph.D.

SINCE 1958 THE OUTPATIENT CLINIC of the Boston Veterans Administration Hospital has been engaged in a multidisciplinary study of 150 veterans of the Spanish-American War. Most of these men originally volunteered for military service and became eligible for total medical services under Public Law 791 of the Eighty-First Congress. The staff assigned to their treatment soon became impressed by the success with which these men were coping with the problems of aging. As a group they appeared to be above average in intelligence and physical condition. At an average age of 81, they were already 14 years beyond current life expectancy. They were all living outside of institutions, with 76 percent in their own homes. Sixty-one percent were still married, and 91 percent were members of at least one organization. It is understandable that these men soon became the objects of a longitudinal research study aimed at determining what factors contributed to their success in managing the problems of aging.

As the study progressed, the present author, who was not a participant, along with others began to notice an interesting countertransference phenomenon in the researchers. They referred to their subjects with pride and in terms which suggested that they were studying a group of supermen. This attitude not only threatened the objectivity of the study but aroused concern lest the subjects might be reacting to it by minimizing their symptoms. It was for these reasons, interesting and worthwhile in themselves, that the author was asked to interview some of the subjects. The first few interviews, it developed, called attention to another factor: the subjects' preoccupation with the past. Much of the content of the interviews consisted of what is commonly called reminiscing.

Reminiscence is defined as "the act or habit of thinking about or relating one's past experiences" (*Webster's International Dictionary*, 2nd ed.) especially those considered to be most personally significant. Although reminiscing is not limited to old age, it is well recognized as characteristic of this stage of life, an observation that contributes to the impression that old people live in the past. It is popularly regarded as a sign of increasing mental deterioration. Clinical evidence for such deterioration was absent in these subjects, and previous studies had already established them as well above average in both intelligence and physical condition (Dibner and Cummins, 1961). These facts suggested that reminiscing in some way might be related to the success of this group in coping with problems of later life.

A significant number of recent studies of successful adaptation to life's crises have applied the concept of "coping" to certain behavior. Coping is a more general and inclusive concept than defense. It has two aspects: an externally directed one, judged for its effectiveness in social terms, and an internally directed or defensive one, judged for its adequacy on the basis of how it protects the individual from disruptive degrees of anxiety or depression.

[65]

Does the increase of reminiscing in the aged signify a coping behavior and, if so, how does it facilitate adaptation? With these questions in mind, the formulations of ego psychology provided the framework for conceptualizing senescence as a phase of life presenting specific problems which require specific changes in the ego for their solution (A. Freud, 1936, 1958; Rapaport, 1959).

Some of the problems often mentioned as crucial to senescence are the maintenance of self-esteem in the face of declining physical and intellectual capacities; coping with grief and depression resulting from personal losses; finding means to contribute significantly to a society of which older persons are still members; and retaining some sense of identity in an increasingly estranged environment. Erikson (1959) states, "Identity formation neither begins nor ends with adolescence. It is a lifelong development, largely unconscious to the individual and to his society" (p. 113). Senescence presents the last but probably not the least crisis in the struggle for identity.

With these problems defined, the investigators then decided to use the criterion of freedom from depression as an index of successful adaptation and to attempt to relate it to the degree of reminiscing within the group.

PROCEDURE

The 25 subjects of this study were selected at random from the population already described. Their average age was 84 and ranged from 78 to 90. The author interviewed each subject for an hour. The interview was nondirective; the subject was instructed to talk about whatever he wished. It was preceded only by the explanation that this was one aspect of an over-all study of his group. The interview was tape-recorded, and the interviewer said as little as possible to influence the content of the interview. The transcription of each interview was then analyzed in the following way. Each sentence of transcription was designated as a unit of measurement, and the subject's responses were classified according to whether the content referred to the past, the present, or the future. Responses were classified as present responses, if the content referred to aspects of the subject's current life situation—even when the events described had occurred in the recent past. Responses referring to the remote past were classified as reminiscences.

During the interview, the subject was also rated by the author on the presence of depression. The rating was based on the clinical criteria of prevailing affect of depression, evidence of loss of self-esteem, and expressed feelings of hopelessness and helplessness. On the basis of these criteria, the subjects fell into three groups. Those rated as clinically depressed exhibited all three criteria; those rated as suspected of depression exhibited at least one but not all; and those rated as not depressed exhibited none of these criteria.

Because reminiscence has often been ascribed to intellectual deterioration, the subjects were rated with regard to the degree of intellectual deterioration, using the deterioration quotient derived from the Wechsler-Bellevue Intelligence (WBI) Test (Wechsler, 1944).

As an afterthought, because these interviews were conducted from 1960 through mid-1962, the investigators were able to resurvey the group in June 1963 to determine which subjects had died in the interim and to attempt to relate this fact to other data.

We were interested in the relationship, if any, between the tendency to reminisce and (1) the degree of intellectual deterioration, (2) the presence or absence of depression, and (3) survival since the interview.

RESULTS

When the total number of responses were classified as to temporal reference, 66 percent of all responses referred to the remote past; 32 percent to the present or immediate past; and 2 percent to the future. Thus, when the subjects were given an opportunity to discuss whatever they wished for an hour, two-thirds of the total responses elicited referred to the remote past, clearly indicating their preoccupation with the past.

Because the data were nominal or classificatory, they were cast into chi-square tables. In cases where observed frequencies were too small, those who were clinically depressed and those who were suspected of depression were grouped together for statistical analysis.

A Spearman rank-order correlation coefficient was calculated for past responses (reminiscence) and WBI full-scale IQ scores, yielding a nonsignificant value of $+.15$. Because of the common assumption that reminiscence represents intellectual deterioration in the aged, the deterioration scores obtained for each subject were compared with responses relating to the past (reminiscences). A nonparametric Spearman rho was computed and again yielded a negligible relationship. These findings indicate that reminiscing in the subjects is not related to the level of intellectual competence or to the decline of intellectual abilities with age.

When the depressed and nondepressed groups were compared according to the frequency of reminiscence responses, the resultant chi square of 5.58 was just short of significance at the .05 level. This finding suggests that if additional cases were to be studied and the same proportions found, the tendency for the nondepressed group to reminisce more than the depressed group would reach statistical significance (.05).

When we resurveyed the group of subjects one year after the completion of all the interviews to determine how many had died in the interim, we found that three of the four subjects rated as depressed had died; four of the five subjects rated as suspected of depression had died; and only one of the 16 subjects rated as not depressed had died. A chi-square table was constructed which compared the depressed and the nondepressed subjects with retrospective mortality. The obtained chi-square value of 10.624 was significant at greater than the .01 level, clearly indicating a strong relationship between a rating of depression or suspected depression and subsequent death. This finding was independent of age.

DISCUSSION

The statistical results indicate, first of all, that the tendency to reminisce is not directly related to either intelligence or intellectual deterioration in these subjects. Several recent studies of the functioning of memory in the aged (Inglis, Shapiro, and Post, 1956; Shapiro, Post, Löfving, and Inglis, 1956; Kral, 1958; Van Zooneveld, 1958) have encountered difficulty in explaining the apparently greater impairment of recent memory as compared with remote memory on organic grounds alone and have suggested that emotional and motivational factors contribute significantly to this finding. In senescence, there appears to be a complex interrelationship of physical and emotional factors at work which affects both memory and learning (Gitelson, 1948). No doubt we cannot yet disentangle all of the strands, but let us consider some of the many emotional factors in senescence which probably encourage reminiscing.

[69]

A. W. MCMAHON, JR.—P. J. RHUDICK

In his description of the effect of emotions on memory and learning, Stern (1930) remarks that an essential function of remembrance is to secure one's past in a form appropriate and necessary for oneself. The emotional condition in the present, and hopes, fears, and expectations directed toward the future, determine the form in which the events of the past are revived or are prevented from being revived (repression). Anything which lacks this relation to the present is forgotten because it is personally meaningless. Events which are forgotten under certain circumstances presumably can have an unexpected revival when a personal situation or phase of life favors it. Decreasing gratifications in the present and the awareness of failing capacities contribute significantly to what has been described in the aged as the process of disengagement (Cumming and Henry, 1961), or a turning away from the present. The resulting lack of interest and avoidance of new learning disproportionately affects memory for recent events. Remote events, on the other hand, were better learned initially, unhampered by the process of disengagement, and are associated with pleasanter memories of the unimpaired capacities of youth (Hunter, 1957).

Rapaport (1961), in his survey of the relationship between emotions and memory, concludes that emotions are as important a determinant of what is remembered as they are of what is forgotten. Memory, then, not only serves a sense of continuity but is selective, with the purpose of creating and preserving a sense of personal significance. For the aging person, his personal significance attaches mainly to events in the past, and these events become increasingly the subject of his conscious awareness. In our achievement-oriented society, the old person's reminiscing is a constant reminder to himself and others of his achievement of longevity.

Another factor in senescence which probably contributes to a tendency to reminisce is the positive increase in narcissism (Deutsch, 1936; Benedek, 1952). The loss of family and friends, with its resulting withdrawal of libido, combined with the increasing difficulty of finding new objects, favors the reinvestment of libido in an ideal image of oneself in the past. The enhanced self-centeredness itself further contributes to a tendency to reminisce.

Freud comments that when "we do not use our psychic apparatus to fulfill indispensable gratifications, then we let it work so as to derive pleasure out of its own activity" (Freud, 1905). This exercise of psychic function for its own sake in the face of decreasing opportunity for real gratification may explain the positive pleasure accompanying reminiscing in some of our subjects, who expressed great pride and satisfaction in their ability to remember events of long ago with great clarity. These are some of the factors which may help to explain why older people reminisce.

At this point, an analysis of the content of the interviews may further clarify how reminiscing contributes to adaptation. Our analysis revealed that reminiscing is a complex mental activity, the function of which seems to vary with the personality of the subject. Pear (1922) states: "The selective factors in memory are determined primarily by the personality makeup. The mind never photographs; it paints pictures." And Rapaport (1961) remarks: "Generally it is agreed that memory processes are subject to the activities of affective forces related to the deep strata of the personality. Remembering is understood as an active process of reconstruction in which selective forces are of greater importance than the elements of the material; that these selective forces are related more or less intimately to the emotional makeup of the personality."

[71]

The subjects in the present study can be separated into four groups on the basis of their personal use of reminiscence. The following example of reminiscing is typical of one group. A patient who was formerly a semiprofessional football player contrasted present-day players with those of his own day. "I remember the really great players who did everything well. The players nowadays fall asleep on the job. They're good players; but there's something missing there. They seem to fall apart; don't have the spark; don't have the pep the old-time players used to have." It is striking that in his description of the present-day players, he attributes to them his own symptoms of old age. This projection helps him to reinforce the denial of his physical decline and identifies him with the players of the past who represent the greater capacities of his youth. This halo effect is a conspicuous element in those reminiscences which depreciate the present and glorify the past. It is associated with the attitude that one has seen and been a part of the best and has nothing to regret. The reminiscences of this group of subjects are full of stories of unexpected recoveries from illness and miraculous escapes from danger, suggesting fantasies of invulnerability. Hartmann (1958) has emphasized that fantasy can have positive adaptive elements and contrasts it with dreaming in its attempt to solve the problems of waking life. He maintains that there are avenues of adaptation to reality which at first lead away from the real situation and defines this process as regressive adaptation. There is a strong component of fantasy in the type of reminiscing just described. It is characteristic of the more hysterical of our subjects, in whom defenses of denial and repression are prominent. This type of reminiscence not only serves to maintain self-esteem and reinforce a sense of identity but also appears to allay, if somewhat regressively, the

[72]

anxiety associated with signs of decline with its reminder of approaching death.

A second use of reminiscence has been suggested in articles by Butler (1963b) and Von Vischer (1958), who believe that the aged person has a need to review his life preparatory to death and that reminiscences serve to provide the material necessary for this review. Several of the subjects in this study seemed preoccupied with the need to justify their lives, and their reminiscences reflected themes of guilt, unrealized goals, and wished-for opportunities to make up for past failures. Though this attitude was not typical in our study, it appeared characteristic of the more obsessive-compulsive subjects who, we may suspect, have been reviewing their past behavior in the same judgmental and evaluative way all their lives. It may be significant that the subjects described by Butler (1963b) were psychiatric patients who showed evidence of obsessive rumination and clinical depression. Some of the interview material quoted in his article suggests the break-down of repression and the return of the repressed rather than the organized quality characteristic of the reminiscences of our subjects. The majority of the subjects in this study more closely resembled Busse's (1959) normal elderly population living in the community, who did not seem preoccupied with guilt or with the need to come to terms with the personal past. This observation is corroborated by investigators currently working with dying patients (Hackett and Weisman, 1962; Weisman, personal communication).

A third group of subjects may be best described as story-tellers who recount past exploits and experiences with obvious pleasure in a manner which is both entertaining and informative. They seem to have little need to depreciate the present or glorify the past, but they do reminisce actively.

[73]

Hartmann (1958), in describing defense mechanisms, stresses that they simultaneously serve to control the instinctual drives and to promote adaptation to the external world. Anticipating the concept of coping, he explains that adaptive behavior can serve not only personal ends or the goals of society but in the happiest instances may serve both simultaneously. The older person's knowledge of a bygone era provides him with an opportunity to enhance his self-esteem by contributing in a meaningful way to his present society. This group of subjects seemed best adjusted to senescence. They showed no evidence of depression or excessive denial.

In primitive societies the reminiscences of older men provided the main link between the past and the present, contributing to a sense of group identity. Simmons (1946) emphasizes the importance of storytelling in the adaptation of the aged in primitive societies:

> Another popular and very common function of the aged in primitive societies is storytelling, a pastime that serves a threefold purpose of entertainment, instruction and admonition. Anyone who enjoys modern facilities for entertainment can hardly appreciate the enviable position held by the old men and women of primitive societies who have an ample supply of interesting legends and tales. They are almost invariably in great demand and profit thereby. Among preliterate people memory is the only repository of knowledge, skills and rituals. There are unlimited examples of the role of the aged as custodians of folk wisdom [p. 82]. . . . Few conclusions concerning the aged in primitive societies can be made with greater confidence than that they are generally regarded as the custodians of knowledge par excellence and as the chief instructors of their people [p. 83].

[74]

From this description it is abundantly clear that the function of reminiscing was even more adaptive in nonliterate societies. Modern society, with its sophisticated means of communication and the breakdown of sharp lines of group identification, has contributed to a decreasing respect for the storytelling function of older people.

Simmons (1946, pp. 88-90) also describes the relationship between respect for the aged and the belief in magic in primitive societies. "The respect for the aged rested in large degree on their shamanistic powers both to cure disease and to return as angry spirits in retaliation for neglect or disrespect by the younger generation. The aged who relate legends often embellish them to enhance references to their own power, and primitive legends often have the theme of calamity befalling youth who disrespect their elders" (pp. 88-90). The development of science in modern society has further contributed to the decline of the influence of the aged by robbing them of their roles as medicine men. Simmons concludes: "The properties of the elderly who remain active, productive and essential in primitive societies is much higher than in advanced civilization for they succeeded much better in providing cultural conditions which utilize the services of their older people, giving them greater opportunities to be regarded as assets" (p. 94).

The advances of science and modern methods of communication have contributed to a decreasing respect for reminiscing behavior in the aged. With the steadily increasing numbers of aged in our modern society, it seems essential that we find new ways to provide opportunities for them to contribute their knowledge of the past. Anxious relatives sometimes discourage reminiscing behavior within the family group because they consider it a sign of deterioration in their loved ones. It would appear, quite to the contrary, that this behavior should be encouraged; we should create occasions for older people to reminisce and not expect their reminiscences to conform to the standards of accuracy of historical texts.

The last group of subjects was clinically depressed. Statistical results suggested a tendency for the depressed group to reminisce less than the nondepressed group, and analysis of the interviews bears out this trend. Depressed subjects showed the greatest difficulty in reminiscing. Their excursions into the past were interrupted repeatedly by anxiety and concern about their physical health, failing memory, personal losses, and sense of inadequacy. They seemed to have given up hope and to have lost self-esteem.

It will be recalled that a follow-up of all subjects one year after the completion of all interviews revealed the surprising fact that three of the four rated as depressed had died, four of the five rated as suspected of depression had died, and only one of the 16 rated as not depressed had died. An explanation that immediately suggested itself was that most of the depressed subjects, although they had not appeared so, must have been severely ill physically at the time of interviewing, a condition that would account for both their depression and their subsequent death. In the hope of clarifying this possibility, the investigators reviewed the dates and causes of death in the eight subjects who had died and found that only one had died within a year of the interview (five months later) and, as it happened, he was the one who had been rated as not depressed. The average time that elapsed between interview and death was 21 months, and the causes of death were varied. These subjects were not close to death at the time of interview, and it is thus unlikely that their depression was secondary to a terminal physical illness.

[76]

Relationship of Reminiscing to Mourning

We know that an essential part of normal grief consists of repetitive recollections of the lost object. In discussing the normal process of mourning, Freud (1917) describes the reactions to the loss of a loved person or the loss of some abstraction as characterized by the loss of interest in the outside world insofar as it does not recall the lost object; the temporary loss of capacity to adopt a new object; and the turning from every active effort that is not connected with thoughts of the lost object. "It is easy to see that the inhibition and circumscription in the ego is the expression of an exclusive devotion to its mourning which leaves nothing over for other purposes and other interests." This description of the working through of a personal loss emphasizes preoccupation with the past as it pertains to the lost object. It implies that the process of mourning is adaptive, eventually working through the loss, and differs from melancholia in that there is no loss of self-esteem. Freud describes the adaptive purpose of mourning in terms of the struggle to withdraw libido from objects realistically perceived as no longer existing. "Each single one of the memories and hopes which bound the libido to the object is brought up and hypercathected and the detachment of the libido from it thereby accomplished." A strong similarity between mourning and reminiscing is suggested by this description. The attempt of the ego to cope with loss through repeated recollections, the absorption of the self in this process, the relative lack of interest in the present—these elements are all characteristic of reminiscing behavior. Perhaps the relative absence in senescence of new objects for cathexis extends the mourning process beyond that seen in normal grief. The absence of reminiscing in our depressed subjects resembles the absence of mourning in the interrupted grief reaction.

[77]

SUMMARY

Reminiscing appears to be a complex organized mental activity operating under the control of the ego and varying with personality structure. It is positively correlated with successful adaptation to old age and appears to foster adaptation through maintaining self-esteem, reaffirming a sense of identity, working through and mastering personal losses, and contributing positively to society.

This paper has suggested the similarity of reminiscing to the normal adaptive processes of fantasy and mourning and to the traditional storytelling role of old people in primitive societies.

We have speculated on factors in senescence which favor reminiscing. The findings of this study indicate that reminiscing is not directly related to intelligence or to intellectual deterioration and suggest that it is positively related to freedom from depression and to personal survival.

The apparent contribution of reminiscing to successful adaptation to senescence calls for more active research; it also has therapeutic implications which suggest that our modern society should attach more significance to reminiscing and provide more opportunity for its legitimate expression.

Denial as a Social Act

AVERY D. WEISMAN, M.D.
AND THOMAS P. HACKETT, M.D.

A GENERATION HAS ELAPSED SINCE Anna Freud (1936) first demonstrated how everyday clinical observations of psychoanalytic patients could be understood as defense mechanisms. This conclusion allowed her to bring clinical data into closer relationship with the theoretical issues propounded by Sigmund Freud in his metapsychological studies. Although she recognized ten distinct "mechanisms," she dealt almost exclusively with the prototype mechanism, *denial*. In so doing, she also accepted the familiar formulation which asserts that the ego's efforts to contend with instincts, reality, and conscience may produce anxiety and that extensive use of denial is an antecedent phase of defenses against anxiety.

Before Anna Freud, the study of the ego and its efforts to contain danger from outside and to control anxiety from inside had a history at least as old as psychoanalysis itself. Her

Although Dr. Hackett was not a participant in the Panel, the conclusions of this article are based upon data which he and Dr. Weisman collected during their study of *Death and the Denial of Death,* a project supported in part by the Foundations Fund for Research in Psychiatry (62-247). Their findings will be reported more completely in a monograph now in preparation.

contribution was unique, however, not only because it was unusually lucid, but for two other reasons. First, she brought the attention of psychoanalysts back to the germinal "first phase" of ego psychology, as Rapaport (1959) terms it, and, secondly, her conclusions were based upon actual observations of children under more or less pathological conditions. Thus, by turning to source material and away from questionable, unverifiable generalizations, she demonstrated that denial is not simply a negation of an objective reality, but is really something that people may *do* in order to contend with a potential danger. Although it was apparent from her description that various types of denial were used for the avoidance of objective pain and objective danger, clear exposition demanded that she examine each type of denial under more or less isolated conditions. Consequently, although she pointed out that defense mechanisms could become obsolescent, be modified, or be replaced in the course of development, she described their operation as though it were based largely upon a fixed inner mechanism. As a result, even today, many clinicians continue to regard denial as a mechanism which can be set into action almost independently of other factors in the system. Some of these unspecified factors include (1) the context in which denial occurs, (2) the object denied, (3) the purpose of the denial, (4) the implications of the denied reality, (5) the form or vehicle of the denial, and (6) the subsequent fate of the remaining "undenied" portion of the cognitive and emotional field. In short, clinicians still tend to speak about denial as if it were an unambiguous fact that is open to public inspection, and they often overlook the complexities of what we call the *act of denying*.

Since the publication of what could have been called *The Ego and the Mechanisms of Denial*, clinicians have expanded the concept of denial so that it now covers almost any situation in which patients avoid direct confrontation with reality—at least with that reality which their physicians deem to be relevant. In his *Psychoanalysis of Elation,* Lewin, (1950, p. 51ff.) describes denial as a major component of the "pleasure ego." This idea implies that in order to achieve pleasure, strong denial is imperative. In our opinion, Lewin's major contribution to the study of denial has been to link avoidances with mood-enhancing experiences and to associate elation with fantasied acts of eating, sucking, sleeping, and dying. He assumes that the patient who truly experiences manic delight is one who believes that he feasts again at his mother's breast, and, having done so, slips into the oblivion of dreamless death. Although this image may be a prototype for denying reality, it is questionable that the "oral prototype" helps to clarify denial as a process.

Fenichel (1945, 1953, 1954) discovered denial in diverse, protean forms of psychopathology: in schizophrenia and fetishism, in memory defects and anxiety spells, in sleep and seizures, in symptoms of practically every kind. According to his view, wherever unwelcome ideas and threatening emotions are found, there too is denial.

Although many other psychoanalysts have written about denial, they have usually concentrated upon the metapsychology, a term which indicates that actual clinical situations are to be subsidiary to more theoretical discussions. The *concept* of denial usually has been invoked to explain a heterogenous group of clinical events. Having done so, clinicians then tend to abandon discussion, as if the *process* of denial needed no further elucidation.

There is little wonder that denial and repression have so often been linked (Jacobson, 1957). Because repression acts to inhibit potentially disruptive internal forces and denial acts to protect against potentially destructive external forces, the two have often been treated as if they were analogous and irreducible units of psychic behavior—an attitude which may stultify further understanding. Although denial and repression permeate many of our acts and attitudes, their components are still obscure. A similar obscurity exists with regard to other mental functions, such as memory. While we all agree that memory is an important *fact* of mental life, few would agree that the *act of remembering* is a unitary mental function. Before the process called memory can be fully understood, factors such as registration, storage, scanning, and retrieval of information need to be clarified. So it is with denial and repression, each of which has its subconcepts and auxillary processes.

In a recent series of sophisticated papers, a group of child psychiatrists, teachers, and therapists, led by Furman (Barnes, 1964; Furman, 1964a, 1964b; McDonald, 1964), has extended the approach pioneered by Anna Freud. They documented and described the responses of two young children to their mother's death, and, in the process, clarified the social context in which this event occurred. The attitudes of classmates, teachers, and relatives were carefully delineated. Although much of the actual behavior and affective responses were reported in the idiom of denial, the process of adaptation was not attributed to the unassisted operation of an internal psychic mechanism called "denial." In the context of complementary responses of everyone who interacted with the children, the *affirmative* aspect of grieving and coming to terms with irrevocable loss emerged with unusual clarity. Moreover, the reports of these investigators demonstrated anew that to regard denial as a mechanism is to ignore the exquisitely human, adaptive purposes which are simultaneously being served.

Denial can be studied more readily in children because their way of managing distress is more demonstrative and less convoluted than is that of adults. Defensive operations of adults are usually snarled with negations, circumlocutions, and complexities imposed by different kinds of character styles. In fact, under everyday circumstances, the subtleties of an adult's predominant defenses are often difficult to detect. As a result, the terms that we use to designate individual defenses are deceptively oversimplified, terse slogans. These, in turn, may often be interpreted as literal descriptions of what occurs in nature. Terminology may obscure the dynamic manifold that typifies mental life. The unity of any event may be the result of *unifying* processes, but not of *unitary* processes. Psychic processes draw together many kinds of experience, as Whitehead (1925) implied, just as any event has a past, a present, and a future. When, therefore, we attempt to describe heterogenous events only according to their overall defensive or adaptive significance, we may also force them into categorical pigeonholes, and then treat the compartment as equivalent to its contents. Even such familiar defensive operations as "sour grapes," "rationalization," "masochistic surrender," "reversal of passive into active," "identification with the aggressor," and so forth, require extensive revision, review, and reduction of information simply to be recognized. For example, a woman patient was habitually friendly, modest, and encouraging to her friends when they were distressed, and apparently was willing at all times to undergo sacrifices for the benefit of others. She was devoted to her husband, who had turned to her for both advice and financial support during the early years of their marriage. His business ventures finally succeeded, but he still relied upon her advice and support—a fact that gave her as much pride as when she was consulted by her friends. One of her outstanding traits was an unflagging optimism; she could find goodness in practically every situation, and never, to her recollection, had she even been irked when people mistreated her and abused her generosity. Although her assets, in fact, were admirable, the patient became periodically depressed. Under these circumstances, it became clear that her customary optimism also served as a defensive operation. From this point of view, the patient was a "Pollyanna"—a rubric for one who is extravagantly liable to find good in everything. This example is significant because the Pollyanna defense did not become apparent until the patient got into trouble. When she became depressed, and reported how she had never been angry despite frequent disappointments, provocations, and betrayals, and, in the course of psychotherapy, disclosed how she had used her "good deeds" to pressure people into doing what she wanted them to do, the complexities of her Pollyanna character were revealed. In fact, her "helpfulness" often involved undermining a person in order to effect a rescue.

Psychiatrists are familiar with the various inhibitions and avoidances that prompt people to shun many ordinary situations and to withdraw from everyday activities. When patients recognize their own inner restrictions, or become painfully aware of their inappropriate emotional responses, their complaints are called *symptoms*. But symptoms can also serve defensive purposes, and certain traits are defensive measures against inner conflict, even if patients do not complain about them. Character traits may be regarded as *strategies* by which a person can alter a particular social context, circumscribe a range of motivated action, or influence the behavior of other people. As in the above example, unless a patient gets into trouble, it is exceedingly difficult to appraise the psychodynamic significance of some of his more active defensive operations. Finally, in the flux of daily life our ordinary behavior

[84]

is so complex that it is almost arbitrary to single out one mode of behavior and decide that it alone is the predominant adaptive or defensive operation. At best, psychiatrists can only observe the way in which random events and responsible conduct shape themselves into general styles of voluntary action, habits, and idiosyncrasies. These fragmentary impressions are then stitched together by the psychiatrist with tenuous threads of inference about social context, interpersonal relationships, motivations, and values.

An ironic factor in determining how difficult it is to make absolute judgments about what patients really say or do is that the distinctive ingredient of our work, *emotion*, often slips through the net of our formulations. What we call affects —such as anger, sadness, fear, joy, and guilt—are often only extreme forms of emotion. In fact, the more diligently we search for the inner nature of another person, the more apparent it becomes that we track a quarry which has just left. To know another person in his totality means that we must be acquainted with the world he lives in, acts upon, conjures with, and, in short, creates. This is clearly an unending task. However sagacious our interpretations, they are only incomplete opinions about another person's strategies and motives.

By this prologue we dispute the tendency to see denial as an irreducible, unitary defense mechanism that people can call upon when all other means of contending with stressful events have been exhausted. The concept of denial as a separate mental mechanism is an oversimplification brought about by atomistic attempts to describe accurately the different ways in which behavior becomes intelligible. Of course there is nothing inherently wrong about *calling* some act or attitude *denial*, unless we are lulled into believing that further inquiry is unnecessary. Merely to state that denial *voids* potentially dangerous realities by *avoiding* their perception is both true and tautological. Such a statement confuses the *process* of denial with its *purpose*. Moreover, it does not indicate how denial may be related to other defensive operations or psychological processes.

When an immediate reality is too immense, people may withdraw and try to avoid further contact with it. If actual physical withdrawal is not feasible, they may alter the shape of the threat by substituting more congenial and less threatening interpretations of what the event signifies. Denial, therefore, does not merely avoid. Although the *negative* aim of denial is to increase the distance between a perception and the person who perceives a threat in the object perceived, there are other aims, served by related acts which have predominantly *positive* goals. After all, the broadest interpretation of human purpose is that we seek to bring about change while preserving integrity, to gather fulfillment while eluding danger, and to insure that any change is for the better.

Despite its familiarity, the phrase "using denial" is misleading. It implies that denial is a mechanism which can be counted on to respond in a fairly predictable way to an appropriate stimulus, much as a spinal reflex may be elicited. But even were the analogy correct, the spinal reflex itself is not an isolated mechanism. It is a schematic abstraction from the nervous system as a whole. Similarly, although denial may be one purpose among many served by a hierarchy of mental functions, it is not "used," but rather *is* a use or a result of numerous acts that have a variety of other uses and results. Weinstein and Kahn (1955, pp. 124-125) studied denial associated with various types of brain damage. They concluded that changes in brain function tended to alter the *patterns* in which symbolic expressions of denial occurred, but did not

[86]

alter the *elements* which enter into the process of denial. In other words, disorganization of cerebral function can bring about gross forms of denial, such as delusion and disorientation. But, even so, a strong factor of reintegrative and adaptive purpose always persists. In effect, what clinicians tend to call denial is derived from many levels of biological, social, and personal operations. It is a highly incomplete *version* of a series of purposeful acts which may be both aversive and appetitive (Weisman, 1959). There are many ways in which man can qualify his aversions, avoid the potentially painful, and repudiate his perceptions. In doing so, however, he can also strengthen his quest for fulfillment and fortify his appetites. For example, a man who makes a sexual fetish of female shoes will shun an undressed woman, but prefer her shoes. Despite the ostensible denial of certain basic features of the woman's anatomy or of her personality, the man finds his way to her and to sexual fulfillment through the intermediary of an inanimate object with which both he and she have had contact. It is unfortunate that in describing sexual perversions like this one we tend to underscore only the deviant form in which the appetite is expressed. We do not emphasize the kind of aversion that the perverse behavior represents, although perversions may be considered as strategies of the ego and forms of denial. In a parallel sense, a scientist who ignores some data and emphasizes others in order to further his pet theories may be expressing his aversions by denying potentially painful perception of damaging data. This process even can be diagnosed as a kind of intellectual perversion.

On the whole, defenses are generalizations based on what individual patients do and do not do and on what they say and do not say under a variety of circumstances. Defense mechanisms are the *generic properties* of a panorama of

[87]

diverse acts which seem to have similar effects. For example, the defense mechanism called *repression* is the aversive property of a set of different kinds of acts in which forgetting is a key element and recollecting brings about anxiety. Different kinds of defenses, such as *reversal of affect, displacement,* and *reaction formation,* are named according to the explanation which is postulated to account for the relationship between different acts. These acts are thought to share a common motivation, and different defense mechanisms are proposed to explain how transmutation and transformation occur between one form and another.

What, then, is denial, and how shall we speak of it? Denial is not a mechanism among other mechanisms; it is a *process* and a *product* emerging from other processes and products—symbolic and literal—that *affirm* what a person is or would like to be in a particular context. Nor is denial concerned solely with external perceptions. The over-all *purpose* of denial is to alter the meaning of events within a social field. One of its over-all *effects* is to preserve a pre-existing relationship. By word, attitude, or deed, denial is a readily available way to reassert control, to forestall threats, and to maintain a favorable version of reality. Patients do not deny reality once and for all, nor do they resolve problems by denying them. Although each of us may find it necessary to avoid certain situations, we must also either carry out our objectives by alternative means or find alternative objectives.

The public world of reality is as much created as contended with. If a man changes the meaning of events and then acts according to his new version, he also expects to share this new meaning with others. When his new version conflicts with the version held by others, however, they often say that he "denies reality" or is "unrealistic." On the other hand, if his new version still falls within the accepted norm or conventional meaning of events, outside observers may overlook the less conspicuous ways in which he violates or denies accepted, public meanings. For example, a 45-year-old man with chest pain believed that he was suffering from cancer of the lung. He did not consult a physician, but continued to work until the pain became intolerable. Because the patient had chosen to accept a pessimistic version of reality, it would be difficult to believe that he showed denial at this stage of his illness. Indeed, if the avowed purpose of denial is to insure survival and to reassert mastery by changing the meaning of threatening events, this patient did not appear to be denying his painful predicament. Nevertheless, after an extensive workup, it was discovered that the patient's father and two older brothers had died of coronary thrombosis and that the patient himself had suffered from repeated anginal attacks. His belief that he had cancer was therefore based upon a denial of what he had perceived to be coronary thrombosis, and his reluctance to consult a physician was related to fear of having this diagnosis confirmed. From his point of view, it was preferable to live and work with a supposed diagnosis of cancer than with a diagnosis of coronary thrombosis, which he considered to be a mandatory and imminent death sentence.

This patient illustrates how denial may be only one phase of a protracted strategy whereby a patient changes the meaning of different events in order to maintain a measure of control over what happens to him.

While we advocate a *dynamic interpretation of denial,* some investigators prefer a more atomistic point of view in which significant variables either are excluded or assumed to be constant. This view may be termed the *static interpretation of denial.* Among the assumptions made under the static interpretation are the following:

[89]

1. What a patient says or does at any given moment is both constant and objective. This assumption means that the patient may be expected to deny the same thing in the same way to anyone else. It also means that what he expresses at the time of evaluation is both typical of the patient and unrelated to the interviewer and his means of obtaining information.

2. Facts and objects in the public field of perception have a normative range of meaning, and substantial deviation from their accepted meaning is evidence of denial. Thus, it follows that when the denied reality is replaced by another version, the *degree of deviation* from the normative meaning will determine whether, in the observer's opinion, the patient has merely erred in judgment or is suffering from a delusion.

3. Patients are always able to report their feelings accurately, so that their statements can be judged literally according to a norm.

The static and dynamic interpretations of denial share an assumption that there is a range of meaning within which people can talk about objects and events belonging to a common social field. Ultimately, our judgment about what constitutes denial depends on the difference between another person's *negative* report and our own *positive* perception of common objects and meanings. This fact is characteristic of both kinds of interpretation. The static interpretation is greatly oversimplified, however, in that it reintroduces the mechanistic point of view, and denial becomes merely an exercise in correcting misperceptions—a task which resembles a "true and false" examination about reality. From the static point of view, a person who says, "true," when we, the outside observers, believe that a statement or perception is false, may be thought to be mistaken. Unless his declaration deviates so widely from the norm that it violates our canons of reality, he is usually judged to be capable of revising his report and correcting his misperception. If, on the other hand, he rejects our judgment of what is true and, instead, calls it "false," we will often say that he denies reality. Nevertheless, just as a man who resists revising his report will confirm our judgment that he is denying, it is possible for us, the observers, to be so unrealistically confident about our own judgment that anyone who disagrees with us is alleged to be denying.

The dynamic interpretation of denial emphasizes the *process* of denial because it heeds the content, the operation, and the occasion—the *what,* the *how,* and the *when*—in which denial occurs. We recognize two aspects of the process of denial. These may be termed the *act of denying* and the *fact of denial.* The crucial distinction is that the *act of denying* arises from one person, while the *fact of denial* is a *judgment made by another* person about that act.

It is rare for a man to deny in utter solitude. One of the confusing products of dealing with denial as an unequivocal, intrapsychic mechanism is that it is then viewed primarily as an isolated event and is not seen in the social context wherein it arises. As a rule, we declare our aversions in order to forestall isolation and abandonment, to maintain our personal image against disfigurement, and to prevent victimization by alien forces. Even though we may be unaware of it, our intention when we deny something is usually to influence someone else.

There are *four steps in the act of denying* a common reality, or a shared knowledge. First, there must be an initial *acceptance* of a mutual field of perception. It is necessary not only that people be able to communicate but that they talk about the same things. Second, a portion of the available, common meaning is altered or avoided. This step is one of *repudiation* of part of the shared reality. It may be conveyed by means of a statement, an act, a demonstrative affect, an interpretation, a fantasy, or any combination of these. Third, the repudiated meaning is then replaced, more or less extensively, with a more congenial meaning. As a result of this *replacement,* affirmative action is reinforced. Finally, there is a *reorientation* of the person who has survived—for the moment at least—a threat to his position within social and libidinal fields; once again he can maintain mutual interaction and familiar operations with others.

The *fact of denial* requires a fifth step: *the judgment by one person that another person has denied an event within their common reality.* People do not know when they have denied a reality, except in retrospect. To them, any act—even one of avoidance or repudiation—is affirmative, because it is designed to carry out an inner program of effective performance.

Whenever we judge that another person's act is one of denial, we may also communicate to him that we dispute the reality of his affirmations, as well as of his avoidances. This is a crucial step, because it may become the basis for still other acts of denial. Acts which deny another person's reality may propagate an entire series of related and escalated denials compounded of our own wishes, fears, fantasies, and affirmations.

The fact of denial forces us to examine the unspecified factors on which the act of denying depends. As noted earlier, some of these factors include the context of denial, the object denied, the purpose of the denial, the implications of the denied reality, the form or vehicle of the denial, and the fate of the "undenied" portion of the cognitive and emotional field. It is not enough to declare without qualification that another person is intransitively denying. Instead, we must be able to assert, "He—repudiates—this reality—to me—here in this place—now—and replaces it—with something else." This statement is then open to searching questions. Why does he not recognize this portion of our common reality? On what basis do *I* judge him? What will he do with the reality that he has replaced?

Those who deny tacitly ask us to accept their modified version of an event, *A,* and to believe that *A* is not *A*. In fact, patients often want us to believe that *A* is *B*. Many patients with coronary thrombosis, for example, refuse to believe that they have had a heart attack. Even after their physician demonstrates how ill they have been, and shows them every conceivable piece of evidence for heart disease, some patients adamantly will preserve an attitude of strategic disbelief. "Maybe the doctor made a mistake," or, "Doctors don't tell you everything," may mean, "I doubt everything that doctors say and do." One man, 24 hours after the onset of severe chest pain, still had not called his family physician. Instead, he telephoned another doctor who 12 years previously had mistakenly said that his wife was suffering from "nerves," whereas she had died of a cerebral hemorrhage a few hours later. The patient had not spoken to this doctor since his wife's death and called him now only because he was sure that the diagnosis of "only nerves" would again be made. Another man, who had already experienced heart attacks, sustained severe chest pain while eating a large dinner in a restaurant, went into the men's room, and collapsed. He kept repeating to a physician, "I'm all right—it's just indigestion—I'll be all right in a few minutes!" This man acted as though he always went into the men's room and sprawled out on the floor when he had indigestion.

[93]

These examples are of patients who have managed to conceal from themselves the facts of life-threatening illness. There are other people who may believe so firmly in the reality and truth of their own ideas that anyone else's deviation or dissent may be construed as a personal rejection. The *content* of a denial may represent merely a short-lived and limited avoidance during moments of stress, or it may represent a lasting distortion of a person's entire perception of himself and of the world.

When psychiatrists speak about a patient's denial, they usually refer to his refusal to accept another version of a shared reality. Such refusal may be termed *cognitive denial,* provided that the autonomy and separate existence of the other person is never in question. Cognitive denial is an interpersonal event by means of which a relationship can still be maintained. Denial may be so extensive, so dogmatic, and so determined by inner necessity, however, that the judgment that someone else is "wrong" actually becomes a repudiation of that person. In our previous examples, the patients expressed only cognitive denial. After all, they did seek help from someone, even though they were not prepared to accept the diagnosis of heart disease. But for some people denial may become a way of life. Amanda, in *The Glass Menagerie,* distorted her everyday life according to images she had carried over from the past, and by doing so repudiated the autonomous reality of her son and daughter. Her act of denying, in other words, ceased at the step we have called *repudiation.* The denied realities were not replaced with more constructive meanings, and a disabling social and emotional situation was perpetuated rather than corrected. We suggest that this kind of predicament—which invokes egregious self-deception —be called *ontological denial* because the denial of a common

[94]

reality goes beyond the repudiation of the reality and becomes a more drastic *act of repudiating another person*. Amanda repudiated the reality of her son and daughter, except as figments of her fantasies. Her attempts at replacement and reorientation were minimal. She could doubt and avoid, refuse to listen, and rebuke, but when she denied the fact of her children's version of themselves and of their mutual plight, she challenged their existence, not merely their perceptions.

Bullies, braggarts, and bigots are specialists in ontological denial: they attempt to destroy another person's autonomy simply because they feel challenged by his dissenting version of reality. Those who perpetrate ontological denial do not tolerate the independent acts of other people. A bigot will not merely dispute the validity of the protests of Negroes; he will deny the reality of individual Negroes as human beings who are capable of wanting and using freedom.

Interpretation of denial as a social process implies that there are different levels of denial, just as there are different levels of affirmative values and affirmations. Haley (1963) has demonstrated how significant communication during psychotherapy can be affirmed at one level and contradicted completely on another. These interpersonal factors become especially relevant when we study the different ways in which patients come to terms with imminent, inevitable, or threatened death.

For the past few years, we have been investigating patients in different life and death crises who have shown an extraordinary ability to turn away from the more fearsome facts of their plight (Hackett and Weisman, 1962; Weisman and Hackett, 1962). These studies have enormous practical value, because a patient who cannot acknowledge urgent issues of

[95]

life and death when directly confronted with them, by that fact alone, may jeopardize his treatment and his chances for survival. We have also realized that denial takes place in a particular social context, at a particular time, in a particular personal idiom, and for a particular purpose. For example, an experienced social worker reported that a middle-aged woman who suffered from terminal cancer had asked no questions about her illness and treatment when she was admitted to the hospital. In fact, the patient seemed more concerned about her husband's duodenal ulcer than with her own symptoms. Although she talked readily about her domestic problems, she seemed serenely unaware that she was seriously, even terminally, ill. Her first question to the psychiatric consultant was, however, "Is it true, Doctor, that Grade 3 carcinoma of the cervix is more malignant than Grade 1?" What prompted this woman to deny concern and to avoid discussing her disease with the social worker, but to disclose both to a psychiatrist whom she had never seen before? What factors —to revert to the old terminology—activated denial in one instance and suspended it in the other?

Another woman acknowledged concern about her fatal illness only to a casual acquaintance whose life would not be substantially affected by her death. Encounters with patients like these have prompted the hypothesis that one of the purposes of denying obvious facts and of mitigating the meaning of threatening events is to preserve a relationship with another person. What appears to be a sweeping rejection of facts may be an effective strategy whereby one person can be confronted with the facts while another is spared. As a rule, the attending physician is given only favorable, even innocently optimistic reports by his patient, whereas nurses, social workers, medical students, and occupational therapists may hear

[96]

more authentic information. A partial reason for this is that patients depend upon their physicians for hope and believe that a downhill course, coupled with failure to respond to treatment, will discourage their doctor, and he will then have nothing more to offer them.

Neither a patient's previous experience with illness nor his medical sophistication precludes denial. One apparently sophisticated man declared that, despite severe chest pain which the doctor diagnosed as a manifestation of heart disease, he could not be having another heart attack. He had followed his doctor's instructions punctiliously ever since a coronary thrombosis several years before, and had believed that his doing so would prevent a recurrence. Besides, he argued, at the time of his first attack pain in his left arm had extended down to his finger tips; this time the situation was entirely different because the pain went no further than his wrist.

Lest we be misunderstood, we should point out that the act of denying is not wholly a social strategy. In fact, there are *three dimensions of denial*—biological, personal, and social. Each is related to the others much as the dimensions of space and time are related to each other. Although different clinical situations are apt to be polarized according to one dimension, such as the biological, the other two dimensions will also be represented. For example, some patients who are right-handed and sustain injury to the right cerebral hemisphere will be unable to recognize the ensuing disability on their left side. This condition, called *anosognosia* (Weinstein and Kahn, 1955), probably results from impaired synthesis of various perceptual cues due to lesions in higher thalamic and parietal centers (Denny-Brown, 1958). Patients afflicted with anosognosia frequently will deny paralysis on the disabled side, and, in some cases, will even deny that the paralyzed limbs belong

[97]

to them. In addition to denying disease, some patients will also confabulate about their social situation, the circumstances of their illness, and their personal attitude toward being ill. One month before she was to be married, a 22-year-old woman sustained a left hemiparalysis as a result of a ruptured intracranial aneurysm. The wedding, of course, was postponed, but her fiancé became more and more reluctant to undertake marriage with someone who, in all likelihood, would be chronically incapacitated. During the recovery period the patient not only denied her paralysis, but went even further and talked as though she were already married, pointing to a nonexistent wedding band on the ring finger of her left hand.

Personal and social dimensions of denial, as a rule, are most apparent during the acute phase of a potentially disabling illness. Olin and Hackett (1964) found among patients with acute myocardial infarctions that delay in seeking treatment may be related to an initial misinterpretation of chest pain. Even when a patient has had considerable experience with coronary thrombosis because of previous attacks, or has lost close relatives from it in the recent past, he frequently will minimize his early symptoms or find ingenious but incorrect explanations for his pain. During the recovery period some patients persist in rejecting the seriousness of their illness, or, indeed, the heart attack itself.

A colleague who knew a great deal about heart disease suddenly developed severe pain in his left shoulder while walking along the beach during his vacation. He thought to himself, "I must have bursitis," and, cradling the painful arm, continued to walk. His wife insisted upon calling the local physician later in the afternoon when his pain persisted. Not until the physician took the blood pressure cuff out of his bag did it suddenly occur to him, "Good God! I may have had a heart attack!"

During acute medical and surgical emergencies, patients seldom voice a fear of death, although they may allude to the significance of persistent chest pain, shortness of breath, agitated concern shown by members of their family, and having Last Rites. A 61-year-old woman developed chest pain, shortness of breath, and incipient loss of consciousness before coming to the emergency ward 24 hours after the onset of her symptoms. She conceded that she "probably had had a small heart attack." When asked about being worried, she promptly denied any concern about survival. "Oh, I wasn't worried about myself. Dying was the very last thing I thought of—I just wanted to go quickly!"

Patients fear death when threatened with abandonment, isolation, and loneliness, but, in general, they are not afraid of death when they are in imminent danger of dying, unless dying also entails *incapacity plus loss of familiar relationships*. An elderly widow was brought to the hospital by the police after she had called a neighbor to say that she was ill. Although suffering from an extensive myocardial infarction, she denied serious concern about dying. Within the first 24 hours, she reported a dream in which there was an empty grave. Years before she had lost an infant son as a result of diphtheria. In describing her dream, the patient said that the empty grave was to be hers, and added that there was also an empty coffin in that grave. She was perplexed because the empty coffin also seemed to be her son's. While the full significance of her dream may be unclear, we can hardly dispute that the patient was more concerned about dying than she was able to acknowledge and that her fantasy of death included a reunion with her son and therefore a triumphant survival.

We have met patients frequently whose first comments, after being told that they have cancer, have harked back to earlier incapacities or to recollections of lost relationships. One man began to talk of having been unable to find work during the depression of the early 1930's and of having been ashamed when his family had to be supported by welfare agencies. He now wanted to spare his family further pain and looked upon his prospective death as another way in which he had failed them. A young woman seemingly ignored the urgency of her rapidly growing carcinoma of the breast. Instead, she talked about her mother, who had died when the patient was in her early teens. She wondered wistfully how different her life would have been if her mother had lived. A middle-aged man with cancer of the lung recalled how he had disappointed his father when he flunked out of college and then left home. He was troubled that now he would also disappoint his own children, because he was no better as a father than he had been as a son.

Some patients develop intense fears of death in circumstances that are related to being spared from death. A 45-year-old truck driver had survived many months of active combat during World War II and had been discharged after fracturing several vertebrae in a jeep accident. During a storm 20 years later, his truck went off the road and turned over. He was trapped in the cab, covered with motor oil, and, believing it to be blood, he panicked. Although he was quickly rescued, the patient thereafter was never able to dismiss a persistent fear of death and of imminent disaster. He also developed a painful contracture of his right hand which made truck-driving impossible. When we saw this man, who had vigorously denied worry about being killed during wartime, he had become a chronic invalid primarily because of his fear of death. Although there was much about this patient's history that was unknown, it was clear that previously he had

survived far greater dangers without developing either con-
version symptoms or fear of death.

Another patient who developed an intractable fear of death
after being spared from death was a 36-year-old mother of
two children. She had had three symptom-free years following a hysterectomy for carcinoma of the cervix. Throughout
this time, however, she had many hypochondriacal preoccupations. When doctors told her they found no tangible evidence of recurrent carcinoma, she thought they were deceiv-
ing her. She examined herself for subtle changes in appearance—swollen glands, abdominal distention, and so forth.
Despite absence of physical distress, she was convinced that
death was certain and that she was being duped. In the course
of psychotherapy, it was discovered that her persistent psychiatric complaints were associated not with her cancer, but
with the loss of her mother. Ten years before, her mother had
died of cerebral hemorrhage, but the patient had never fully
accepted this fact. Her denial was so intense that she kept her
mother's clothes still hanging in the closet, ready to be used
when her mother "returned." She explained to her young
daughters that an angel had come and had spirited their
grandmother away. She told her story so vividly that one of
the daughters developed a fear of kidnappers. In short, the
patient believed that death was a kind of heavenly imprison-
ment and that sooner or later the hostage would be released.
Belief in her mother's ultimate return was neither a psychotic
symptom nor an article of religious faith. She was wholly
aware of the irrationality of her convictions, but she could
not release herself from the embrace of her mother and from
her painful grief at having been abandoned. The patient
had been excessively attached to her possessive mother and
had refused to marry until her husband promised to take

care of her mother. She demonstrated, by word, act, fantasy, interpretation, and affect, that denial as a social act can be extremely persistent. The apparent cure of cancer spared her life, but intensified her conflicts about her mother's death. She feared both death and survival; her preoccupation with being deceived seemed to be related to the disbelief she had felt in the past, when physicians had told her that her mother was really dead.

Denial of the imminence of death sometimes takes the form of one final human affirmation, such as a positive gesture of independence. A 46-year-old man, who had been thoroughly acquainted with his hopeless prognosis from the onset of his illness, stated during his final hours that he still expected to be an old man. Whether we call this regression or denial, the fact is that it occurred in the recognized presence of death. He had guarded his independence militantly during long months of progressive incapacity. From time to time he demonstrated various forms of denial, but only in circumstances which threatened him with hopeless and helpless dependence upon others. For example, after a relatively tranquil, even hopeful, period was shattered by an unexpected pathological fracture, the patient was reproached by a physician for needing regular doses of narcotics. He interpreted this remark as an accusation that he was too dependent. This reproach occurred at a time when he was also no longer able to provide funds to buy food for his children. He responded by lapsing into dreamlike, unrealistic fantasies and plans for a future that would never come.

Despair may be brought out by circumstances surrounding the experience of dying rather than by the imminence of death itself. A young woman was pinned beneath her automobile following an accident. As she waited for the police to lift the car, she heard bystanders say that if they raised the automobile it might kill her. Her breathing then became more labored, and she began to expect death momentarily. But it was not the dread of dying and of never seeing her family again that tormented her. Instead she thought, "What a way to die! I never imagined I would die like this—what a mechanical, meaningless. . . ." There is a clue to be found here that is valuable in the psychiatric management of dying patients; dying patients can be helped to find some meaning in their death. To find a meaning in death, we believe, is of greater help to some patients than are mechanical aids to temporary survival.

The threat of death usually elicits its own denial. Even in the face of almost certain disaster, we may believe that we will be spared, either by some magical intervention or last-minute reprieve or simply because it is natural to think of ourselves as exceptions. The fear of dying is quite different from the dread of being dead. Dying is the ultimate in impairment of ego functions and in deprivation of human relationships. Death itself is an institutionalized concept that we must often be prodded into remembering, because we are so likely to forget it. How to take care of patients who are dying is a practical problem with so many factors that no glib psychological formula will solve it. We should realize, however, that "death agonies" are rarely observed in dying patients, and probably represent, to a large degree, derivatives of theological concern for lost souls. Saunders (1959) noted that, with sufficient medication to relieve pain, and a dignified appreciation of patients as people, dying can be accepted as an inevitable fact of life.

In many patients the fear of dying is less intense than other fears which they have experienced. A 52-year-old business-man became blind in his right eye as a result of thrombosis

[103]

of the central retinal artery. Two years later he sustained a severe myocardial infarction. Five years after that he developed the first symptoms of the cancer that would ultimately take his life. In addition to these grave and incapacitating illnesses, he had also been deeply depressed during the early stages of his eye disease. He believed that he had abandoned his family, that his wife had become insane, and that people avoided him because of a foul odor emanating from him. During his final days, before he actually succumbed to cancer, it was possible to talk with the patient about his many illnesses, and, in spite of his terminal state, to learn which had been the most frightening. Without hesitation, he said that the abrupt blindness in his right eye had been the most disabling. He was afraid that visual loss in one eye would shortly be followed by total blindness, and he was alarmed lest he become a helpless invalid. The melancholia that followed disrupted his life, and he despaired of ever returning to a productive existence. After so many years, however, he could scarcely recall the depth of that depression. Following the coronary thrombosis, he again became depressed, but did not feel hopeless, because he had known other men who had had similar attacks and had recovered. Later on, when he became aware of the unchecked invasion of cancer, he still clung to a remote hope that the diagnosis was incorrect. "After all, Doctor, they weren't at all sure what I had when I came in here. Maybe they're wrong now, too." This patient had survived several serious illnesses and now was dying, yet he maintained that his fears were greater in the presence of threatened blindness than in the presence of certain death. As if to verify this claim, his final days were painless, almost serene, as his life literally seeped away.

[104]

This man's case illustrates how denial need not be the central factor, nor does it necessarily determine the psychological management of the dying patient. The patient apparently experienced more fear in response to his blindness than to the threat of death, which he accepted with only tangential and transparent wishes that the physicians might be incorrect in their prognosis. Most of his final days were spent regretting that he would not see his oldest son graduate from college. Curiously enough, there was an illusory claim to survival which appeared in a few dreams, indicating that affirmation accompanied him to the brink of death.

We have proposed that denial is largely an interpersonal event, with, however, biological and personal components. No one can deny in isolation, and the over-all purpose of denial is often to stabilize and to define a relationship. This means that the *act of denying* will arise in the patient who seeks to establish the relationship; the *fact of denial* is a secondary judgment by an outside person. Moreover, we have distinguished between *cognitive denial* and *ontological denial*. Cognitive denial refers to modification of the meaning of a common reality. Ontological denial repudiates the reality of the other person in order to substantiate one's own beliefs and convictions. The difference between cognitive and ontological denial determines whether disputed decisions, differing perceptions, and alternative actions lead to reordered points of view or to permanent alienation. After all, a patient whose complaints defy our ability to explain them challenges our knowledge, but a person who denies our version of reality challenges us as human beings.

In less academic and more practical terms, there are two kinds of denial: denial *by* the patient and denial *of* the patient. The first—denial by the patient—has been the principal topic of the preceding discussion. But the second kind—denial of the patient—is a form of ontological denial that may arise in the physician and in anyone else who is charged with caring for the dying patient. It is brought about by abandonment, withdrawal, and loss of accessibility imposed by the living upon the dying. To be sure, there are few physicians who will abandon their patients knowingly when therapeutic efforts fail. It is wholly possible, however, for a doctor to observe the amenities of daily visits, to prescribe medication, and to treat complications while further increasing the emotional distance between himself and the patient. In other words, as the patient becomes less and less capable of autonomous decision, his physician may unwittingly tend to deny the patient's personal reality and to view him primarily as a biological unit or a sick organism. A physician may know a great deal about disease and death and still not want to know anything about how dying patients feel. It is also possible—indeed, it is frequently true—that physicians experience more despair about inevitable death than do their dying patients.

We have encountered the fear of dying more often among patients who are relatively well than among patients who are moribund (Weisman and Hackett, 1962). Gravely ill patients, once their pain has been adequately controlled, are more concerned about the severance of relationships and the indignity of dependence than they are about survival for its own sake. Consequently, when a physician, or any other responsible person, exerts unwarranted, unrealistic, and well-intentioned but ill-advised efforts to strengthen denial, he may impose greater suffering upon patients. Whenever a physician knows that he is deliberately circumventing a truth, and the patient knows it, too, there can be only one result: an emotional isolation even in the physical presence of each other. Although such a consequence occurs more often in the relationship between physician and patient, it is not limited to the medical milieu. In the presence of fatal illness, actual or implied, all human beings are caught up in crisis, conflict, and disease (Weisman and Hackett, 1962). Being only human, a physician may shun the dying patient, and, in so doing, deprive him of his distinct dignity and reality. Although a doctor's tendency to reinforce a patient's denial may be an expression of his own discouragement and impatience, it is not as serious as capitulating to the inevitable by abandoning the patient before his death.

All of these factors also apply to death as it occurs among aged patients. Although most aged patients do not eagerly anticipate death, neither are they afraid of death. It is not unusual, for example, to find some aged patients openly expressing envy of another patient who has died quietly and without complaint during sleep. In their earlier years, patients are naturally most concerned about serious or disabling illnesses, whereas those in middle years tend to be depressed about failure to achieve lifelong objectives. In contrast, aged patients seem to have come to terms with both of these problems. Many reasonably well-adapted patients in their 80's and 90's retain an interest in the events of the world, but derive more satisfaction from reminiscences (McMahon and Rhudick, 1964).

It is somewhat paradoxical to observe that whereas the very old are usually quite willing to talk about their remaining days, and to admit that these days are few, younger persons find it more difficult to acknowledge this fact when speaking with their elders. In other words, persons with many years of life ahead tend to be more afraid of death than are those on the threshold of death. Moreover, these younger persons may shrink from the reminiscences of the aged, and, in effect, deny the autonomy of the very old. Too often the elderly are not deemed capable of cogent, relevant observations about "today's world." Actually, today's world is always about the same, as far as human problems are concerned, and each generation seems to be no less baffled than the generation it succeeded. There are many ways in which the aged reach forward to younger persons, even while reaching backward to embrace bygone generations.

Isolation and abandonment may threaten aged patients, although fear of death is more intense in younger patients. One factor mitigating the fear of death in the aged is that incapacity and waning powers are already familiar to them. Partial loss of function, actual or implied, is usually more threatening than complete loss of a special function. This is true for both interpersonal and biological functions. On the whole, older people are threatened by loss of dignity and independence. Without these, an aged person then becomes an object or a statistic which fills a slot or a category, while experts talk about the "problem" of old age.

Weisman and Kastenbaum (data unpublished) have studied the social and emotional circumstances surrounding the death of aged persons in an institution. They have discovered that frequently an important personal loss has occurred in the weeks preceding a patient's final illness. For example, one fairly hearty man had anticipated a brief reunion with his sons and daughters on Thanksgiving Day. When the holiday arrived, no one called for him. He waited in vain, even for a word of explanation of why their promise was broken. Although he did not complain, neither did he resume his customary activities within the institution. Day after day he refused both food and drink, and it became increasingly difficult to mobilize him for ordinary hygienic care. His chronic respiratory ailment worsened, and, after a mild infection, he died.

Few older persons confuse longevity with rejuvenation, although most will agree that longevity is never long enough. Fewer still look for a magical undoing of past mistakes or for a second chance. Nevertheless, abiding interests usually continue unless secondary illnesses supervene. One nonagenarian spent his days reading books he had enjoyed in adolescence and young adulthood, rediscovering some of the pleasures he had forgotten during his working years. In contrast, men who have made their living as craftsmen or artisans rarely continue their work as an avocation or as a hobby. One explanation is that their pride in having achieved a high level of competence will not allow them to function at less than full capacity.

In summary, we are all victims of the common prejudice that death is always, under every circumstance, an evil. Consequently, despite the reassurances and fantasies of personal survival that some religions offer, death is still a bleak and inevitable fact to be avoided as long as possible. But if it were possible to live forever and to forestall death indefinitely, that might be an even greater evil. It has been said that before man opts for immortality, he ought to be sure about what he is getting into (Pelikan, 1961, p. 23).

We have proposed that denial, like illness and health, has its representatives in the biological, social, and personal dimensions of human existence—all of which may be overlooked by oversimplified interpretations of denial as a defense mechanism. The act and fact of denial is not a single unilateral event, designed to muffle the impact of unwelcome knowledge or imminent disaster. It is a social process in which avoidances are expressed in order to reaffirm and to revise familiar

[109]

versions of reality. In this sense denial is a social act which arises from the attempt to establish reciprocal communication between two people. Frequently the process of denial originates in one person, but, as a mutual strategy, it is encouraged by another person who feels the challenge that is presented. Crises that evoke denial are also capable of activating many kinds of defensive operations. These crises challenge a person to defend his integrity, to readjust dislocations of meaning, to stabilize his style of being, to reaffirm his status, to prevent agonies and anxieties, to restore subjective responsibility, and to renew his control (Weisman, 1965).

Unrestricted use of denial as a goal, without recourse to affirmation or other means of contending with stress, will not further these objectives. Actually, in coming to terms with death, single-minded denial will often interfere, and may even encourage isolation and abandonment. Unless physicians can face truth with their patients, patients will not be able to use truth. After all, how shall any of us contend with imminent disintegration? The answer to this question depends solely upon whether we recognize a genuine distinction between man, the mechanism, and man, the mortal.

The Physician and His Patient Who Is Dying

EDMUND C. PAYNE, JR., M.D.

To focus on the dying patient is entirely pertinent in a symposium devoted to aging. Although the dying patient is not necessarily an old person, the emotions surrounding death and dying are never far in the background in any consideration of aging. As people age, they are made more aware of death by the loss of the people in whom they have important emotional investments and by a growing appreciation that they are nearing the end of their own lives. In addition, the elderly are more likely to be among the patients who come to psychiatrists with the chronic, incurable diseases, such as heart disease and cancer, which have a fatal termination.

The observations that are to be discussed in this paper were made primarily in the setting of a tumor clinic in a general teaching hospital on patients with metastatic disease. The issues that are involved in a terminal illness are especially clear in patients with malignant disease. The course of metastatic cancer is sharply delineated. Although there may be fluctuations in the symptoms, in general there is implacable progression of the disease. It is not possible for the patient to escape from his knowledge of the disease, whether this knowledge is admitted to consciousness or is kept primarily on a preconscious level of denial. Thus, the nature of the dread inspired by the disease and by the prospect of death, the defenses used to cope with this fear, and the various stages that the patient passes through in his adaptation to dying stand out more sharply than under other circumstances. Although the course and nature of a particular illness influence the patterns of the emotional responses that we see in reaction to it, it is possible to extrapolate from the particular situation and to derive valid impressions of the significance of dying that apply to other situations.

As is true of all the major universal crises—such as puberty, aging, and loss—that are encountered by man, dying, when closely inspected, proves to have complex psychological accompaniments which reach into all areas of personality development and structure. The focus of this paper will be on only a few aspects of this general problem, especially the fear aroused by dying, the defenses that are especially prominent in meeting this fear, and the stages of adjustment that the dying patient passes through.

THE FEAR OF DYING

Most people experience intense fear when they realize that they are dying. This fear is seldom absent, although it is dealt with in different ways by patients with different character structures. An apparent exception is the reaction seen in acute, life-threatening situations. Persons involved in a dangerous accident, in mortal combat, or in a similar peril frequently report that they felt no fear during the period of danger, but instead felt only a clear alertness accompanied by highly efficient functioning. Such emergency situations, however, are commonly followed by a marked affective reaction, in which anxiety or its equivalents are discharged. The fear that would have been experienced ordinarily in such a situation is dealt with by the mechanism described by Edward Bibring (1953): "The anxiety which threatened to overwhelm the ego was blocked in statu nascendi, or 'bound' (anti-cathected) as long as the danger lasted, and liberated only when the danger subsided" (p. 28). This mechanism can be observed in many circumstances of life-threatening illness. For example, a man with an acute myocardial infarction may bind his anxiety not only during the initial period of the attack but throughout his hospitalization, only to experience a severe attack of anxiety when he leaves the protection of the hospital to return home. A similar mechanism undoubtedly operates in situations where a man deliberately meets his death rather than admit to cowardice (the admission of which unconsciously would represent passive surrender or the acceptance of castration) or sacrifices his life in the performance of an heroic act in the service of others. Then fear is bound by a massive anticathexis during the period of action. In these circumstances an additional factor that makes dying acceptable is the narcissistic recompense of acting in accord with strongly held ideals or the satisfaction of making a supreme gift to a cause or to a person who is loved. In most other cases, however, dying is accompanied by strong feelings of pain, anxiety, and distress.

The dread of dying is difficult for us to understand fully. We can say, "Who should not be afraid to die?" Or we can agree with Socrates:

> . . . either death is a state of nothingness and utter unconsciousness, or, as men say, there is a change and migration of the soul from this world to another. Now if you suppose that there is no consciousness, but sleep like the sleep of him who is undisturbed even by dreams, death

[113]

will be an unspeakable gain . . . for eternity is then only a single night. But if death is the journey to another place, and there, as men say, all the dead abide, what good, O my friends and judges, can be greater than this? [from the "Apology," *The Dialogues of Plato*].

Is the fear of dying a unique fear, a drawing back specific to the event, or is it a dread that originates in the developmental anxieties of our infancy? In order to answer this question, we have to consider not only observations of dying patients but also the development of the concept of death and of the fear of death from early childhood.

Of the psychological observations that have been made of children, relatively few studies have concerned themselves with the development of children's ideas of death. Among these few, observations by Anthony (1940) and Nagy (1959) stand out. In his own analysis of children's ideas of death, the author has used the case material published by Anthony and Nagy, although his conclusions may differ in some respects. Their material, which was obtained by questionnaires and by reports made by parents of their own observations of their children, is confirmed in many details by observations made in play sessions with children (Rochlin, 1963).

Anthony, who studied younger subjects than the other authors, demonstrates clearly that a stage exists with children in which they have no knowledge of death. These young children, usually aged two or three, are clearly puzzled when they encounter dead animals, such as poultry or game in a butcher's shop. They are unable to understand the changed state of these creatures from the active, responsive form in which they are accustomed to encounter them, and they ask many puzzled questions about them. An even more striking

[114]

example of the absence of knowledge of death is provided by a three-year and three-month-old girl whose mother had suddenly died while alone with the child. When the father returned home, he discovered that the child had peacefully curled up beside the mother. She reported: "Mother lay down upon the floor and went to sleep, so I went to sleep, too." This little girl had no understanding of death as a specific state or of its significance. She showed no instinctive recognition that her mother was dead, and her experience and the development of her concept of death were not adequate to the correct interpretation of this experience. Instead, she related her mother's closed eyes, immobility, and lack of responsiveness to the state of sleep, with which she was more familiar. Some degree of denial, defending against fear aroused by an appreciation of an unusual, ominous quality in her mother's condition, may also have been operative, without being the determining factor in her interpretation. Even though she could not immediately understand that her mother was dead, we can be sure that her concepts of death and sleep were both profoundly affected by this experience. We can predict that her ideas of death and dying were tightly bound to the painful emotions of loss, grief, and abandonment which must have accompanied her realization of the tragedy that had befallen her. The linking of sleep and death, common even without such a dramatic experience, could provide the nucleus for severe disturbance of sleep.

The first awareness of death as a definite and specific state usually develops between the ages of two and four, after speech is reliably established. The concept is usually formed around an explanation by the parents in response to questions by the child, and often in association with the child's experience with a dead or inanimate object. This development is

[115]

illustrated by a friend's description given to me of her child's discovery of death. Her two-year and four-month-old little girl became frightened that an African mask, the mouth and teeth of which were prominent, would bite her. Her mother explained that it could not hurt her because it was not alive. "What is *alive?*" was the child's question. After the mother's explanation, which pointed to some of the differences between living and inanimate objects, the little girl generalized this knowledge to other objects of her environment, and kept asking: "Is the bench alive? Is the fire alive?" Then she came to the question of death. One day, while having duck for dinner, she asked: "Is the duck alive?" The parents explained the concept of once alive, but no longer so, but the little girl showed a marked reluctance to eat her duck. That night she awoke, crying out, "No more duck! No more duck!"

This typical sequence of events illustrates a child's initial absence of any knowledge of death. Typically, the first distinction is between animate and inanimate, and this concept serves as the basis for understanding the difference between living and dead. Young children consistently note the absence of functions possessed by the living in defining what is dead. "Can't move, can't see, can't hear, can't breathe," are common expressions in answer to the question: "What does it mean to be dead?" As the concept is further elaborated, children also make a consistent connection between death and absence or separation. The dead have gone away. They are in Heaven, or in the graveyard, or in the coffin, or in some special world of their own, but they do not return. This linking of disappearance and death is made by children old enough to have had enough experience with dead animals or with the death of persons in the environment to realize that the dead are seen no more.

Young children conceive of death as being the result of violence. Death is produced by biting, shooting, stabbing, bombing, burning, automobile crashes, or being flushed down the sewer (Anthony, 1940; Nagy, 1959; Rochlin, 1963). Death, especially in somewhat older children, is frequently personified as a man who kills people. Even when they speak of death as a natural process accompanying old age, young children in their play most often picture death as caused by violence; it is as if they express verbally the explanations given them by adults, but play out their own conception. A link has been forged, it seems, between the concept of death and dying and the child's primitive aggressive impulses.

Several factors further this linkage. Infantile aggression is expressed in impulses to bite, tear, smash, squeeze, and pinch off, but not, in the earliest stages of development, in wishes to kill. The child is surrounded, however, by examples of death resulting from just such actions; the animals that he eats, the flies in the house, and the dog that is hit by a car have all been killed. Thus, his observations connect death with violence. The idea of death's occurring from natural causes is too abstract a concept to have real meaning at this stage of development. The integration of the child's observation that death is the result of violence with his own aggressive impulses is cemented when he, through his own aggressive act, kills a living creature by squashing a beetle or roughly handling some small pet. A gradual transformation takes place, through which angry impulses and wishes for the disappearance of the object are experienced as wishes to kill or wishes for the death of the person toward whom these impulses are directed.

A major step in the development of children's ideas of death is the association of the concept of dying with the self, and the resultant recognition by the child that he too may die. The recognition of the possibility of dying or of being killed, as a danger, precedes the recognition that some day he will surely die, as a natural consequence of being alive. This latter step can only occur much later, at an advanced stage in the development of the capacity for logical and abstract thinking. Anthony's observations indicate that young children regularly pass through a period in which they express anxiety about dying. This association of death with oneself occurs sometime between the ages of three or three-and-a-half and six years, with considerable individual variation (Anthony, 1940; Harley, 1951). This step is undoubtedly built on earlier mechanisms of fearing retaliation in kind for one's aggressive impulses or turning aggression against one's self. An example of these forerunners is given by the little girl who ate the duck and awoke with a nightmare. Though we cannot know the exact content of her anxiety, we can speculate, with some assurance, that it concerned not a fear of dying or being killed but some primitive fear that the duck she had eaten would in turn eat her. In order for the fear of dying to arise, several further steps must occur. The concept of death, of course, must have been sufficiently elaborated. In addition, a representation of the self must have been defined adequately before the destruction of the self can become a meaningful danger. At the stage in which the fear of dying is usually first observed, there is a rudimentary formation of the institution which will become the superego, with the capacity to direct threats of punishment for unacceptable wishes toward the self. Above all, the child's instinctual development has carried him into the Oedipal period, into a deep involvement with his rivalry with the parent of the opposite sex. Now his hostile wishes for the removal of his rival are experienced as death wishes, and the resultant fears of retaliation are experienced as fears of dying.[1]

The utilization of the concept of death for the expression of instinctual conflicts of the child is greatly facilitated by the animistic nature of the young child's thinking (Anthony, 1940; Laurendeau and Pinard, 1962; Nagy, 1959; Piaget, 1929). Without exception, children below the age of seven on whom sufficient data exists to make a judgment attribute the properties of the living to the dead. A little girl of four years and ten months states that the dead would like to come back, but can't because they are nailed in their coffins and can't root up the sand. Other children describe the dead as sad, or lonely, or troubled by the cold. Often the concepts expressed are not consistent. A little girl of five begins by saying that the dead are like wood, their eyes are closed, they can't speak; but then she expresses the idea that the dead continue to grow. This reaction is not the same as the denial of death, although children who are afraid of dying also can use denial. Rather, these animistic concepts represent both a normal developmental stage of thought and the limits of the child's conceptual capacity at this particular age. In some cases these notions can extend well beyond these ages. Freud (1900) quotes a highly intelligent ten-year-old boy as saying: "I know Father's dead, but I can't understand why he doesn't come home for supper." Because of this animistic attribution of emotions to the dead, the dread of death becomes associated with the dread of separation and abandonment. The child

[1] In the interests of brevity, this description of the instinctual conflict of this period is grossly oversimplified. Death wishes, of course, may exist not only toward either parent but toward siblings and other persons. Other fears of retaliation, especially the fear of castration, are also important.

[119]

feels: "The dead are alone, cold, and lonely; they cry because they are afraid. This is what I would experience if I were dead."

The child's magical, animistic view of death and dying is gradually supplanted by a more realistic, causally determined concept as intellectual development proceeds. We know, however, that more primitive mental processes and beliefs remain alive in the unconscious, overlaid by later acquisitions, and retain the capacity to be revived under appropriate circumstances. In dreams and in the metaphors of poets, death is invested with the significance that it had in childhood. Animistic views of death may persist relatively unmodified into adult life. For example, a man with an obsessive personality structure and conflicts around his aggressive impulses was tormented after his father's burial by the thought that his father was cold and soaked by the rain. He had the obsessive thought that he himself might be buried alive by mistake, and he pictured himself as cold and lonely and unprotected in his grave. Most people do not show such open, conscious persistence of infantile modes of thought; still, an animistic view of the dead is one of the foundations of most religions. And although an adult may base a more abstract contemplation of dying on faultless logic, his present ideas are still intimately connected to these early views.

Another model around which ideas of dying can form, in contrast to those discussed above, can provide the basis for a more positive acceptance of the inevitability of dying. This is the state of sleep, in which consciousness, voluntary control over motility, and contact with the outside world are temporarily given up. Indications of the equation of sleep and death are found in common usage, in literature, and in some phobias

[120]

of sleeping. In infancy, falling asleep, especially in the nursing situation, is associated with pleasure and the cessation of a frustrating need, and throughout life sleep can retain this quality of withdrawing from the demands of reality to the peaceful state of oblivion. This notion sometimes serves as a prototype for dying in persons who see death as a welcome release from a life that has lost much of its meaning, a life in which pain outweighs gratification. It can be true especially for some elderly persons who feel that they have finished their task and have lost the people for whom they cared the most, and are waiting impatiently to die.

Thus, we learn certain things from looking at children's views of death. They have no innate knowledge of death; the meaning of death is learned, like any other intellectual concept, through experience, and by elaboration of earlier models. Important components of the concept of dying are the disappearance of the object, loss of motility and other functions, and the view that death is the result of violence. Derivatives of the instinctual drives attach themselves to this constellation, and dying becomes linked with the central danger situations of infantile development, such as the fear that the infantile ego will be overcome by instinctual drives or external stimuli, the fear of object loss, of loss of love, of castration, and the fear of these dangers as they are embodied in the threats of the critical superego. Equating death with the disappearance of the dead object forms a link to the child's fear of separation and abandonment, with the animistic attribution of feelings of helplessness and loneliness to the dead. The idea of death as a result of violence forms a connection with the child's aggressive impulses on all levels of development, so that the fear of dying may express the fear of retaliation for these impulses. The enforced passivity of the dead and the loss of functions provide a link with various aspects of the castration complex (Freud, 1926).

By the time the child reaches the peak of the Oedipal period, the concept of death is well formed, although still animistic in nature. The rivalrous, aggressive wishes of this period are experienced as death wishes, and it is in this setting that the idea of death and dying seems to become associated with the self.

When a person is dying, his fears comprise the various meanings that death has acquired for him in the course of his life, as well as his responses to the physical and psychological changes that accompany the process of dying. The infantile contributions to the fear of dying are reawakened by the regression induced by illness and by the threat of danger. The prominence of this element is influenced by the degree to which the infantile conflicts have been solved and by the individual's susceptibility to regression, but it is never absent. Most prominent are the fears connected with separation, abandonment, and helplessness, and the fears of retaliation connected with conflicts around aggression.[2] These considerations can best be illustrated by brief clinical reports.

The problems of separation appear in the case of Mrs. W. The author first saw this middle-aged, somewhat masculine, awkward woman in the tumor clinic after the discovery of metastases from a cancer of the breast that had been removed five years earlier. Although obviously very frightened, she kept herself under tight control and remained aloof during the interview. She was unable to ask for or accept any support from the physician. Initial attempts to establish a relationship

---

[2] The focus of this paper has not permitted a thorough discussion of the important role played by the superego, which represents the internalization of these threats of punishment.

with her were met with curt, abrupt responses which effectively blocked any exploration of her anxiety. Much of the
anxiety that was expressed in her behavior was the result of
recognition of the seriousness of her illness, but it also reflected
the lifelong discomfort that this woman had felt in situations
that required closeness to another person or in which her
dependency needs were heightened. It became apparent as
her history gradually unfolded over long contact that she had
always defended herself against experiencing and revealing
her strong oral-dependent needs by maintaining an exaggerated attitude of self-sufficiency and independence. She had
been able to sustain these attitudes, for the most part, except
for a period of time after her marriage had been traumati-
cally terminated by her husband's suicide. Under the impact
of this loss, she had begun to drink heavily, but after some
months she was able to reconstitute her defenses and bring
the drinking under control. She had lived with her mother
until several months before the metastases were discovered, when the mother had required hospitalization because
of increasing senility, and now Mrs. W. lived alone.

Shortly after the discovery of the metastases, an oöpho-
rectomy was performed in an attempt to control the cancer.
She was tense and relatively uncommunicative with her social worker, who saw her daily in the hospital, and she was
completely unable to talk with the author, associating him
with the psychiatrists involved in her mother's commitment.
The only outward expression of her anxiety at this time was
a persistent diarrhea. She was discharged to a convalescent
home, but left after one day, finding this further dependency
intolerable.

Over the next several months, Mrs. W. experienced mount-
ing anxiety. Much of it focused on being alone. When she returned home at night from work, her empty house seemed

[123]

"like a dead place." Immediately upon entering her room, she would turn on her radio in order to hear another human voice. She could not tolerate the dark, and she feared falling asleep. Sometimes she stayed up all night, watching television and dozing in her chair. Sleep symbolized death to her, and she had frightening dreams of being with her father, who had died in her adolescence. She also turned to alcohol again, as she struggled with her great need, but also her great reluctance, to accept help from the physicians and the social worker. Although she constantly and unconsciously maneuvered herself into situations where she had to be dependent, she was then unable to tolerate this dependence and had to rebel and flee. She would stop taking medicine that was essential to her well-being, quickly reach a state of medical emergency, and precipitate admission to the emergency ward. As soon as she had partially regained her strength, she would insist on leaving the hospital against her physician's advice.

During the summer vacation her social worker and the author were away simultaneously for a brief period, and Mrs. W.'s struggle became even more frantic. After our return, she became hypersensitive to the slightest delay in our response to her needs, in spite of a previously increased trust resulting from our readiness to be available to her at any time. She began making superficial cuts on her wrists and telephoning for help. Finally, this behavior became uncontrollable, and she forced a brief hospitalization in the same state hospital where her mother was a patient. While in the hospital, she felt less anxious and spent her time helping to take care of other patients. It was clear in subsequent discussions that the relative peace she experienced there was in no small part the result of being close to, although never in direct contact with, her mother.

[124]

Following this crisis, when she had tested our reliability and interest in her to the limit and had found us still willing to help, her panic subsided to some degree, and she was able to use support from us more freely. She returned to part-time light work. When she was able to work, her anxiety subsided; when her illness prevented work, it mounted again. Her disease, with the accompanying weakness, gradually progressed, however, and her sense of loneliness once more became intense. Her mother died, and shortly afterward her father-in-law died of cancer. Fear again threatened to overwhelm her. Admission to a chronic hospital was urged on her, but for a little while she clung to her apartment, which, with her belongings, remained the last symbol of her independence and the last link to the people who had been meaningful in her life. At last, however, her physical and emotional need for care outweighed her fear of dependency, and she accepted hospitalization. Upon entering the protective atmosphere of the hospital, where she was surrounded by interested nurses and doctors, her panic, stemming mainly from her fears of abandonment, subsided dramatically in spite of the steady progression of her disease.

This woman's unconscious conflicts centered around her strong dependent needs, the helplessness that they implied, and her expectation that she would be deserted by the very people on whom she relied for the satisfaction of those needs. This was the central meaning of the fear that she experienced when she realized she was dying. This unresolved infantile conflict was intensely mobilized by the threat of separation which is part of dying. The problem of loss, of separation from the world and the persons to whom there are emotional bonds, is an issue confronting all persons who are dying and is one

[125]

that exerts a profound influence on their adaptation to terminal illness, especially in the final phase of the illness. But the threat of dying in some patients may also mobilize other important fears. The case history which follows illustrates how the threat of dying can be experienced primarily in terms of conflict surrounding aggression.

Mr. M., a successful, perfectionistic man in early middle age, was followed in psychotherapy after he had experienced two attacks of myocardial infarction in close succession. For ten years prior to this illness he had been treated for hereditary hypercholesteremia and had lived with the fear of heart attack, from which his father had died.

When Mr. M. was one and one-half years old, his mother committed suicide. He at first said that he was informed of this fact in puberty by his father, and was also told that injuries produced in giving birth to him had caused the depression that led to her suicide. He was aware of some feelings of guilt, but of even stronger feelings of resentment toward his father for burdening him with this blame. As therapy progressed, however, it was clear that he had established the connection between his birth and his mother's death much earlier.

Mr. M. suffered from migraine headaches from early adolescence on. They were provoked by situations in which anger was mobilized, but could not be expressed. This anger was directed especially at his father, who was self-centered and manipulative. But it could not be expressed toward his father, who had coronary heart disease, because, as the patient's stepmother said, "If you upset him, it will kill him." The patient's need to control his strong emotions, which he accomplished partly by means of the reaction formation of helping others, was strengthened as a result.

[126]

During and after his first heart attack, Mr. M. thought, "I might die." The anxiety accompanying this thought was handled predominantly by isolation and denial. He even felt mildly euphoric during his hospitalization until, on the day preceding his discharge, he had a second myocardial infarction.

When I first saw him, two or three months after his discharge from the hospital, he said that he had accepted the possibility of dying and indeed was able to discuss it quite philosophically. It was apparent, however, that his confidence had been badly shaken and that he was quite afraid. To a great extent, this fear was kept from his awareness by the continued use of the mechanism of denial.

The point to emphasize in this case is the connection that existed between the fear of dying and aggression. To Mr. M., dying was associated with attacking or being attacked. This fear was stimulated in him by any situation in which he felt anger or the need to behave aggressively; the occasion could be a competitive situation in business, anger at an associate or friend, or sexual relations with his wife. He would keep himself unaware of his growing anxiety until it reached a high level and broke through his defenses. Then he would be caught up in an acute anxiety attack, typically expressed somatically, and he would be swept by the fear that he was dying. He tried to avoid any situations that might produce "tension," greatly reduced his activity, and babied himself. Another old conflict was reactivated by this defensive pattern, however and he felt that his fear was weak and feminine. The chief task of psychotherapy lay in working through his conflicts around aggression, and the equation he had made: "Anger kills—you die from anger." He believed, in spite of his denial, that he had killed his mother through the act of being born. He feared that his wish to attack his father angrily would kill its object, a fear confirmed by his environment. Therefore, he turned his anger into an attack on himself, by means of his headaches. On at least one occasion he was convinced that the headache was produced by a brain tumor and that it would kill him. When he developed heart disease, his identification with his father was increased, and any aggression that he experienced became even more the source of a fatal attack on himself. As he became aware of the guilt and fear provoked by his aggression, his anxiety diminished and he returned to a full, active life.

THE ADJUSTMENT TO DYING

It is important to consider not only the fears associated with dying, but also the factors that make it possible for some people to come to terms with their fears and reconcile themselves to their death. We are aware that, at one extreme, various inner problems can result in a person's wanting to die and either actively seeking death in suicide or stoically waiting for it to come. But more important for the issues which we are considering are those traits that make it possible for a man to want to live and to find dying painful and still to accept his death as an integral part of his life. Two broad related areas are of particular importance here. They are, first, the degree to which the important developmental conflicts have been resolved and, second, the nature of the emotional commitments that a person has been able to make during his life to people and to productive endeavors.

Each developmental phase sets tasks which the person must meet. Successful solution of these tasks results in increased autonomy and resilience of the personality; failure to solve them successfully requires the continued expenditure of energy for the maintenance of rigid defensive attitudes. Thus, if the resolution of the child's normal early, intense dependence on his mother has resulted in the development of a confident and trustful attitude, he develops increasing self-reliance and is able to tolerate a greater degree of separation from his mother. It is the development of a true sense of independence, as opposed to the need to maintain a rigid attitude of overindependence as a reaction against still pressing, but unacceptable, dependent needs. Such a person can permit himself to be dependent under appropriate circumstances without becoming anxious, and therefore can better tolerate the enforced dependency and passivity of a terminal illness. He can face the separation imposed by dying because it does not so strongly signify a dreaded abandonment. Similarly, if aggression has been directed into channels that are compatible with the individual's standards and ideals, if close relations are possible without excessive ambivalence, if, in a word, the major infantile conflicts have been adequately resolved, then old irrational fears and reactions, although still present, are less likely to predominate, and adaptive, appropriate regression can be permitted. Under these circumstances, the person is freer to come to terms with the reality of dying rather than having to struggle with archaic situations of danger.

A man's life is enriched by the people and things that he has loved and by what he has been able to contribute of himself to them. If he has not been capable of this sort of commitment, if his efforts and interests have been confined chiefly to himself, then his life becomes increasingly sterile, and the end of his own life means the destruction of everything of importance to him. For such an individual, death is truly the end, and his sense of futility and the realization that it is now too late to choose another course engender hopelessness.[3] By contrast, the man who has been able to make a commitment to other people, to his work, or to a cause is sustained by his knowledge that something of meaning will continue after his death. This attitude is manifested in the accomplishments of some creative persons who use the experiences of their illness to deepen their insight and make a further contribution to the field to which they have devoted their lives. Rather than dissipate their energy in futile efforts to prolong their lives, they may spend it to complete the contribution they wish to leave with the world.[4] When this attitude is possible, those things which are valued most do not die with the individual, and, therefore, some of the desolation is removed from death.

Various stages of a terminal illness can be observed, beginning with the patient's first recognition of the fatal disease and of its implications. This initial recognition may be handled in many ways. There may be a clear intellectual recognition of the danger, as in the case of Mr. M. In others, the perception of the disease and its implications may be blurred or even completely rejected. The patient may feel the full impact of fear and shock, or it too may be blunted by various mechanisms of defense.

The middle course of a terminal illness varies according to the disease. It is clearest in patients with metastatic malignancy who suffer a relatively steady progression of their illness, accompanied by increasing ill health. In the effort to master the fears and conflicts that are evoked during this

[3] The despair that a man with a primarily narcissistic orientation experiences when faced with death is vividly pictured in Tolstoy's (1886) short novel, *The Death of Ivan Ilyich*.

[4] An inspiring example is the fierce determination with which the dying Béla Bartók devoted his strength to completing his last commissions.

phase of the illness, a person employs the methods of defense that he characteristically relies upon in other situations of danger. Examples of this are numerous and familiar (G.L. Bibring, Dwyer, Huntington, and Valenstein, 1961; A. Freud, 1936) and need not be illustrated. But there is one defense, the defense of denial, that stands out so prominently and is employed with such frequency in this situation that it calls for special attention. It is seen in striking form in the patient who can come into a clinic clearly labeled "Tumor" and speak of his metastatic disease as "arthritis." The power of denial to block out an unpleasant reality was demonstrated by a 58-year-old man who was answered in the affirmative when he asked his physician if his weakness and weight loss were caused by cancer. At first he seemed to accept this information with equanimity and took realistic steps to make the most of his remaining period of life. Soon, however, he stopped speaking of cancer and instead began to talk of the time when he would recover completely. In spite of continued emaciation, he would comment that each day he seemed a little stronger. His persistent knowledge of the true state of affairs, now kept at a preconscious level by his denial, was expressed only in his dreams. In a recurrent dream, he walked through a dark tunnel with a door at the end; he always awakened, with anxiety, before he could open the door.

Denial is a defense that is predominantly directed against the perception of external dangers, in contrast to most other defenses which operate primarily inwardly against the instinctual drives. The very young child's mental processes are governed by an imperative need for gratification and for the reduction of painful tension. He repudiates that which is painful and primarily accepts and acknowledges that which gives pleasure. It is only gradually, as the ego becomes stronger with maturation and through repeated successful, adaptive experiences with the environment, that the child develops an ability consistently to acknowledge and be governed by what is objectively real, even though it produces displeasure. Even after the ability to test and evaluate reality is well developed, children still actively mitigate reality's painful impact through denial in fantasy and play. This activity becomes less and less important as normal development proceeds, and the habitual, prominent use of denial in an adult often indicates a severe disturbance in the organization of the ego. In times of great stress, however, especially when the person is himself helpless to combat the danger actively, as is true with the dying patient, denial can again become an important defense and is then more clearly adaptive.

Denial operates in a massive way in some patients, as was illustrated above. Other persons fluctuate between a realistic and an unrealistic appraisal of their illnesses. Such patients may accept the fact that they have a fatal illness, but unrealistically overestimate the length of time they still have to live. Others may cling to any temporary sign of improvement as an indication that there is hope for recovery.

A young man who had been informed that he had lymphosarcoma described how he was trying to work and plan as if he had a normal life ahead of him. When his disease was first discovered, his physician had disguised the true diagnosis and had given a euphemistic explanation of his symptoms. Subsequently he was inducted into the Army. He was soon hospitalized for recurrent symptoms, and this time he was fully informed of his diagnosis. He reacted with a feeling of shock but also with a feeling that he had somehow known this all the time and that the information which he now received only confirmed his suspicions. He attempted to master his fear through intellectual control by reading whatever articles he could find about his disease. He seized upon a statement in one of these papers that an occasional person has lived for as long as 20 years with lymphosarcoma, and he attempted to reassure himself that this was not such a serious illness after all. Upon receiving a medical discharge from the Army, he threw himself into activity, working long hours, pursuing his earlier intentions of studying optometry, and planning to marry and have children as soon as possible. He retained an intellectual recognition of the nature of his condition, but his activity helped him maintain the illusion, especially during the day, that he did not have a fatal illness, and he was thus able to achieve a feeling of considerable equanimity for long periods of time. At night, however, he would sometimes awaken in a cold sweat, intensely afraid of dying. Like the child who indulges in denial through play and fantasy, his activity helped him to deal with the affect evoked by his situation. A number of the patients seen in a tumor clinic clearly know the nature of their disease but, like this young man, deny the implications of this knowledge with greater or less facility. The successful use of this defense most often occurs in the setting of a positive relationship with the physician, and is supported by the feeling, "So long as the doctor takes care of me, everything will be all right."

Denial is closely linked to perception and operates by blocking or negating a perception. If the stimulus increases in intensity, the effectiveness of the denial diminishes. During this middle course of a terminal illness, denial tends to break down when the symptoms of the disease increase. This breakdown is especially likely when the progress of the disease is accompanied by pain, which is an insistent stimulus that

[133]

forces itself into awareness. At such times, patients are especially prone to confront their physicians with questions about the nature of their illness. The unwary physician may mistake this inquiry for a genuine wish to be enlightened, but experience indicates that such a period of heightened anxiety is seldom a good time to confirm the reality of the patient's approaching death. The dangers of doing so are illustrated by the case of a relatively young man with painful skeletal metastases from a bronchiogenic carcinoma who, during a time of increased symptomatology, put heavy pressure on his physician to tell him the true nature of his illness. The physician responded to this appeal by revealing the diagnosis. For several days afterward, the patient was very much agitated and was preoccupied with a wish to commit suicide. Only when his physician was able to soften the implications of the diagnosis, restore some measure of hope, and outline a program of palliative therapeutic measures did this extreme anxiety subside. During this period the patient disclosed that his father had died when he was seven years old and his mother two years later. He compared the feeling of fear and aloneness that he had experienced when confronted with the seriousness of his condition with his desolation after their deaths.

Although some patients use massive denial and seem never consciously to admit to themselves that they are dying, and others seem to rely on denial hardly at all, the most typical course lies somewhere in between. Denial seems to be an emergency defense to handle intense feelings of fear and helplessness, and it serves to give the patient time to adapt to the reality that he is dying. As exacerbations and remissions of symptoms occur and disability slowly increases, the patient gradually accommodates to his illness. This accommodation is often easier in the very old, who already have slowly adjusted themselves to accepting the end of their lives and who have important ties with people already dead. It is much more difficult for a vigorous person who, until the onset of his illness, was actively striving for the gratification of his needs and ambitions. In such a man the readjustment demanded is much more far-reaching and the terror generated is much greater. The use of denial in such a person gives time for this massive adjustment to be made and for a new identity,[5] that of a person who is dying, to be assumed, with all the shifts of cathexes that this process involves.

What to tell a patient with a fatal illness is a common question, and it is appropriate to discuss it in connection with denial. In deciding what course to follow, the physician should always remember that a blunt confrontation with the prospect of inevitable death can mobilize great terror. On the other hand, the adoption of an attitude of false optimism by the physician and by the patient's family can increase the patient's feeling of isolation and cut him off from the support that he could receive from the physician and from the people whom he loves. The dichotomy between these two points of view is actually more imagined than real, however. A physician does not have to pretend a false cheerfulness in order to permit a patient to maintain his denial, if this defense is necessary to him. He can establish a relationship that permits

[5] The central core of a person's identity, which maintains a sense of continuity and a sense of being a unique "I," does not disappear even when death is imminent. A marked shift of a person's perspective of his existence occurs, however. The future is drastically foreshortened and now truly finite, and emotional investment is withdrawn, in varying degree, from the environment and displaced onto the inner representations of the people loved in early childhood.

[135]

communication and can convey his serious appreciation of what his patient is experiencing without demolishing a defense that may be essential. This procedure was followed with the patient mentioned earlier who, when told that his symptoms were due to cancer, at first seemed to accept this fact with equanimity, but later reinstituted an extensive denial that enabled him to talk of complete recovery. When he stopped speaking of his illness as cancer and talked of getting well, the physician tactfully followed his lead. On the other hand, the doctor continued to show interest in all of his symptoms, discussed with him his concern about his failure to gain weight, and helped him to plan activities that were still within the scope of his diminishing strength. The doctor also soberly told him that he had a chronic debilitating illness, and that progress would be very slow and accompanied by setbacks, but that the doctor remained ready to be of assistance in any way that he could. These intentions were demonstrated by the maintenance of an active interest and frequent visits. The way was left open for the patient to express his fears, even though his denial was supported. He was encouraged to discuss the doubts that beset him during restless and uncomfortable nights when he was unable to sleep.

When the physician contemplates telling a patient the nature of his fatal disease, it is always important for him to proceed cautiously, evaluating the response to the information that is given and always leaving the way open for retreat, if this is necessary, and for some possibility of hope. A crucial factor in the decision to tell or not to tell should be the evaluation of the patient's habitual ways of dealing with internal and external dangers. If he is relying heavily on denial and is obviously looking to the physician for protection, these defenses should be supported. On the other hand, another person may be made more anxious if he feels that important information is being withheld from him. The withholding of information can be threatening to someone who has a strong need to be in control of a situation and who uses intellectual mastery in dealing with conflicts. In every case the course to be followed should be the one that offers the greatest assurance of maintaining an effective relationship between the doctor and the patient. The frequent raising of this question of whether or not to tell a patient that he has a fatal illness is probably more of an indication of the doctor's anxiety over a dying patient than it is of the importance of the issue in the total management of the patient. The doctor can block communication as easily by telling as by not telling. This result is especially likely when the doctor takes the attitude that he has discharged his responsibility to the patient by telling him "the facts" and that now it is up to the patient to deal with them as best he can. On the other hand, the doctor can follow either course and still make himself available for support to his patient. The type of support that will be effective in a particular instance will be determined by the individual personality structure of the patient. The information that he imparts about the illness will be only one part of the physician's total approach. It is important to remember that denial is a fragile defense, but often one which the patient clings to stubbornly. If the physician feels that it is important to support the denial, he can do so by speaking of the illness in the terms of the patient's choosing. The terms themselves will vary widely; diagnoses such as arthritis, chronic pancreatitis, and pleurisy are frequently picked up by patients to refer to symptoms resulting from metastases to the bones, to the intra-abdominal viscera, or to the lungs, respectively. Patients usually regard the term *tumor* as indicating a benign process and *cancer* a malignant one, and they gain reassurance from using the former. In initially imparting information, the physician can do so in a general way, and if the patient does not

[137]

wish more specific knowledge, he will usually not ask more specific questions. Before answering questions that are asked, it is always useful to obtain some idea of the conclusions which the patient himself has come to and of the fantasies that are associated with them. It is easier to do so than many physicians realize. The physician may often turn the question naturally by a remark such as, "You seem very concerned; what have you been thinking about this?" In the situation where a denial previously has been strongly maintained, but breaks down because of increased symptomatology—as in the case described above of the man who was orphaned at an early age—the physician should always first discuss the patient's anxieties with him rather than quickly answer his questions. Most often the patient is asking for support. If he has the ability to accept the knowledge of his condition, he will often indicate it by stating his question as a tentative conclusion that he has come to himself, and the physician may then wish tactfully to indicate agreement. It is important for the physician to be guided by the needs of his patient rather than to allow his own ideals of the way in which a person should be able to accept his death to dictate his course of action, because all too often his patient will not be able to meet these lofty standards.

A patient's ability and need to face the nature of his illness varies during its course. At one point it may be important for him to maintain his denial, whereas later in the illness he may have come slowly to an acceptance of the knowledge that he is dying and at that point receive more support from being able to discuss it openly. The evaluation of a person's need and readiness to discuss the nature of his illness or approaching death cannot be made on the basis of oversimple generalizations such as, You tell the truth to someone who is strong or psychically healthy; you protect the person who is weak or sick. The decision must come from a careful evaluation of the way in which each individual adapts to his illness. In fact, some patients who appear quite disturbed—suspicious patients or those who use paranoid mechanisms—may need special frankness and openness in their management. This possibility is illustrated by a woman with metastatic cancer who transferred from one hospital to another because of her dissatisfaction with her previous doctors. She complained bitterly and in quite unrealistic terms that they had given her treatment that had made her worse. She expressed much resentment that none of the doctors would tell her anything about her illness. It became apparent that one of her chief defenses was projection and that soon she would be blaming her new doctors for her inevitably worsening condition. It was decided that the only course that would enable her to maintain any trust at all was to be quite honest with her about the nature of her disease. It was explained in a kindly manner, and, at the same time, the measures that were planned to help her deal with her most troublesome symptoms were outlined to her in order to give her something positive to hold on to. Although she continued to express much bitterness and disappointment, she was able to see her doctor as a helpful person and to work with him with benefit during the terminal phase.

So far this discussion has primarily considered the *patient's* reaction to dying. But the physician also can react strongly to his patient's terminal illness. On the day that the author first began to serve as psychiatric consultant to the tumor clinic, he found himself preoccupied with the universal question, "What do I tell a dying patient about his illness?" This question was part of a broader one, "How can I possibly talk to, or assist, these people who are so hopeless and so beyond any help?" It soon became clear that this pessimism reflected personal anxiety. Continued experience observing these reactions and those of other physicians working with patients who are dying has clarified some of the bases of this anxiety.

The physician, like anyone else, has his own conflicts about death, and he may be afraid that they will be stirred up by too close contact with his patient's reactions. He may wish to avoid the sadness that he will feel at his patient's death, if he permits a close relationship to develop. If he is not at ease with strong emotions, he may recoil from the intense emotions of his patient or fear that they will make too great a personal demand on him. The physician's professional role as a healer is important to his self-esteem, and someone who relies unduly on success in this regard can be made to feel intensely frustrated and impotent by the patient whom he cannot cure and for whom he mistakenly feels that he can do nothing. The doctor may have unresolved conflicts over his own aggressive impulses. Such conflicts can lead a surgeon to feel guilty about an operative procedure that was necessary for him to perform, but which has left his patient with a permanent disability. Another physician may retain unresolved grief over the death of his own parents or other persons close to him, grief which is exacerbated by the experience of having his patient die.

The physician's anxiety can influence his behavior, to the detriment of his usefulness to his patient. It may lead him to adopt any of a variety of inflexible attitudes, of which the establishment of an unvarying rule about what a patient is or is not to be told about his illness is only one example. He may adopt a rigidly optimistic attitude, or give explanations instead of permitting his patient to talk, or cut short a patient's visit or make less frequent appointments, or even respond in a manner that causes a patient to change doctors—all in the service of maintaining distance from these patients. Probably all physicians react at times in some of these ways in response to the suffering and the impending death of their patients. If he can tolerate his anxiety without too frequent recourse to these attitudes, however, and can remain in emotional touch with his patient, the doctor will discover that his unique relation to his patient enables him to provide important support, useful for all patients, but essential for the one who is dying. In order to assess the importance of this relationship, it is necessary to return to a consideration of the emotional processes that accompany dying, and in particular the patterns of regression that occur.

Some regression occurs in all illness. The increased anxiety and feelings of helplessness resulting from the threat to the integrity of the body, the shift from usual pursuits to inactivity and preoccupation with bodily discomfort, and the necessity for nursing care and for reliance on the physician for protection all promote regression. All of these issues are more pronounced in the dying patient, for whom the possibility of great danger becomes a certainty and the feeling of helplessness proportionately greater. In this situation a special pattern of regression occurs which plays an important role in the dying patient's adjustment. It is based on a longing for the situation in infancy, when helplessness was shielded by the protection and security provided by the mother's care. In his regression, the dying patient recathects this early period of his life and revives the attitudes associated with it. The process is evidenced in many ways. Dreams of the parents occur with greater frequency; memories of childhood, especially of the special position occupied by the child in relation to his parents, are more vivid and frequent. Many persons with a terminal illness experience a longing to visit their childhood home. One woman who was dying from cancer of the breast paid frequent visits to her mother's grave. She would sit by the grave for hours, experiencing a strong sense of communion with her mother, and come away comforted. She did overtly what many other patients accomplish in their dreams and fantasies.

As a person consciously or unconsciously recognizes that he is in the final phase of an illness, and dying, he prepares to give up the world; in some ways it is a counterpart of the preparatory mourning done by the patient's family. Libidinal interest is detached from the environment which is being lost, a process similar to the freeing of libido from the image of a lost love object in a person who is grieving. In the living, however, there is reinvestment in other people. In the dying, the reinvestment is in the body and its care, and in the early images, especially of the parents. The reinvestment in the body is especially marked when there has been a prolonged period of invalidism. In this final stage patients who earlier tenaciously refused hospitalization because of the fear of separating from their families may welcome it as a situation in which their needs can better be met. The regressive revival of early images reaches its peak at this time, and instances have been reported when it achieved hallucinatory intensity (Deutsch, 1936; Worcester, 1940). At this point, it also becomes especially necessary for the physician to deal with the reactions of the family.

The increased need of the dying patient to be comforted and protected as he was by his parents strongly influences his relationship with his doctor. He attributes to the doctor the wisdom and magical power to help and to hurt which, as a child, he believed the parents possessed. When he regards the doctor positively, the patient can experience a feeling of security with him, even though in reality there is no way to cure his disease. If a close relationship develops, the dying patient can use the doctor as a protecting mother, who can comfort him and help to mitigate his feelings of isolation and dread. The ties with the physician are strengthened rather than diminished in the final stages, because he is the heir of the early relation with the parent which is highly cathected until the end. In order for such a relationship with the doctor to develop, it is often essential for the patient to feel free to express his feelings of fear and doubt and to come to realize that the doctor understands and sympathizes with his distress. During this period the physician, anxious to reassure his patient, may be tempted to minimize the serious import of the terminal illness. The patient, however, may interpret this approach as a rebuff and a rejection. Even when he endeavors to support the denial that his patient uses to avoid facing the pain that a full recognition of his disease would inflict, the doctor should treat the patient's situation with the gravity that it deserves.

The patient's attitude toward the doctor is by no means always positive. Every dying patient experiences disappointment, sometimes intense, with his physician, who in reality cannot fulfill all that is required of him. The patient may blame the physician for the mutilation that is the unavoidable result of a necessary operation. Patients sometimes project traits that were feared and hated in their parents onto the doctor and imagine that he is critical, domineering, sadistic, or rejecting when, in truth, the physician displays none of these characteristics. The patient may provoke negative attitudes and responses from the physician in order to support neurotic patterns of coping with the conflicts aroused by the illness. Thus, unconsciously he may try to make the doctor angry in order to expiate a feeling of guilt, or he may become involved in an altercation that distracts him from the frightening reality of his illness. These negative attitudes may not be evident in the beginning; but may come to the fore as the illness progresses, and the patient finds it more difficult to avoid awareness of his perilous situation. At this time a crisis often occurs in the relationship with the doctor, as the dying man expresses his fear, despair, and resentment openly and with full force and intensity. This is a crucial time when the bond between physician and patient is most likely to be disrupted. Either the patient may seek medical care elsewhere or the doctor may withdraw. If, however, the crisis can be weathered, if the doctor can give sufficient support, the patient's alliance with the physician will be strengthened and will become a renewed source of consolation and protection. Two cases will serve to illustrate these issues. Both patients were middle-aged women with advanced stages of breast cancer. One woman was more openly dependent and relied more upon the defense of denial. The other found strength in maintaining her independence and in facing many issues directly.

The first patient is Mrs. C., the woman already mentioned who sought consolation by returning to her mother's grave. She was born into a Jewish family in Armenia, the youngest of seven siblings, the baby of her family, and her father's pet. Most of the conscious memories of her early life were happy until, when she was six, her father died. While still grieving for him, her family was caught up in the disasters that overwhelmed her country; they lost their home and had to go to a displaced persons' camp. She recalled this period as very traumatic and filled with much hardship. When she was 13 years old, the family was brought to the United States to live with an older brother, whom she idolized and whom she looked upon as a second father. Her mother had bronchial asthma, and Mrs. C. gave up many of her own activities to take care of her. Although she presented this sacrifice as evidence of her love, it was apparent that her feelings were really quite mixed and that in many ways she had remained dependent on her mother. Her pattern of relying on important people in her life, including her doctors, suggests that the death of her father, at a time when her attachment to him and her hostility to her mother were intensified, had interfered with the successful resolution of her ambivalent attachment to her mother, and that this loss and the subsequent disruption of the family had left her with strong feelings of guilt, dependency, and insecurity.

Following her mother's death when the patient was 20 years old, she maintained a close, dependent relationship with her brother. Shortly after his death, when she was in her early 30's, she married an older man, with some awareness that she was looking for someone to replace her brother and to take care of her. In the marriage her feelings of deprivation and resentment became more pronounced. There were many quarrels and several brief separations which were always patched over.

Mrs. C. first entered the hospital at the age of 45 because of an acute myocardial infarction. She was obviously depressed and was frequently seen crying on the ward. Her physicians quickly encountered problems in the management of her case. Initially they had been sympathetic and interested in her difficulties, but their attitude gradually changed to one of frustration and annoyance as they found that all of their efforts to help her were quickly defeated. Instead of responding

and beginning to take care of herself, she clung increasingly
to her attitude of being sick, weak, and suffering. The situation steadily deteriorated as the doctors reacted with impatience, and Mrs. C. withdrew more and more into a position
of hurt and martyrdom. Once her masochistic pattern of pro-
voking rejection could be recognized, however, the physicians,
instead of reacting personally to her provocation, were able
to adopt a more objective attitude toward her. They went out
of their way to recognize her discomfort. Instead of minimizing her complaints, they agreed that she faced many problems. At the same time they encouraged her to rehabilitate
herself in spite of her difficulties. She responded quickly to
this approach and left the hospital on good terms with the
doctors.

A year after this hospitalization she discovered a mass in
her breast which on biopsy proved to be malignant, and a
radical mastectomy was performed. She had always been concerned with the way her body looked and functioned, and she
reacted with shame and depression to this "mutilation." The
loss of her breast reactivated strong competitive feelings with
other women. A recurrent nightmare expressed her anger,
her dismay with her mutilated body, and her envy of women
whose bodies were not damaged. In her dream she would cut
off the breast of a female friend with a knife. Then she would
burst into tears and, sobbing, say, "Your breast will grow
back; mine never will." She was unable to sleep at night without her prosthesis because the site of the amputated breast
felt so empty and bare, and she would not permit any other
woman, not even the clinic nurse, to see the operative wound.
She was also extremely reluctant to let her husband see the
scar because she thought it was so ugly that it might frighten
him. At other times, when she was angry with him, she hoped

that it would frighten him so that he would suffer along with her.

Over the ensuing months, Mrs. C.'s depression gradually lessened and her relationship with her physician in the clinic strengthened as she responded to his recognition of her painful struggle and his attempts to show her that she could still be a worthwhile person in spite of her operation. Her initially intense apprehension that the cancer would spread to other parts of her body also slowly faded. About a year after the original operation, however, this improving adjustment was shattered by the development of metastatic lesions in her lungs and bones. She became more depressed, developed many complaints, and ruminated on the question of whether or not her pain was due to cancer. She felt "dead," and she experienced a loss of interest in her surroundings. Her mother was frequently in her thoughts at this time, and she expressed a great longing for her mother. It was at this point in her illness that she began to visit her mother's grave. She considered buying a cemetery plot nearby so that she could be physically close to her mother after her death.

With this intensified stress, her dependency and hostility increased, her masochistic defenses no longer fully sufficed, and some paranoid mechanisms were at times manifest. She felt neglected and mistreated by the doctors, whom she now began to see as cold, heartless, and indifferent, and she expressed her underlying anger more directly. When a pleural effusion necessitated thoracentesis, she focused her distrust and resentment on the doctor who performed the operation. She felt that he was using her as a guinea pig and blamed him for the pain which, in reality, resulted from the metastases.

This whole period was a crucial time in the doctor's relationship with Mrs. C. Her despair was concentrated in the disappointment that she felt with the hospital and with her doctor. If he did not relieve her suffering, it meant to her that he did not care for her. Anger on the part of the doctor at her complaining or his withdrawal at this time would have confirmed her mistrust and seriously damaged the relationship. Instead, her physician attempted to clarify her distortions and to acknowledge her distress. He maintained an encouraging attitude and proceeded with an active therapeutic program. As her symptoms were more effectively controlled her complaints decreased, and she began to discuss more openly with the doctor her fears of becoming helpless and dependent. As her denial again became more effective, she spoke more consistently of her pain as "pleurisy," developing the theory that it was the result of a tropical germ she had caught from her stepson, who had recently returned from the Army. She became better able to accept her doctor as a good parental figure from whom she could receive comfort and protection, and she sustained this attitude throughout the remainder of the time that she was followed at the clinic. This relationship with the doctor and his skillful management of her particular needs seemed to be the crucial factor in enabling her to deal with her fear of dying. On several occasions her denial broke down, usually following an intensification of her symptoms, and she then spoke more freely of her fears. At such times she anxiously asked, "Do I have cancer?" but on one occasion she said: "I'm not as dumb as I pretend to be, but I don't really want to be told whether this is pleurisy or cancer." With the subsidence of her symptoms, the denial would be reinstated.

The danger of rendering the mechanism of denial ineffective in someone who needs to use it is illustrated by an event that occurred in the final stages of Mrs. C.'s illness. As her discomfort increased she became more concerned with the question of death, but she still clung to some feeling of hope and maintained a degree of equanimity. While still ambulatory she decided to accept admission to a chronic hospital because of her reluctance to become too dependent on her husband. In this hospital she remained aloof from activities that she was physically able to participate in, and in a characteristic way she rebuffed the initial efforts of the hospital personnel to get her involved. According to her report, one of the doctors finally said to her: "You know what you have. Why don't you make the most of the time that you have left?" On hearing this remark, she experienced a tremendous feeling of terror, and she fainted. She refused to eat for the next three days and only began to eat again when told that she must take some food and build up her strength before she could leave the hospital. Her fitful sleep was broken by nightmares of dying. She was very angry at the doctor and at the hospital, but she clearly felt guilty, afraid that she had been a bad patient. Although she very much wanted to leave the hospital, she also felt reassured at having been told that she could return at any time that she wished. After her discharge Mrs. C. and her family made some unsuccessful efforts to find another hospital or nursing home. Eventually she did return to the original hospital and there spent the last few weeks of her life.

Mrs. C.'s denial was fragile and only thinly veiled her fear of death, but as long as she felt protected by her doctor, she could use it with a fair degree of success. The relationship with the doctor was necessary to permit the effective functioning of this defense. When her new doctor became exasperated and confronted her with the nature of her disease, she felt abondoned, could no longer use the denial effectively, and experienced the terror that it had warded off.

In contrast to Mrs. C., another patient, Mrs. K., can be characterized as a woman with a need to stand on her own two feet. Much of her struggle in her final illness was around an attempt to find ways to do so after her legs would literally no longer support her. For her, too, the relationship with the doctor was of central importance in making an adjustment to dying. She was the devoted mother of two children, an attractive woman, friendly, and determinedly cheerful. A striking feature of her personality was her wish to put others at ease, even in a situation which inevitably stimulated great anxiety in her. She had first been seen at the age of 48 when she consulted a physician because of a lump in her breast. When the necessity for an operation to biopsy the mass and, if indicated, to remove the breast, was first discussed with her, she demonstrated an ability to look at the situation realistically with a minimum of denial, saying that she wished to have the procedure done, knowing that such a lump might be cancerous. She was, however, quite distressed that she could not know the results of the biopsy before further surgery was performed, thus expressing her need to be in control of her situation. In speaking with the social worker later, she said that her greatest concern was for her husband. He had had a myocardial infarction two years earlier, had become so nervous that he was unable to work, and had been seeing a psychiatrist since that time. Her son, too, had been nervous and in psychiatric treatment since his recent discharge from the Army. She was afraid that her husband and, to a lesser extent, her son might be upset and made worse by a diagnosis of cancer and by radical surgery. Indeed, she had had some discomfort in her breast for two years but because she had not been able to feel a definite lump and was so concerned about her husband's condition, she had not sought medical care for herself. She had come in at the present time because she could combine her visit with one that her husband was making to his psychiatrist, apparently finding it difficult to do something just for herself. Such avoidance was uncharacteristic of this woman. Her behavior illustrates the way in which someone who ordinarily faces even unpleasant facts directly may find it necessary to employ denial initially under the pressure of anxiety.

Her daughter reported to the social worker that, after the operation, Mrs. K. did not ask to be told the diagnosis and was not told, although it was obvious that she was immediately aware of it from the extent of the operation and from the behavior of the people around her. At Mrs. K.'s request her daughter was informed of the result but neither her husband nor her son, because she wished to spare them any shock. As it happened, however, her husband suffered a cerebral vascular accident and died only two weeks later. The fact that she had been "considerate" was sustaining to Mrs. K. in her grief. She continued to live with her elderly mother and she continued to work, as she had since her husband's illness, in order to remain as independent as possible. After the first postoperative year, she was followed in the tumor clinic on a yearly basis until, on a visit seven years after the mastectomy, metastases to the sternum were discovered. These lesions were irradiated, and hormonal therapy was begun. While her symptoms remained mild, she continued to be active and to show little overt anxiety, saying that by working she was able to keep her mind off her troubles. In order to protect her mother, she did not tell her that she was again having symptoms. She said that her doctors had told her that the radiation treatment was for an infection of the bone. She hoped that they were telling the truth. Soon, however, in spite of treatment, her symptoms progressed, and she developed painful lesions in her knee and shoulders. A year after the metastases were discovered, an adrenalectomy was performed in an attempt to reverse temporarily the course of her illness.

The operation did not produce a remission of her lesions, and when she returned to the tumor clinic two weeks after discharge from the hospital, she was obviously more anxious and depressed. When the doctor encouraged her to express her feelings, she began to weep for the first time. Struggling with the tears that she was unable to control, she said that she was afraid that she was dying. This fear had become worse since her increasing incapacitation from pain in her knee. She was terribly afraid of becoming helpless and dependent, fearful of being a burden and of making too heavy demands on her family. She was also now clearly afraid that there would be no one to take care of her. She felt very much ashamed of her display of emotion, and said that she had never permitted herself to give way to these feelings at home. It was pointed out to her that even the strongest person must have some outlet for feelings when undergoing such frightening experiences as she had had, and she was encouraged to use her relationship with the doctor to express the emotions that she had to hide at home. She was told that the doctor could understand that a person who had devoted her life to helping others would find it very difficult to be in a position of having to rely on someone else to any extent. She was also specifically promised both then and later that she would not be abandoned and would not be left in a position of being totally dependent on her family.

Following this interview there was a marked improvement in Mrs. K.'s mood. She became more cheerful and began once more to wear lipstick and to pay attention to her dress. Shortly thereafter she asked her physician very directly and for the first time whether or not she had cancer and would die. As gently as possible she was told that this was indeed the case. Along with this knowledge she was again given reassurance that she would not be abandoned. After this episode the patient felt much closer to her doctor, was able to express her feelings with him more easily, and was able to accept and appreciate his help with greater ease. An effort was made to maintain her activity as much as possible because activity represented a very important character defense for her. For instance, when she later developed a pathological fracture of her knee, she was taught crutch-walking so that she still could be up and about at least to a small degree. When she was no longer able to come to the clinic, she was followed by the physician and the social worker of the hospital's home care program for the last two months of her life. She very quickly formed an excellent relationship with her home care doctor; it was facilitated by the fact that he was connected with the same hospital as her original physician. She was able to be up some of the time in a wheel chair and to maintain a relatively serene outlook until just before her death.

The contrast between these two women helps to illuminate some of the issues involved in the care of the dying patient. Mrs. C. showed her dependency more openly in her relationship with her doctors and with the important people in her life. Her leading way of dealing with the dependency and the resentment that resulted from the deprivations of her childhood was a masochistic character pattern, which required that any expression of these feelings be disguised under the cloak of doing something for someone else or be justified by assuming the role of the hurt and needy child. When her needs were increased by her illness, she had to hold more firmly to her invalidism in order to justify her demands.

Mrs. K. was also concerned with the question of dependency, but handled it very differently. She possessed more

[153]

strength of personality and had developed a much more effective reaction of independence against her passive needs. The fact that this attitude was to some extent a defensive independence is shown by the rigidity with which she had to maintain it under all circumstances. When a regression occurred under the impact of terminal illness, Mrs. C.'s longing for a protective situation was much more direct and apparent. Mrs. K. initially suppressed any evidence of her need for support, and only under great stress and after overcoming much inner resistance was she able to accept and make effective use of the support offered by the physicians. Even then this acceptance of care was confined to a relationship with her doctors, and she remained self-reliant in other areas of her life.

It was necessary for Mrs. C. to support her denial. This acceptance, however, did not block the communication between the doctor and the patient. She was permitted to express her fears and her doubts, and the doctor, through his attitude, conveyed to her his sympathy and his appreciation of the gravity of the issues that she faced. He did not permit falseness and superficiality to mar the rapport that existed. He did respect what, in his judgment, seemed a necessary way for the patient to deal with her anxiety and did not interfere with her euphemistic attitude toward her illness. His willingness to do so helped to make it possible for the patient to see him as a kind and protecting person.

Mrs. K., however, would have been violating her necessary style of life if she had spared herself by fleeing from the recognition of her approaching death, no matter how painful this realization might be. If the physician had not responded to her needs to be accepted as a responsible, self-reliant person who was honest with herself, some part of her confidence in him would have been destroyed. She would then have felt

[154]

it necessary to pretend a false optimism in order to spare him, and this need would have further increased her sense of isolation. Being honest with her did not mean bluntly telling her, "You have cancer; there is nothing we can do for you." It consisted more of answering her questions in the spirit of, "It is as you think. I want to understand what this means to you," and, on the basis of the doctor's understanding, then planning with the patient an active, constructive program adapted to her needs. This program included relieving her pain, maintaining her activity and self-sufficiency as long as possible, and providing her with the assurance that she would not be left helpless and a burden on her aged mother. It is significant that this patient did not seek direct knowledge of her illness during the stage in which there was some promise of remission through the use of hormones, and knowledge was not gratuitously thrust on her at that time.

The Family of the Dying Patient

In medical practice the members of the patient's family occupy an important position which is not always taken sufficiently into account. Their role is not as likely to be overlooked when the physician often visits his patients' homes, where he is forcibly impressed with the influence for good and ill which the central family members have on his patients' progress. The importance of the family most frequently goes unrecognized when the care of the patient is primarily based in a hospital or clinic, where the doctor is more insulated from the patient's usual environment. In an acute illness from which recovery is relatively rapid and complete, this lack of recognition sometimes may matter little, but in any chronic illness, and especially in one in which the eventual outcome is death, the involvement of the family is crucial. It is not within the scope of this paper to give a detailed discussion of the family's role, but some of the more important issues may be considered briefly.

When a husband or wife develops a fatal illness, the spouse is exposed to intense conflict. He or she usually must face a complete readjustment in crucial areas of his life. When the attachment between the couple has been a good and relatively unambivalent one, he must anticipate the loss of the person who has the greatest emotional significance for him and who is the chief source of libidinal gratification. This anticipation provokes anxiety, especially at first, and then grief. The painful work of mourning must begin at the very time that increased demands are made in the relationship with the patient. In any marriage, each partner finds satisfaction of some dependent needs. When one partner dies, the other must face the loss of this support and also, especially in the case of the wife, often financial deprivation and the restriction of social contacts. When dependent features are prominent in the personality structure of the patient's spouse, the reaction to the threatened loss can be severe, taking the form of a strong sense of helplessness. Anxiety is intense, and it may be difficult to mobilize the resources necessary to cope actively with the situation. Often denial of the threatened loss will be a prominent defense. This denial interferes with the spouse's ability to give needed care and support to the patient. Moreover, the spouse may feel intense unconscious resentment toward the patient who raises the threat of abandonment by being sick or dying, and may even compete with him by developing symptoms of his own in order to obtain the attention and appreciation of the doctor.

[156]

Such attitudes on the part of relatives are often difficult for the doctor to deal with because he, in his concern with the patient and his primary interest in the patient's welfare, may regard them as expressions of weakness or selfishness. But it is in just such situations that skillfully planned support is most often necessary in order to prevent a crisis that can be disastrous for both the patient and his family. The bolstering of even a frail support may be essential to the patient at a particular stage of his terminal illness. Often a display of interest on the part of the doctor, attention to the complaints, and encouragement directed to whatever is the chief area of strength of the family member will permit the latter to continue functioning effectively in relation to the patient.

In addition to the anxiety that is evoked by the anticipation of the death of a person with whom a close relationship exists, and the grief that accompanies such a loss, some degree of guilt is almost universally aroused. This guilt is reflected in the ritualized self-reproaches that accompany burial in almost all cultures. The guilt and self-reproach are primarily reactions to deeper, hostile feelings experienced toward the lost person. Probably no human relationship is completely free of ambivalence, with some feelings of hostility intermingled with feelings of positive affection. This ambivalence is more marked in certain character structures, as in the person with an obsessive-compulsive personality, for whom all personal relationships are characterized by ambivalence and in whom there is a constant struggle between positive, tender strivings and aggressive, controlling impulses. Such a person has a strict, punishing superego which inflicts a heavy burden of guilt. Also, if the relationship to the dying patient has been characterized by a high degree of conscious or unconscious hostility, then the guilt will be intense, no matter what the person's personality structure may be. In these instances the resulting guilt can sometimes lead to a crippling reaction. The author observed an instance of this effect in a woman whose angry wish was suddenly "granted."

This 65-year-old woman had always been a rigid, controlling, self-righteous, self-centered person. Whenever her husband disappointed her, she became angry and abusive toward him. One day during an argument with him, she furiously told him to "drop dead" and refused to speak to him for the rest of the day. That evening her wish came true; he died suddenly of a heart attack. She was consumed with guilt, turned her reproaches back onto herself, and gradually developed an agitated depression. Her most bitter regret was her failure to speak to her husband again after expressing her hostile wish, thus missing the opportunity of taking back or undoing what she had said.

Guilt may be expressed in many forms. It can lead to exaggerated concern and solicitude which betrays its source through its very exaggeration. Often the underlying hostility finds expression through turning what is consciously meant as loving care into restrictive control. This process was demonstrated by a sister who crippled with her kindness.

She was a 60-year-old woman who for a number of years had provided a home for her older, spinster sister, Miss M. When Miss M. became ill with a metastatic cancer, her younger sister's resentment of the burden of her care became more intense, but her reaction against the resentment was proportionately strong. She insisted on accompanying Miss M. into the examining room when they came to the clinic, hovering over her as if to guard her from the clinic personnel. She reported that her sister was very weak and unable to do anything at all around the house, and that she (the younger sister) had to wait on her hand and foot. The patient, however, told an entirely different story. She was becoming increasingly depressed, she said, because her sister would not allow her to undertake the simplest task in spite of her ability and eagerness to do so. As a result, she felt increasingly worthless. This restriction of her activities forced her into premature invalidism and constantly confronted her with the fact that she must have a very serious condition indeed.

Some persons habitually deal with impulses that cause conflict by projecting them onto the outside world. If such a person feels guilty about his relationship with a family member who develops a fatal illness, he is apt to attempt to cope with his self-reproach by finding fault with the doctor. He criticizes the treatment that is given, is suspicious that the patient is being neglected, and holds the physician responsible when the illness takes a turn for the worse. It is as if he is saying, "It is not my fault but yours." This defensive reaction within the family creates a difficult problem for the physician. He should not passively acquiesce in such criticism, yet at the same time it is important for him not to be drawn into a battle with the family. A battle is what they are seeking, in order to avoid facing their own inner conflicts and the problems posed by the dying patient. In such a situation the physician must explain clearly to the family the condition of the patient and the probable course of the illness and must discuss fully each new plan or procedure before it is put into effect. His attitude should be that he is willing to do all that he can to be of assistance, but that the family must decide whether they wish to avail themselves of his help. At the same time he must refrain from retaliating to the many provocations that he will be offered. He thus avoids becoming caught

[159]

up in a diversionary battle and keeps attention focused on the issues of the patient's illness that are actually important.

The various factors discussed above—anxiety, grief, ambivalence, and guilt—all may serve to isolate the family from the dying patient. The defenses of family members against these disturbing conflicts take various forms. Denial may be prominent and may be expressed in attitudes ranging from insincere optimism and forced cheerfulness when with the patient, to actual avoidance—staying out of his presence as much as possible. Some families will discuss nothing but superficial matters with the patient, avoiding any subject that possibly might lead to the consideration of the all-important reality that the patient is dying. Sometimes a family member's anxiety and need for denial are so great that, in an exaggerated way, he attempts to censor whatever the doctor communicates to the patient. When the physician observes such an attitude, it should warn him that a crisis may be approaching for this particular person.

When a close relationship exists within a family, the opportunity to receive love and the continuing possibility of investing love help to mitigate the pain and fear of dying. But when defensive needs interrupt the intimate interchanges that enrich a person's life and sustain his sense of being a part of his social environment, the patient is forced into a solitary world where he feels set apart, no longer one of the living and not yet one of the dead. In Tolstoy's (1886) sensitive novel referred to earlier, Ivan Ilyich's family reacts to his dying by continuing to live their lives as usual and by denying the seriousness of his illness. He is tormented by their indifference, believing that no one feels for him because no one is willing to appreciate his situation.

[160]

Apart from this lying [the denial of his impending death] or in consequence of it, the most wretched thing of all for Ivan Ilyich was that no one pitied him as he yearned to be pitied. At certain moments, after a prolonged bout of suffering, he craved more than anything—ashamed as he would have been to own it—for someone to feel sorry for him just as if he were a sick child. He longed to be petted, kissed and wept over, as children are petted and comforted. He knew that he was an important functionary, that he had a beard turning gray, and that therefore what he longed for was impossible; but nevertheless he longed for it.

The doctor can play an important role in helping the family to cope with the problems and demands of a terminal illness. He should be alert to the indications of anxiety, guilt, and grief and should help the family to face these feelings by providing an opportunity for discussion of them. Sometimes he can relieve a family's feeling of guilt by adopting a benevolent, supportive attitude. His authoritative position lends added weight to his words when he gives judicious praise for their positive efforts and absolution for their failures. By taking the lead in making plans for the various stages of the patient's illness, he may bolster a frightened family sufficiently to allow them to supply essential comforts to the one whom they are losing.

The physician should form an estimate of the central family members' strengths and weaknesses as quickly as he can in order to determine the degree of responsibility that they can assume in the management of the patient. He must decide whether the emotional resources of the family are sufficient to care for the patient at home or whether a chronic hospital or nursing home will be necessary at some earlier or

[161]

later stage. This decision involves estimating the extent to which the central family member is dependent on the patient, the balance between love and hostility, and the intensity of feelings of guilt, among other factors. In some cases a family member can make amends for past hostility and make peace with his conscience by giving devoted care to the patient during his terminal illness. If, however, he does not seem capable of it, the physician should take the initiative and recommend another plan before the failing resources of the family precipitate a crisis in which the patient is rejected and the family experiences a sense of failure and increased guilt. If the doctor recognizes the point at which the strain on the family is becoming too great, simple measures such as placing the patient in a hospital or a nursing home for a week or two will often afford sufficient relief to stabilize the situation and permit resumption of care at home.

The active interest and resourcefulness of the physician, shown in the ways described above, will often increase the morale of a family, which would otherwise collapse, to such a point that they will be able to carry through effectively and realize a sense of satisfaction that will make their subsequent adjustment much easier. And the physician will have the deep satisfaction of having provided truly comprehensive medical care.

SUMMARY

This paper has focused on some of the psychological factors important in the management of the dying patient and has pointed out the importance to the physician of knowledge of these factors. Among them are, as we have seen, the evolution of the concept of death, the components that contribute to the fear of dying, and some of the developments in a person's life that help to make dying bearable. Two adaptive

[162]

mechanisms, regression and denial, are of special importance in coping with the crisis of dying. Anxieties may be aroused in the physician by his relationship with the dying patient and may interfere with optimal management of the patient, or, on the other hand, they may be utilized for increased insight by the physician. What has been stressed is the great importance to the dying patient of a positive relation to the physician. This has been accompanied by specific suggestions for management. Finally, this paper has mentioned some of the problems created for the patient's family by his approaching death and has underlined the importance of work with the family by the physician for truly comprehensive medical care.

PART II: DISCUSSION

Discussion

SAMUEL ATKIN, M.D., MARTIN A. BEREZIN, M.D.,
ROBERT N. BUTLER, M.D.,
STANLEY H. CATH, M.D.,
ARTHUR W. McMAHON, JR., M.D.
EDMUND C. PAYNE, JR., M.D.,
SIDNEY TARACHOW, M.D.,
AVERY D. WEISMAN, M.D.

DR. WEISMAN: This symposium has been concerned with what happens to people in the course of aging and with the relation of aging to adaptive processes that terminate in death. The contributors have described different forms and directions these processes may take. How can we understand the underlying uniformity within these different points of view? What practical effect will these findings have on the actual conditions under which people age and die? If, for example, the aged are advised to continue to be productive and even creative only because there have been notable examples of men and women who have been so long after their official retirement, not only will we be overlooking the more immediate problems of growing old, but we will also be ignoring the blunt fact that, throughout their lives, most

[167]

people are neither creative nor productive, except in an obligatory sense.

Dr. McMahon and Dr. Rhudick indicated that one of the primary purposes of reminiscing is to communicate the problems and pleasures of the older person to the present generation and to transmit to them bits of information and significant experiences about the world in which the aged person grew up. Dr. Butler discussed the concept of the "life review," a survey of earlier life often made by an older person in the course of preparing for death. Dr. Payne considered the plight of a special group of patients who suffer from serious illness and who must therefore consider the likelihood of death within a predictable period of time.

Erikson's (1959) writings about identity crises, developmental periods, and phase-specific problems have encouraged psychiatrists to recognize that the crucial characteristics of personality are not established once and for all in the cradle and playpen, on the toilet, in the mother's arms, in the parental bedroom, or even during early school years. The early, formative years may shape a person's view of reality and may induce more or less permanent distortions of attitude, but the overture is not the finale. Adult life does not consist merely of playing and replaying, with different arrangements and different musicians, the music that was written in early infancy and childhood. Madison Avenue advertising notwithstanding, the contemporary world does not belong only to the young. The significant values for which we strive daily are not superannuated versions of an earlier way of life. How we live and what we do belong to an abiding *now* and are derived only in part from the past. We can demonstrate that there are many turning points and crises throughout life. They occur with such decisive regularity and amid so many

[168]

circumstances that to believe development ceases at any one period of life may itself be symptomatic of resignation, depression, or despair. What follows attempts to show, from a point of view (Weisman, 1965) that introduces *time sense* and *responsibility,* how aging, creativity, reminiscing, and dying may be understood as related solutions to a common problem.

Reminiscing

What is a reminiscence? What is its purpose? We must distinguish between a *true reminiscence,* a *pseudo reminiscence,* and *anecdotes* spun out by garrulous persons of any age. A pseudo reminiscence is a fabrication, designed to enhance the image of the person who tells a story to *any* audience. Some pseudo reminiscences are repeated so often and so enthusiastically that the storyteller ultimately may believe them himself. However engaging, such reminiscences are retrospective fantasies and serve the same purpose that any other kind of fantasy serves. They revise actual events according to what, conceivably, might have happened. Typically, pseudo reminiscences are legends about the "good old days," when everyone was less ambiguous in his intent, more sincere in his declarations, less dependent, more resourceful, and so on.

There are many persons who live out their lives anticipating a windfall or a great stroke of fortune which will alter their bleak circumstances and bring about fulfillment of their fantasies. What happens to a person when years pass, and there is no windfall? Inevitably, such a person is wedded to a fantasy and, more important, to a set of values which were appropriate only for a much earlier phase of his life. Because he is ill-equipped, and reluctant, to change his orientation, it is natural for him to displace the strong sense of reality invested in his fantasy backward in time. His image of the future becomes transplanted into a fanciful past. After all, many persons believe that their failures and disappointments might have been triumphs, were it not for some fluke or technicality. Thus, when disappointment is repeated over and over again and "something" never happens, the difference between the dream of what might have been and the telling of what might have occurred in the past is only a technicality. Psychoanalysts recognize a type of patient called the "as if" personality. Pseudo reminiscers may present a combination of traits that can be termed the "if only . . ." personality. These people recount reminiscences intended to waken admiration by means of tales of triumphs or misfortunes and by shunting aside failures as well as unworthy sentiments. If a reminiscence includes misfortunes or mistakes, they are given such magnitude that secondarily they will evoke admiration. Reality testing may be partially suspended, just as in a stage play. By revising some facts, others may be underscored. The purpose may be revealed by moods of either enthusiasm or self-pity during the recital. The aim of a pseudo reminiscence is consistent with the aims of denial—to maintain a current relationship according to a specific image—and is not at all for the purpose of reaffirming in the present a constant meaning from an earlier era of a person's life.

As a rule, our brief life span does not allow us to recognize the course of historical trends, but we can measure the passage of time by means of objects and events that disappear and by changes in social structures and institutions around us. We tend to weather events in the psychological atmosphere that surrounds us, just as we feel cold or warm, comfortable or distressed, according to local meteorological conditions, quite independently of the more enduring climate that prevails. We may perceive changes within us while the world seems to remain the same, or we may perceive the world around us to change while we seem to remain the same. Most of the time the world appears to change, while we retain a sense of nuclear constancy from one moment to the next. There are occasions, however, on which we are *obliged* to change in response to events that alter our articulation with a world that, seemingly, stays the same. These are *crises of accident,* such as a serious illness or someone's death, or *crises of development,* such as marriage, career choice, or, in fact, almost any crossroad where it is necessary to make a decision. Actually, both the world and the self are always in a process of changing and remaining the same. It is disproportionate change in the one that produces an illusion of constancy in the other. The key issue here is whether we can bring about *desired* changes in our surrounding world or whether the world will act upon us and, willy-nilly, change us according to its inscrutable intent. This issue makes the difference between feeling in control and feeling victimized.

In true reminiscences we may participate in an active, indicative, present tense (*i.e.,* reliving) or in a passive, past tense (*i.e.,* remembering). Not all memories are reminiscences, nor is reminiscing merely another form of recollecting past events. True reminiscing does not always glamorize or justify the one who recalls, even though its intent is to provide a sense of mastery and continuity. The principal purposes of true reminiscing are *to shorten the span of time* between past events and present circumstances and to articulate key episodes from past, chronological time with the *now* of existential time.

True reminiscing is an attempt to cope with change and to draw upon events from another period to illuminate problems of the present. It is not limited to the aged, but it is more obvious among them simply because the discrepancy between the worlds of the past and the present may be more dramatic for the aged, and the older person may be in more need of reaffirmation. Recently I read about a man who took his little girl to see an old Charlie Chaplin movie. He had seen it many times as a child and wanted once more to enjoy it, especially one particular scene. As he watched the film, he became more and more uneasy; he was afraid that his daughter would fail to share his pleasure. Suddenly the scene flashed on the screen, and his daughter laughed spontaneously. He said that at that moment she had *embraced* his memory. For an instant, he was again himself in the past, spanning the years, yet simultaneously in the present.

This is not an unusual event. We have all experienced episodes of false familiarity, and just as past events may penetrate the present, our present moods may permeate and transform the past. We may be simultaneously in both worlds, sharing reality sense and condensing time sense into a single moment. Whereas false reminiscence restores a flagging self-image, true reminiscence, as shown in this incident, may restore a continuity between one generation and the next. The life review described by Dr. Butler may occur in private, but the type of reminiscing that Dr. McMahon and Dr. Rhudick studied not only is most prominent among the aged but requires an audience of another generation in order for it to achieve its full purpose. In hospitals, younger social workers and house officers seem to learn more about the early lives of older patients than do older social workers and staff members. In other words, the greater the discrepancy of chronological age, the more reminiscences tend to proliferate.

In reminiscing, older persons often skip a generation in order to establish a link with younger persons whose lives and experiences could not have overlapped with their own. Furthermore, not only do the aged reminisce more readily to those who are at least two generations removed but the young are far more responsive to recollections of things that happened before they were born. What may be a dull and repetitive story for a middle-aged person may be a verbal tradition or a slice of Americana to someone younger. This observation suggests that older patients may be more effectively studied and treated by younger professional persons, whose relative youthfulness will spontaneously encourage a thriving relationship.

Survival

Survival may be discussed on three levels, each of which has its own tasks. These are (1) *biological survival,* which includes maintenance of physical well-being, adaptation to waning capacities, and avoidance of pain; (2) *pragmatic competence,* the tasks of which have to do with earning a living and with choosing and controlling the ways daily activities are performed; and (3) *responsible behavior.* The level of responsible behavior and conduct presupposes the successful operation of the preceding two factors. *A responsible act may be defined as one that is consciously chosen, competently performed, and has a consummation that is consistent with an ego ideal.*

Responsible behavior includes both the practical values of everyday competence and the values served by the significance of a person's collective acts. Responsible behavior is not to be judged by the effectiveness with which a person follows conventional standards, observes the amenities of local customs, and engages in highly laudatory, worthwhile pursuits. A man may be right for the wrong reasons and good with the

[173]

wrong motives. He may be a failure according to some standards, but still may be a success according to his own prevailing beliefs and values. *Motives* are the wishes and fears that prompt his acts—whether or not his performance is successful —but *values* are the standards which represent to him the distillate of his successful acts. In other words, motives are related to values in the same way that beliefs are related to a hierarchy of rules, definitions, conformities, and principles. If there is any grand design for responsible behavior, it is that the *causes* of voluntary acts are ultimately equivalent to their *end results* and that the *purposes* of behavior are appropriately represented by their initial intent.

How can we prepare for significant survival? When studying for an examination, we can accumulate information in order to be prepared to answer a finite set of questions. It is always possible, however, that we will be called upon to answer questions for which we are completely unprepared, inadequately prepared, or prepared according to obsolete, even irrelevant, information. In preparing ourselves for significant, responsible survival, the latter situation is more than just a possibility. It happens because most of what we believe and do gathers its significance from events which are outside our direct experience. Whatever has *meaning* acquires its meaning by standing for something else, and there are few facts so unambiguous that their meaning can be understood in isolation. In short, familiar ways of contending with events are determined by familiar meanings. When events change or are replaced by fresh events, our familiar world becomes supplanted by a new world in which we know neither the language nor the rules. As a result of this progressive dissociation, communication between one generation and the next may become wholly perfunctory.

[174]

With this background in mind, we can postulate that a true reminiscence is one that attempts to span the lapse of time between generations and thus narrows the breach of communication between two alien worlds. In some instances, reminiscence is the *only* bridge that can reach from one side of this abyss to the other.

In contrast to the true reminiscers, depressed patients, as Dr. McMahon and Dr. Rhudick point out, seldom reminisce. Because they deny that the future can be any different from the past and perceive the present as a bleak and hopeless morass, they have no reason to try to reconcile the meaning of past events with that of the contemporary world. Although melancholic patients will maintain that their guilt and corruption were always there, and that whatever happened in the past had but a single disgraceful meaning, these distortions can scarcely be called reminiscences. Neither can they be called a valid act of responsibility nor an accurate appraisal of time. One of the hallmarks of melancholia is, therefore, that a sense of time and of significant survival have vanished and have been replaced by a meaningless vacuity.

The Creative Act

Dr. Butler has shown that creativity may persist beyond the years of active employment and that chronological age may not close off either productive or creative capacity. In his concept of the life review, he implies that the act of reminiscence parallels the creative act. The act of reminiscence pertains to the past, whereas the creative act is projected into the future. Yet both are efforts to understand the meaning of the present, to comprehend changes of meaning, and to evaluate reality.

We need not concern ourselves here with the underlying forces that make a person creative, productive, or original in order to understand the *function* of creativity in old age; our immediate problem is to find out what it *means* to be creative.

Sick persons usually are unable either to reminisce or to be creative. Indeed, they scarcely may be able to plan for a healthy future. As has been pointed out elsewhere (Weisman, 1965), *being sick* and *being responsible* are opposite states of being. To be sick does not mean only that there are physical symptoms. There is psychological sickness which comes about when a person is incapable of exerting influence or of maintaining customary and appropriate status. Such sickness may occur whenever one's personal meaning is lost—when familiar objects, people, functions, and values have disappeared, when long-cherished rules and principles are violated by others with impunity; in short, when no one seems to *care*, in the far-reaching sense of the term.

If sickness and responsibility are opposite states of being, can we also contrast extreme forms within each of these states? Can we contrast the creative person with the dying patient? What can a creative person do that a dying person cannot? The following suggestions are offered, with an apology that time and space do not allow adequate documentation.

1. An act of creation transforms inner anxiety into an outward triumph. The creative person finds a fulfillment and a resolution of conflict by means of an instrument, medium, or form.

2. The creative person perceives a selected aspect of reality as though it were the entire configuration of what he means and what his world means to him.

3. He has intuitive grasp of events surrounding him. His reality testing not only grasps the world, but reality returns the grasp. In imagination, the creative person embraces the world.

[176]

4. He is convinced that this version of reality is also relevant for others. Moreover, at the moment when it becomes conscious, it is also externalized.

5. The creative act changes his perception of himself and of his location and articulation within time. His perceptions then acquire aesthetic status and may resemble universal principles instead of passive responses.

6. The creative act itself is a work of art because it demonstrates unity of design, symmetry of cause and finality, harmony of material, orderly arrangement of contrasting forces, and systematic patterns of performance.

Needless to say, the concept of the creative act here is being used to include many kinds of aesthetic and analytic events in which fresh meaning is both discovered and expressed.

Now, what happens to a dying person as he approaches death?

1. The dying person undergoes a progressive constriction in his point of view toward the world and in the ways in which he once confirmed his meaning in that world. Outward forms become inner anxieties.

2. He loses control of taken-for-granted functions. Triumphs and capacities diminish as his demands and incentives become limited to highly localized necessities.

3. Instead of grasping the significance of events beyond immediacy, his perceptions become circumscribed by the simple urgency of biological survival for its own sake.

4. He cannot master events or exact freshness from his daily experience. He can only make a pact with reality that will permit him to endure with minimal distress.

5. Motivations are reduced; meanings are blurred; the field of potential acts is narrowed. Symmetry, unity, harmony, system, and order reduce themselves to a here-and-now of isolated fragments.

6. He shares each fragmentation and dislocation of his organs and functions, dwindling with each downward step and awaiting the next episode with resignation.

Few persons are truly creative, but responsible acts are well within the grasp of ordinary persons and are a form of creativity. This does not mean, of course, that we can control the number or kinds of alternative acts that are feasible, nor that we have unlimited capacity to direct our own conduct. It does mean, however, that to be responsible is to choose, from within a narrow, and even progressively narrower, range of potential acts, alternatives which will be consistent with our ego ideal. The creative act is one kind of responsible act. Like the creative person, the truly responsible person may find a kind of exhilaration in perceiving his own determinism.

Several other implications lie in the antithesis between sickness and responsibility, or between the creative person and the dying patient. The first implication is that just as it is possible to be self-destructive without being suicidal, it is possible to be more dead than alive throughout most of life. The second implication has been suggested by Dr. Butler—that creativity, or responsibility, is a high order of survival, one that makes ultimate use of human potential. If this proposition is true—and I believe that it is—then a higher order of survival may be enhanced with the passage of years. Accumulation of significant experience may bind past events to present circumstances, and, as a result, responsible acts are not necessarily destined for extinction. A third implication is that a dying person may retain some capacity to operate on a level higher than that of a sick organism. He may even be able to transform his inner anxiety into an understanding of his own significance.

In the light of these considerations, it is apparent that the major therapeutic effort of the psychiatrist who works with dying patients will be directed away from fostering denial at every turn and for as long as possible. It would seem that those who advocate blanket denial as an antidote for dying patients incorrectly assume that the only alternative is to maintain a constant litany of *memento mori*. Actually, unflagging denial and incessant talk of death amount to the same thing. They only tell a patient, over and over, in their own ways, that he is extremely ill—which the patient already knows. Just as anyone must strive to understand his own state of being alive and to fathom the problem of inevitably becoming something other than what he is, the dying patient also needs help in finding significance for himself (Weisman and Hackett, 1962).

Many of these conclusions have been anticipated by Hanns Sachs (1942) in his reflections about "Beauty, Life and Death." He looked upon beauty as the opening of two alternative doors—one leading to death and the other to life . Art, and creativity in general, possess the power to effect a compromise between two antagonistic forces—motion and immobility, life and death. He derived the "sadness of beauty" from the relationship between the creative unconscious and both life and death. According to Sachs, the absolute absence of anxiety is the hallmark of beauty and signifies that the superego has relaxed its demands, that the distance between the ideals of the superego and of the actual ego—with all of its vices and infirmities—has become diminished and that there is no objection even to the id and its drives (Sachs, 1942, p. 233). The superego shares this triumphant feeling and enters into the activity leading toward it. "Death brings with it the striving after permanence, stability, immobility. The presence of death makes itself felt in the sadness of beauty which, in its fullness, is more than ordinary mortals are able to face in their everyday life" (p. 240).

[179]

Have we come so very far from our original instruction and intent to discuss the relation between people who reminisce, those who are persistently creative into their old age, and those who are confronted with imminent death? The proper function of denial is to serve the ultimate purposes of affirmation and reaffirmation, and denial is, among other things, a social act. It is a strategy which enables a person to mobilize his resources in the presence of potential disaster. Some of these resources depend upon the ability to maintain a favorable relation with other people during the period when adaptation, affirmation, and revision are taking place. Reminiscing may serve a similar purpose. Furthermore, as a technique of affirmation that closes the gap between generations, true reminiscing may be a low-key method of simulating what a creative person does in a more enduring way. Both creativity and reminiscing, at some stages of development, may be prompted by similar motives and related psychodynamic processes.

Finally, we must remind ourselves that we derive most of our opinions about old age and dying only partly from clinical observation. To a far greater extent, our understanding depends upon our innate appreciation of the dynamic unconscious, particularly of the way in which its harmonious workings direct and illuminate the tasks inherent in both life and death. To state it another way: Given the *facts* of life and the *inevitability* of death, what does it take to become responsible for ourselves, and how shall we go about it?

DR. TARACHOW: I believe that the projects envisioned by Dr. Butler are excellent. The relationship of creativity to phases of the life cycle and the multiple factors which enter into both aging and creativity should certainly be studied.

My principal criticism has to do with definitions and methodology. First is the definition of creativity itself. Felix Frankfurter, mentioned as being in the creative group, strikes me as perhaps a not too felicitous choice. Although Frankfurter was a remarkable lawyer, judge, and teacher, I am not certain that these functions should be classed as creative. First of all, then, the researcher has the task of presenting a definition of creativity (and of selecting people who are creative and who could be studied) which is acceptable to psychological as well as social scientists. The next issue concerns use of the term, psychoanalysis. Dr. Butler indicated that his mode of investigation was psychoanalytic, but the procedure he described seems more like a passive, undirected, free-association technique. This is not analysis, nor is it an analytic method. In psychoanalysis the analyst actively points out connections, trends, and relationships, and this activity plays a real role in the elicitation and selection of material which is to come from the person being examined. For these reasons, another expression should be found for Dr. Butler's "psychoanalytic mode of activity." Furthermore, I am not clear as to how Dr. Butler uses the expression "countertransference."

Next is the issue of the tape recorder. As it happens, I am making a tape-recorded study of the supervision of psychoanalytic candidates, and I find that many distortions result from the use of this technique. These distortions should be evaluated in each study. In my own work I am aware of distortions which arise from my side. I find that I tend to respond to some future audience which might listen to the tape and that all my interest is not directed—as it should be—to the problems of the candidate and the person whom he is analyzing. The student with whom I am working also may have reactions to the recording process; I have not yet had an opportunity to isolate or to study them.

The matter of a life review is another issue which deserves comment. I have the impression that Dr. Butler's subjects engaged in a life review only after they had been indoctrinated in a number of interviews, so that they came to know what the investigator was searching for and tried to comply with his interests. I do not believe that a person spontaneously engages in a life review of himself at any age unless he is in a pathological depression.

I might also take issue with Dr. Butler's implication that man is superior to animals. Certainly in one respect, at least, he is not. Man is one of the few animals who kills his own kind. This is a phenomenon which is rarely found in nature.

Dr. McMahon's paper has a most interesting central thesis, the problem of reminiscence in the aged. The aged certainly do libidinize the past, and this must be a great factor in their defective memory for recent events. There are a number of clinical syndromes with which reminiscences might be compared or contrasted.

First, the relationship of reminiscences to confabulations is seen, for example, in Korsakow's psychosis. There the element of denial is very prominent, as anyone who has studied confabulations will notice. An interesting phenomenon evidenced by both confabulatory and senile patients is the relationship of the symptoms to insomnia and to nocturnal agitation. I should be very much interested in knowing at what hour the researchers into reminiscing interviewed their aged patients. Some years ago I made a study of Korsakow's psychosis and compared interviews conducted during the daytime and at night. I found that certain patients who seemed quite lucid, oriented, and clear during the day had very active confabulatory syndromes[1] at night. A similar type of diurnal variation can be found in senile patients.

[1] The confabulatory syndrome is closely related to the syndrome of manic denial. In fact, many years ago Foerster and Gagel (1934) demonstrated that

The other comparison I should like to comment on is the relationship of reminiscences to *déjà vu* phenomena. A study by Jacob A. Arlow (1959) a few years ago suggested that the principal function of the *déjà vu* phenomenon was to enable a patient to go back to something that he had mastered in the past in order to help him overcome an anxiety in the present. This dynamism, if you will, seems to be true both of the *déjà vu* phenomenon and of the reminiscences of the aged.

There is a third comparison or contrast between reminiscences and certain kinds of obsessional thinking. Even though the obsessional neurosis is so closely connected to the control of aggression, there are some types of obsessional thinking which have a different function altogether. For example, there may be obsessive reversion to previously mastered activities. A patient in his earlier life might have had a strong musical interest which was superseded by an intellectual or mathematical interest. This patient, later, when faced by difficulties in his current actions, might find himself obsessively preoccupied with some musical activity of the past which he had been able to master successfully. This is an obsession based on regressing to an activity mastered in the past. A similar mechanism may be seen in traumatic neurosis, and some of the phenomena of old age might even be considered as a variety of traumatic neurosis in which certain stereotyped ways of attempting to find an area already mastered are observed. Reminiscence is both a reminder of longevity and a reminder of past mastery.

In studying advancing old age one has to consider not only the problem of increasing narcissism but also the effect of

---

one part of the brain could produce either confabulations or manic states in human beings.

progressive loss of objects, together with the two-sided problem of aggressive object relations and libidinal object relations.[2] Let me make a few comments about the progressive
loss of objects and the search for some type of object relationship even under the most difficult circumstances. I recall a
documentary movie which dealt with a man facing execution.
During his prison stay this man had developed a strong and at
least partly affectionate relationship with the warden of the
prison. It was the prisoner's request that the warden be the
person to pull the switch at his execution. Interestingly
enough, the warden understood the object-seeking aspect of
this request: when interviewed, the warden explained it in
terms of the prisoner's attachment to him. We also know of
hospitalized patients who are facing death and who insist that
they want to go home to die. They want a last reunion with
objects close to them.

As to the difference between mourning and reminiscence—
there is a difference. In reminiscence there is a clinging to
the object, not an attempt to work through separation. The
patient in reminiscence returns to early object ties. In mourning there is a working through of separation from a previous
object. Mourning is the acceptance of the sadness of separation, the fact of separation, and the renunciation of the object. Reminiscence is just the opposite. A well-known phenomenon which has been imperfectly understood is found in
people who believe they are drowning. They often report
that in a flash their entire lives have passed through their
minds. This is a kind of acute emergency reminiscence, if
you will, in which there is a desperate return to all objects of
one's past life at the moment of fear of losing the tie to these

[2] We should also differentiate between the apathy of the aged, the depression
of the aged, and the paranoid reactions of the aged.

[184]

objects. The crucial difference is that reminiscence is a process whose function is to deal with attempted *reunion* with past objects, whereas mourning is a process whose function is to deal with *separation* from past objects. Dr. McMahon suggests that the aged be given an opportunity to reminisce without being treated contemptuously, but such an opportunity perhaps might be replaced by a different, a more productive, process. Instead of being given the chance to reminisce, perhaps the aged could be helped to do something productive and creative, to work, and to maintain lively object relationships in the world about them.

I should now like to comment on some suggestions that have been made about the countertransferences of doctors and of others who deal with the dying patient. Some appear to handle such a situation well; others, not so well. This raises the question of what accounts for the difference. I think the answer lies in the issue of the unconscious desire provoked to kill the dying patient. On the general principle that masochism provokes sadism in others, just as helplessness provokes aggression, such an unconscious desire would seem to me to be the chief occupational hazard for the doctor or attendant, Thus, the success with which reaction formations against impulses to kill develop, or have been developed in the past, would be the prognostic indicator of the success with which a person could then deal with the dying patient. Twenty years ago Bertram D. Lewin (1946) neatly pointed out in a paper on the countertransference of the doctor to his patient that the ideal patient is the cadaver: he is absolutely submissive to the doctor's orders, does whatever the doctor wants, and gives the doctor no trouble. The point is valid, and there is something here with which healing impulses, maternal impulses, have to contend: ambivalence.

[185]

A relatively unsuccessful play by Tennessee Williams, *The Milk Train Doesn't Stop Here Anymore,* illustrates the problem of death wishes and ambivalence provoked in those who take care of dying patients. In this play, the chief character is a young man who turns up wherever there is a rich old woman who is dying. The play has a highly ambiguous quality; at the end, the audience is left unable to decide whether the young man is a murderer or whether he really loves old women and wants to be with them and help them in their last days. I think that the excessive closeness with which the play approaches the death wishes of the attendant is probably the chief reason why the play was not a success.

Dr. Weisman and others have mentioned the topic of denial. It has been commonly observed that convicts retain the belief that they are going to "beat the rap." This observation is supported by a study made at Sing Sing prison, where Bluestone and McGahee (1962) studied men sentenced to the electric chair. They found that these men did not believe they were going to die; almost all of them showed massive denial. Furthermore, most of them became psychotic before execution in their disbelief in their own death. This fact does not generally receive legal or medical attention.

To return to a more general topic, the fear of death has been treated in this symposium as though it were universal. It exists, I think, universally in the Western world, the Christian world, but it does not exist in many other cultures which are more archaic and more primitive and where death is accepted with much greater equanimity. There the separation between life and death is far less sharp than we in our culture make it.

I should like to call to your attention a paper by Henry Alden Bunker (1951). It was one of the last papers he wrote;

he had a carcinoma, and it is my belief that he knew he was dying and wrote this paper in anticipation of death. In any case, in this very interesting paper, he discusses problems of development and maturation. The point of view he puts forward is that life is a series of renunciations. The infant must first renounce union with the mother, renounce omnipotence and symbiosis with the mother, and develop a separate ego structure. Next comes the renunciation of the breast, and after that comes the renunciation of the mother as the sexual object in adult life. Then there is the renunciation of sexuality, and finally, there is the renunciation of life itself. Life, Bunker thus postulates, is a series of renunciations, and the maturity or health of the individual depends on the extent to which these various separations, these various renunciations, have been mastered.

To this paper of Bunker's may be added two early papers by Ferenczi (1913; 1926). Though simple, they are fundamental; they are the two papers in which he discusses the development of the sense of reality. The infant's ego structure originates at the moment of separation from the mother—at the first disappointment. This single hypothetical moment is crucial, for it marks the point of origin and connection of many different elements: the separation from the mother, the formation of the ego, the first stages of object relationship, the sense of reality, the first thought. The first thought, it should be noted, is an angry one, a painful one, not a pleasant one. The first feeling is hatred, not love; here is born ambivalence. Ambivalence, aggression, ego boundaries, object relations, sense of reality, and separation from the mother all originate at this crucial moment. Ferenczi's second paper on this subject emphasizes ambivalence and has an interesting title, "On the Acceptance of Unpleasant Ideas"—the development of the sense of reality and of ego boundaries. The ego boundaries of which we are so proud are something which we have accepted reluctantly, along with object relations. Thus, to pursue this idea, our object relations from their inception and almost by definition are ambivalent, and ambivalence can always be read as aggression. There is a powerful current of aggression, therefore, in our basic relations to objects.

Along with these papers by Bunker and Ferenczi, there is a paper by Winnicott (1958), "The Capacity To Be Alone," which is also useful as a background for thinking about the dying patient. Winnicott makes the point that the problem at bottom is not the separation from objects which makes it difficult for the individual to tolerate loneliness (separation from objects is the principal task of death); the problem lies in the previous object relations to the mother. If the object relations to the mother in childhood have been basically affectionate and friendly, the individual will be able to tolerate object loss; if the original separation has been made from a mother toward whom he had many aggressive impulses, there will be murderous feelings toward the objects which have been introjected. In later separations he must struggle with these many internalized problems of aggression. He cannot tolerate loneliness, object loss, because of the aggression within himself. If the original relationship had been a more friendly one, on the other hand, he would have been able to tolerate loss and to get along without the mother.

These, then, are the general considerations which seem to underlie the problems that the dying patient faces; primarily the patient is going to lose his objects. I have suggested that if a patient is burdened by aggression, his ability to tolerate object loss, to tolerate impending death, will be seriously impaired. On the other hand, however, everyone needs aggression in order to meet problems and even to face death. A patient of mine had a series of dreams that illustrate how aggression, or a mixture of aggression and love, can help someone to face dying.

This patient was a woman who had been operated on for an ovarian tumor. She had been told that the biopsy showed malignancy and that she was to be given a series of cobalt treatments. She was an intelligent woman, with a depressive temperament, and she knew that her illness might possibly have a fatal outcome. She was released from the hospital on a Sunday evening, after the operation and before the cobalt treatments were to begin. On Monday her husband was to go to work and leave her alone; she faced this prospect with depression and dread. That morning, after having had a dream, she awakened depressed. In the dream she was looking at a large new dome and at a man digging a hole. The man went down into the hole and then came out of it. The associations to this dream indicated that going into the hole and coming out of it represented going into the grave and coming out again—a looking at death and coming out alive. The dome in the dream was immediately connected to anatomy, to the idea of a skin over a skeleton; if it were pricked, it would collapse. Thus, in the dream, the patient was looking at death and at anatomical dissolution. At noon that Monday, her husband telephoned her and was very comforting. After this conversation she took a nap, during which she had two more dreams and awakened feeling cheerful. In the first dream she behaved aggressively toward a woman who had criticized her; she pushed and bumped the other woman. In the second dream, she and a beautiful woman were rivals, and the patient said, "My body's skinny, but it's as good as yours." Her dreams thus reflected concern with anatomy and with aggression. The initial dream, which she associated with bodily disintegration and death, was evoked in a mood of depression. The subsequent dreams in the cheerful mood showed successful aggression and anatomical intactness. It is significant that it was her husband's telephone call that changed her mood. In other words, after being loved, this woman could then mobilize the aggression necessary to turn back disintegration and death. One might have expected that the feeling of being loved would have produced libidinal themes in her dreams, but such was not the case; the love mobilized aggression, and the cheerful mood was connected with successful aggression and rivalry.

There is a similar theme in Monsarrat's novel, *The Cruel Sea,* later made into a movie. A group of men are adrift on a raft at sea. Some of them survive and some of them succumb, and the action consists of flashbacks to their previous lives. It becomes clear by the end that the men who had something to live for, the men who had someone they loved, could invoke and deliver sufficient aggression to remain alive and to fight against the dangers of the sea. Those who had no one to love did not have enough aggression; they succumbed. The role of aggression is peculiar; aggression may play a destructive role, but, on the other hand, it may play a saving role in the patient who is faced with the problem of death.

The fear of desertion which the dying patient faces should not be oversimplified. It must be regarded in the light of the vicissitudes of the aggressive feelings within the dying patient and the possibility that these feelings can be turned against the self. For example, statistics show that the aged are the

[190]

group with the highest incidence of suicide. There are also many instances of active persons who retire and who die very soon thereafter.

The reactions of the dying patient to the doctor may vary. So far I have mentioned aggressive reactions, depressed reactions, paranoid reactions; I would add hysterical reactions. I know of a woman, aged 88, dying of a malignancy, who developed what I would call an hysterical delusion that her doctor was secretly in love with her; she read off every action and word of his in terms of this delusion.

One last comment on the denial of death: it is very widespread. Almost every religion offers the denial of death, and the heaven and hell of our Western mythology are busier and more bustling with activity than the earthly life span. In the heaven, the activity is mostly oral; in the hell, it is mostly anal. In either case, it seems, we are doomed to a pregenital existence after we die. Apparently death can be denied, but at the cost of a regressive sacrifice of genitality (Bunker, 1951).

Dr. Payne: I recall from my childhood the memory of an aunt toward whom I had curiously mixed and ambivalent attitudes. My recollection of her is generally mildly unpleasant and associated with the drab circumstances in which she lived with her elderly, chronically ill husband. Set apart from these impressions, however, are memories of vivid, magical sessions in which she would recollect the world of her youth, singing the old-fashioned songs that she sang then, and re-creating the people whom she had been fond of and their romanticized adventures in the semifrontier setting in which she had lived. Undoubtedly she would fall into the third group of Dr. McMahon's subjects, those whose reminiscences are most adaptive, serving to maintain their own sense of identity and to mitigate present unhappiness, while at the same time furthering a current object relationship by giving pleasure to the listener and conveying to him a sense of his own history.

Dr. McMahon and Dr. Rhudick's interesting study clearly indicates that reminiscing is indeed an activity under control of the ego, which aims at adaptation to the vicissitudes of senescence, and is not the result of deterioration of intellect or personality. The style of reminiscence and the ratio of narcissistic and object libido involved in this cathexis of memories of the past are correlated with the individual's personality structure and style.

Dr. McMahon notes the positive correlation between reminiscing, freedom from depression, and survival, but the data do not clearly indicate the manner in which each of these variables affects the others. I would speculate that the presence or absence of depression is the most significant determinant. Reminiscence is interfered with by depression, as are other ego functions. The most challenging aspect of this part of the investigation is the support it lends to the hypothesis that, in the aged, depression exerts a direct influence on failure to survive.

The suggested similarity between mourning and reminiscing is not convincing. The hypercathexis of memories connected with the lost object is, in mourning, part of a process that eventually leads to decathexis. Loss and mourning are certainly prominent in senescence. Reminiscing, however, represents a recathexis of the past, not for the purpose of eventual detachment of libido, but rather to fill the vacuum left by the loss of gratifying objects, abilities, and situations in the present. It is these which must be mourned.

Dr. Weisman has performed a valuable service by carefully explicating the adaptive maneuver that we call denial, in terms of (1) the context in which denial occurs, (2) the object denied, (3) the purpose of the denial, (4) the implications of the denied reality, (5) the form of the denial, and (6) the fate of the undenied portion of the field. Most psychoanalysts will agree with the importance of each of these components and with the relevance of the four steps that he subsumes under the "act of denying." The social context in which the process of denial occurs, in particular, deserves further painstaking study. As is true in most areas of psychoanalytic observation, it is the adaptational point of view that most recently has been made explicit and that consequently is the least developed.

In order to define the "dynamic interpretation of denial" more sharply, Dr. Weisman describes an antithetical point of view, the "static interpretation of denial." This "static" view is characterized by the following assumptions:

1. The patient may be expected to deny the same thing in the same way to anyone else.

2. Substantial deviation from the accepted, normative range of meaning of facts and objects is evidence of denial.

3. Patients are always able to report their feelings accurately.

Although this antithesis serves its rhetorical purpose admirably, the context in which it is stated suggests, inaccurately, that the "static interpretation of denial" is the point of view expounded in psychoanalytic theory and held by a majority of analysts. The reader inadvertently may be led— by the linking of "static," "atomistic," "mechanical," "mechanistic," and "mechanisms of defense"—to believe that this "static interpretation" was advanced by Anna Freud in her pioneering contribution (A. Freud, 1936). Those familiar with her work, of course, will realize that nothing could be

[193]

more foreign to her sophisticated observations than this type of formulation.

Our judgment that another person has denied, in the special sense in which we use the term, is *not* based on our observation that he repudiates a part of the mutually *available* reality. All great social, religious, and scientific innovators repudiate some segment of the reality that they share with their society and replace the commonly accepted meaning with a meaning more congenial to their personal vision. Our observation that their reports differ from our own perception and that of the rest of the world does not establish the fact of denial. On the contrary, in order to make the judgment that another person utilizes denial, we must demonstrate that what he repudiates is a belief, true or false, to which he also adheres. The man who uses a sexual fetish is not so much attempting to deny that women have no penis, but that they have *lost* an important part of their body—an unconscious belief which, though erroneous, threatens his own sense of bodily integrity. To justify labeling his actions as denial, we must demonstrate that his behavior and communications contain indications of both the belief and its repudiation.

An important and probably universal aspect of the context in which denial occurs is a situation of relative helplessness. When a person is confronted with an imminent threat which he is unable effectively to master or avoid, he is in danger of succumbing to discouragement, or even despair, and to subsequent paralysis of his adaptive efforts. Denial permits the impact of the threat to be delayed, preserving hope and gaining time for more effective means of coping to be mobilized or developed. Dr. Weisman's example of the truck driver who panicked when trapped in his truck contrasts beautifully the nondisruptive effects of a threat when it

[194]

can be actively combated with its disruptive effects when it is experienced passively and helplessly.

The child, because his ego is immature and weak, experiences more frequent helplessness in coping with his environment and consequently relies more extensively on denial. In adulthood, situations that induce feelings of helplessness vary according to individual vulnerabilities; two such situations common to most men, however, are the anticipation of object loss and of dying. The threatened loss of centrally important loved persons usually mobilizes immediate efforts to circumvent the danger. Denial usually will be minimal as long as a course of appropriate action is possible, because the denial would interfere with such action. However, when the person who is threatened with loss feels helpless to prevent it, he may rely on denial until the initially unbearable pain becomes acceptable.

Certain persons are predisposed to deny traumas which are similar to those that evoked a sense of helplessness in childhood. A woman whose mother died during her early childhood, and who was subsequently disappointed in her relationship with her strict and grieving father, systematically denied any evidence of withdrawal by later love objects. This maneuver interfered with more finely attuned interpersonal responses, but, by postponing the experiencing of powerful, crippling, depressive affect, served the adaptive purpose of preventing her from prematurely despairing and abandoning the relationship.

Patterns of denial are complex and individually structured in patients threatened with loss of life, as Dr. Weisman has indicated. When patients are first confronted with a life-threatening disease, their patterns of denial frequently differ from those manifested later. The massive blocking of fear

[195]

often seen initially usually can be maintained only for relatively brief periods of time and may require the additional support of a protective situation, such as hospitalization. Experience with a home-care program for patients who are discharged from a hospital after serious illness has alerted us to the regular exacerbation of anxiety that accompanies such discharge. Whereas the implications of even dramatic, acutely painful symptoms may be successfully denied at the onset of illness, sudden intensification of symptoms at later stages most often causes some breakdown of denial. Concomitant with this breakdown the patient may become increasingly absorbed with the advancing illness, his adjustment to a drastically altered life situation, and his increasing dependence on his doctor.

A psychiatrist cannot work with dying patients without being impressed, as Dr. Weisman has been, with the multiplicity of factors that determine the circumstances in which a patient's deepest concerns will be revealed or concealed. An unrealistically cheerful, uncomplaining attitude is often shown to the physician because the patient fears discouraging or angering him. The physician is not merely a chief source of the patient's hope but, in modern medical practice, the one person with authority to confirm or dismiss the patient's fears. The *risk* of receiving an answer to questions is therefore greater with him than with other personnel. Dissimulation may also be employed with members of the family because of a wish to protect them from pain and to avoid their withdrawal. On the other hand, a relaxation of defenses is more apt to occur with those people, whatever their official role or personal relationship, whom the patient intuitively senses to be unthreatened.

The introduction of a new term for a familiar phenomenon can be both provocative and troublesome. I have two reservations concerning the use of the term *ontological denial*. First, it implicitly divides denial into two types: "good," affirmative acts, and "bad" acts that repudiate another person. Such value judgments are not the same as statements concerning the adaptive significance of denial. All acts of denial no doubt are attempts at adaptation. Some acts of "cognitive denial" are successful; others fail in their purpose, with damaging effects to the subject or to others. On the other hand, total repudiation of an enemy may be not only effective from an adaptational point of view but also necessary for survival. Second, a more serious objection is that the term *ontological denial* distorts the more specific meaning that we have hitherto conveyed when speaking of denial. Ontological denial, as defined, refers to the denial of rights to another and does not depend on the intrapsychic process of denying a percept or a belief. The faulty capacity of bullies, braggarts, and bigots for appreciating the rights of others as human beings is perhaps better understood as a failure in the development of object relations. A person cannot deny that which he is unable to understand in the first place.

Dr. Weisman briefly discussed the biological dimension of denial, relating it to the hierarchical organization of the central nervous system as revealed by organic lesions. Although the process of denial that we observe on the psychological level cannot yet be specifically related to biological processes, this relationship may be a rewarding area for future investigation. One model that may be relevant to the physiological basis of denial is the withdrawal of cathexes from the perceptions and representations of the external world that occurs during sleep and their replacement, during dreaming, with representations organized according to certain fundamental principles. Observations made by Stone (1964) on *blindisms* in retarded blind children also provide a link between the automatic regulation of cathexis during sleep and the more deliberate use of similar mechanisms to control perceptions during the waking state. He uses the term *withdrawal blindisms* to designate intense, rhythmic, repetitive, completely involving behavior, such as intense rocking from the waist while vigorously pressing the eyes with the fist or thumbs. These blindisms typically were provoked by contact with a stressful reality, such as being placed in restraint or being tripped over by another child. A typical blindism had a completely preoccupying quality and was accompanied by marked reduction in awareness of and reaction to the environment. Electroencephalographic tracings "revealed an association between the withdrawal 'blindism' (rocking and eye-pressing), and slowing of the wave pattern. In addition to generalized slowing, typical 4-6 per second waves appeared which are characteristic of the drowsy state in children of this age. These specific changes occurred as quickly as 10 seconds after the onset of the 'blindism.' " Such studies suggest that further investigation of the relationship between shifts in cathexis and activation or blocking of various hierarchical levels of the central nervous system will result in closer integration of psychological and biological conceptualizations.

DR. BUTLER: Apropos of Dr. Tarachow's discussion, I should like to make three comments. First, the use of the tape recorder need not (although it may) interfere with the use of psychoanalysis as a method of research. Shakow and his associates (Sternberg, Chapman, and Shakow, 1958) have made some relevant comments on this point. In my experience, the use of the tape recorder has never appeared to be an insurmountable impediment to the freedom of expression (Birren et al., 1963; Butler, 1963d). Freud, of course, considered psychoanalysis itself a method of research and a theory of the nature of man as well as a mode of treatment.

Secondly, present and past definitions of *creativity* and *creative* vary and have always varied. Most psychoanalytic studies of creative persons have been of persons long dead. By selecting a variety of persons of recognized achievement for study, one might go beyond traditional pathography. Raw data has great advantages over armchair theorizing.

Thirdly, I do not agree with Dr. Tarachow's views on reminiscence in the old, unless I have misunderstood him. It is not sufficient to refer to reminiscence as "libidinization of the past." I can only reassert that I have repeatedly observed a recurrent process of life review occurring in healthy as well as in troubled old people. One will not always directly find evidence of "castration anxiety," "penis envy," and the like. One must be alert to the process of life review itself and to defenses against it. Many old people show "libidinization of the present" as well as of the past, as may and do people of all ages. My postulation of a life review is derived from my studies of the healthy aged and from clinical work at Chestnut Lodge and in private practice. My experience has been that all old people have recollections, thoughts of the past, and that they are prompted to question and consider their lives as they have lived them by the realization of the proximity of death.

I do not think that reminiscence should be regarded as sickness. The psychoanalytic process itself is not an unnatural, sick process, although it might be described as artificially

[199]

(professionally) induced in order to counteract opposing in-
ertial processes (defenses and symptomatic adaptations).

An aspect of the five-year follow-up of our study of healthy
aging at the National Institute of Mental Health (Birren et
al., 1963) is relevant to Dr. McMahon's paper. Although clinical depression per se does not correlate highly with mortality, certain clinical features show very suggestive associations
with mortality. Both the original psychiatric ratings of individual adaptation and some social psychological ratings
showed such suggestive associations (Birren et al., 1963).
Widowhood was also associated with mortality, but the more
general experience of losses was not.

The process of life review has been observed in the healthy
elderly resident in the community as well as in the disturbed
elderly (Butler, 1963d). The concept was originally formu-
lated as a normative process with varied outcomes (Butler,
1961b; 1963b).

There is a progressive preparation for death or grieving or
mourning which a person experiences as he grows older. In
our emphasis on denial, we perhaps lose sight of the fact that
a more synthetic or constructive development can take place.
This development in part may account for the fact that unlike
younger people threatened by death, older people, no longer
able to maintain notions of personal invulnerability, increasingly do prepare themselves for their inevitable demise.

In our work as physicians, there is a great deal we can do
toward utilizing the constructive possibilities inherent in the
realization of dying. For example, there is such a thing as the
defensive use of dying, either by the patient or by the doctor.
The element of countertransference has already been mentioned, but beyond that there is the fact that dying can
be used as an excuse, consciously or unconsciously, to exploit

the environment or to exploit other persons. This mechanism, however, is likely to have unconstructive results. It may stand in the way of more meaningful interpersonal relationships between the patient and those who will be surviving him—children, grandchildren; or it may interfere with religious faith, with many tasks, and with a number of features of life, including even such practical matters as finances. If the physician does not permit the elderly patient (or perhaps also the younger patient) to use dying defensively, he may be able to open the patient's eyes to more constructive possibilities and more meaningful interpersonal relationships.

The comments that have been made about the desire to kill and the other primitive aspects of reactions to dying patients or older persons remind me of the kind of remark that parents often make to children, "You're giving me gray hair!" or "You're wearing me out!" It is as though in order to survive, we must all risk the aging and death of other living things, including our own parents. In other words, we have to eat other forms of animal life and living matter to survive, and our very parents also wear out as a consequence of our growth.

One aspect which, so far, has not been stressed is our attitude toward time and the utilization of time. In a sense, life itself is an incurable disease. There was a very witty English novel of a few years back called *Memento Mori* (Spark, 1958), in which nearly all the characters are over seventy. Each one of them at some point in the story receives a telephone call in which an unidentified voice says, "Remember, you're going to die." The question of what one does with one's time and the realization that one never knows when that time will end is important both therapeutically and in relation to the whole psychology of later life.

[201]

DR. McMAHON: Reminiscing can be understood from several points of view. In our paper, Dr. Rhudick and I were concerned mainly with its adaptive aspect. The discussants have enriched the concept of reminiscing by the addition of dynamic, economic, and experiential points of view. In this discussion I shall try to relate some of these aspects to our findings and to call attention to some relevant observations from genetic theory.

We share with Dr. Butler the belief that reminiscing is an ego activity with a primarily adaptive purpose, but I think that his interpretation of its function is too narrow. In defining his concept of the life review, he describes a universally occurring resurgence of past experiences, "especially unresolved conflicts," under the stimulus of approaching death for the purposes of a final synthesis. This interpretation presupposes that all the elderly experience a discontinuity between the past and the present. It also suggests an analogy with the return of the repressed, in relation to which reminiscing is a manifestation, an adaptive means of recovering the past, and part of a therapeutic process. Although reminiscing may function in this way for some people, it is an unwarranted generalization to assume that it does so for all. When Thoreau was on his deathbed and was asked if he was ready to make his peace with God, he answered, "I wasn't aware we had quarreled." Most of our subjects seemed to share with Thoreau a sense of continuity which required no further synthesis, but they did reminisce actively. We found reminiscing employed in a variety of ways, including defense, communication, and self-affirmation, as well as in the life review. It may be that most of our subjects were neither especially guilty nor especially creative, but I suspect that the differences in the quality and function of reminiscing among our subjects were determined mainly by their personalities and identifications, which influenced their individual experience of the past.

Dr. Weisman's phenomenological distinction between pseudo reminiscing and true reminiscing corresponds to a major difference in the quality of reminiscing observed in our subjects. Whereas the denial maintained by pseudo reminiscing seemed to be functioning adequately as a defense, the value of the reminiscences as communication suffered. The listener felt excluded and slightly depreciated by the repeated emphasis on the "good old days." In Dr. Weisman's terms pseudo reminiscing tended to widen rather than to bridge the gap between the past and the present.

His comments about the greater receptivity of younger people to reminiscing are supported by the enthusiasm of the younger staff working with these men. As a matter of fact, it was concern about the potentially distorting effect of this enthusiasm that originated the request from which our study evolved.

Dr. Tarachow and Dr. Payne have commented on some psychodynamic aspects of reminiscing and their relation to mourning. Dr. Tarachow distinguishes between mourning, as a cathexis for the purpose of separating from the object, and reminiscing, which he believes is an attempt to cling to it. I do not believe that this distinction is valid.

Freud did not return to a systematic rethinking of his theory of depression, as expressed in *Mourning and Melancholia*, in the light of his later formulations in ego psychology. In the chapter, "The Ego and the Super Ego," in *The Ego and the Id* (1923a), however, he did turn to the subject with some brief but penetrating observations (pp. 28-31). He commented that melancholia has been explained as due to the reinstatement of the lost object within the ego, or an object

[203]

cathexis has been replaced by an identification. He explained that this kind of substitution has a great share in determining the form taken on by the ego, expressed in the idea that the character of the ego is a precipitate of its abandoned object cathexes; by undertaking this introjection, the ego makes it easier for an object to be given up. "It may be that this identification is the sole condition under which the id can give up its objects" (p. 29).

In these comments Freud calls attention to the increasing role of the developing ego in coping with loss and indicates that it acquires this ability through the process of identification. Perhaps in order to distinguish between the situation of the melancholic and a more normal state of affairs, he adds, "We must also take into consideration the case of simultaneous object-cathexis and identification—cases, that is, in which the alteration in character occurs before the object has been given up. In such a case the alteration in character has been able to survive the object-relation and in a certain sense to conserve it" (pp. 29-30). This suggests an alternative to the cathexis-or-identification situation: an ongoing process which occurs not just under the stimulus of loss and which has a sustaining quality at the time of loss. Freud also comments in the same chapter that the effects of the first identification made in earliest childhood will be general and lasting.

Many later studies of the developing infant have indicated that the infant's capacity to tolerate separation from the nursing mother is in direct proportion to the ability to substitute for her presence a satisfying memory or a mental representation of their interaction. Rapaport (1958) has called these mental representations the first manifestations of thought. They

[204]

also represent the beginning of the infant ego's capacity for impulse control. Lichtenstein (1963), Jacobson (1964), and others have referred to the mental representation as the rudimentary form of identification. Significantly, they occur under the stimulus of the alternating presence and absence of the satisfying object which, with beginning self-object differentiation, become the first experience of loss. Edith Jacobson (1964) in *Self and the Object World* traces the role of self-object differentiation and the process of identification through the various stages of personality development. She describes in great detail the circular process whereby self-object differentiation reduces the degree of narcissism in object relations, facilitating identifications of the kind which stimulate further self-object differentiation until a relatively stable sense of identity is established at the end of adolescence. The idea recurs throughout these formulations that the satisfying qualities of the early object relationships become an essential part of the memories of the interaction, providing incentive for and giving a satisfying quality to subsequent identifications and eventually providing a sense of identity and continuity which can exist independently of the object. True reminiscing appears to have this quality and function and is both a manifestation and reaffirmation of the experience of continuity which Dr. Weisman describes. I believe that the process of mourning shares with reminiscing these essential functions and quality.

The depressed subject, on the other hand, seems unable to derive satisfaction from memories of the past. It appears that his object relations have not provided the kinds of identification necessary to bridge the gap between the past and the present. Loss forces him back on earlier identifications which seem to provide no acceptable substitution for the lost object, and no sense of continuity can be maintained.

DR. ATKIN: I should like to approach the fear of death and of dying from two aspects: (1) the fear of death and of dying as anxiety, rooted in emotional conflict or guilt, and (2) the fear of death and of dying encountered in serious illness or old age and rooted in the biological process.

What are the attitudes of human beings toward death and dying in Western culture? Remarkably enough, fear is not the most striking feature; rather, it is the relative equanimity of most people to the inevitability of death. Sometimes we encounter this equanimity in persons who are actually dying. Although in the minds of most people the knowledge, in the cognitive sense, that they will die someday is always present, this knowledge ordinarily is not accompanied by fear.

Built into the human psyche is a process of counteracting, in a quantitative sense, traumatic factors—those factors in a situation that seem very threatening and confront us with major problems of adjustment—with psychological devices of equivalent force to put them in abeyance. The degree of anxiety in response to threats differs widely in different persons. In some, because of their history, it may reach an extreme of intensity. To illustrate: Analysts have commonly noted that certain patients who readily express anxiety over weekend separations are remarkably able to repress and keep out of communication the fact of an approaching vacation or other long separation, which is much more threatening. The termination of an analysis is sometimes delayed for years because of the patient's difficulty in facing the fear of separation. It is hardly surprising, then, that the threat of death should be similarly handled.

It is apparent that denial and other flight mechanisms are used frequently to deal with the threat of death. Before I became a psychiatrist, my interest in this subject was aroused

[206]

by my experience at Montefiore Hospital in New York—it was then an institution where patients were kept until they died—where I observed hysterical fugue states in patients who were abruptly confronted by the shocking truth of their condition. I recall one patient with lung cancer who overheard a surgeon carelessly speak out the truth about his illness; he completely repressed and denied the entire episode. Another callous physician, without preparation, discussed amputation in the presence of an elderly patient, who immediately repressed the whole experience.

Without ignoring the mechanism of denial, I should like to stress another mechanism, one that belongs in the general category of narcissism: the fact that all of us harbor notions of invulnerability and grandiosity. These notions sustain our existence. Perhaps without a great deal of narcissism, we could not live. Certainly it helps us to brush aside the ignominy of death.

Some clinical examples come to mind in which attitudes toward death, which Dr. Tarachow and Dr. Weisman have mentioned, were found to originate in early childhood. I analyzed a woman with a mild transference neurosis who, at two and one-half years of age, lost her father in a violent death—he was killed in front of his home by a speeding car. At the time presumably she could not conceptualize the idea of death or loss. However, she developed interesting and fantastic notions centering around the resurrection of her father, ideas resembling those that appear in some religious and philosophical systems dealing with death, transfiguration, and resurrection. During latency she performed actions like those shown in the striking French film, *Forbidden Games*: she would find dead animals and bury them. Sometimes she would even kill and bury them, then go back later and dig them up to see if they were alive.

Another patient illustrates the close relationship between the fear of death and the childhood fear of separation. This patient was abandoned before the age of two in a distant country and was adopted shortly thereafter by a wealthy American family. She reacted to any separation, no matter how brief, with psychotic depression and paranoid symptoms For her, separation was tantamount to death. Her relationship with doctors adds a curious angle. A few years ago she moved to New York from another city and needed to re-establish her medical menage It was utterly impossible for her actively to find a doctor to take care of her in her illnesses. It was something that just had to happen to her as a passive object of parental concern, as if she were still a child.

Now to the second aspect of the fear of death, that which occurs in serious illness or old age and stems from the biological process. I have had experience with a number of patients who have come to me for analysis in situations of severe and threatening illness, either because of their extreme fear of death or because of other anxieties precipitated by their state of physical danger. There is a recurrent factor in these patients which I present as a problem because I have no answer to it, but which seems to me to have some bearing on the wider problem of growing old: the actual biological factor and the consequent threat of death. A patient, an internist, was suffering from severe polycythemia vera and as a consequence lived for years with the threat of early death. He came for treatment because of severe anxiety, much of it of a neurotic nature. In recent years, measures of control had been found for his physical disorder, comparable to the introduction of insulin for diabetes. Consciously he was convinced of the efficacy of the treatment. Yet the fact that medicine had apparently conquered his illness had not helped him. He behaved as if he still had a disease with a rapidly fatal prognosis, and he still suffered from very severe anxiety, which remained untouched by psychoanalytic therapy. I could quote other cases that illustrate the fact that even where medicine offers an answer, it is not possible therapeutically to decrease severe anxiety in the case of a deep biological threat originating in the soma.

A more favorable response to psychoanalytic therapy usually occurs when the biological threat is not based upon a physical illness. I have had patients whose family history was extremely bad—patients whose fathers had died in their early forties of cardiac disease and several of whose uncles or siblings, perhaps, also had died of cardiac disease in their early forties or fifties. With such patients, where there was no actual biological threat of death in the somatic sense, it was possible to achieve considerable therapeutic success. Currently I have a patient, now in his forties, who came to me with some very severe manifestations, the end result of an old anxiety over his family's history of early death and the constant emotional turmoil this anxiety kept him in. His fears were well grounded; his family history was really very bad. Here the illness was on a cognitive level. There was no actual biological threat of death in this man, and the analysis is proving to be successful.

Dr. Payne mentioned an interesting contrast between the middle course of a terminal illness, where the patients suffered from severe anxiety and even showed some psychotic reactions, and the final stage, where these same people made some kind of peace with dying and showed a marked decrease in their anxiety. He suggests as an explanation that they have been through some sort of cognitive process, perhaps including a process of regression, by which they have accepted themselves as dying patients, and with it there has come a decrease in the fear of dying.

I do not altogether agree with this formulation, and I think it requires more elaboration and explanation. Felix Deutsch (1936) made a contribution to this issue. He used the term *euthanasia* somewhat differently from the usual sense: not to indicate the right of a person to die painlessly, but rather to describe the person who dies more or less happily and peacefully. The examples that he gave imply a double process. On the one hand, there may be a regression, mostly along narcissistic lines. On the other hand, the person who dies peacefully does so because he has paid the ultimate price to his conscience, to allay his guilt, and, having paid this price, he can now return to forbidden objects and reunite with them—if sufficiently regressed, he can even have fantasies of gratification with incestuous objects. In the three examples which he gives, as I recall, the woman returns to her brother in fantasy, and the two men return to their sisters. In the last stage of life, when the cards are down, so to speak, a final price has been paid to one's conscience and, if there is sufficient regression in the narcissistic sense, there is a possibility too of returning to objects of gratification forbidden in early life. Euthanasia has been achieved.

In my old days at Montefiore Hospital I worked in cancer wards, wards of diabetics before the era of insulin, and wards of cases with the most advanced form of pulmonary tuberculosis. I have thus had a broad overview of masses of dying patients. Whatever the explanation, I must agree with Dr. Payne's assertion that there is a final stage of equanimity that is seen in a great many dying people. As you all know, however, there are not only individual differences in dying, but

[210]

differences associated with the type of illness. The TB patient may show a certain euphoria; the cancer patient, depression. On the whole, however, I could not help being impressed by the number of patients who showed equanimity in the last stages of existence. There were occasional patients in whom a paranoid outburst occurred in the final days or hours, even when up to that time they had shown the more usual tendency toward complacency or equanimity. This sudden use of projection, this burst of aggression, this abrupt paranoid reaction to their environment would tend to confirm Dr. Tarachow's remarks about the power of aggression in the dying patient.

Dr. Tarachow's remarks about aggression also remind me of Dr. Alvin Goldfarb's discussion of suicide (at a previous meeting of this Society) and its possible relation to aggression. Dr. Goldfarb presented some charts which showed that the rate of suicide for white males rises gradually with advancing age, levels off to a kind of plateau, then rises again sharply after the age of 65. For women, on the other hand, the rate drops after 65. The same drop occurs, remarkably, for nonwhite males. Dr. Goldfarb did not stress the point, but I would venture the interpretation that in white males, with presumably stronger superegos than the other two groups, the combination of age and decreased capacity and opportunity for expressing aggression could account for the great increase in suicides.

Dr. Berezin: Dr. Payne's paper and the discussions following it remind us that although all old people die, not all people who die are old. Concepts about death and dying are applicable to every period of life, for people die at all ages from all sorts of terminal illness. In discussions with surgeons, internists, and psychiatrists who have worked a great deal with the terminally ill patient, I find that they recognize a period in which they have to readjust themselves in order to deal effectively with this kind of patient. There is a working-through period for the doctor with respect to his own attitudes and emotional reactions. The physician requires this period of working through in order to develop an empathic attitude which will enable him to deal with a very trying situation. Some doctors develop considerable skill in handling the complex emotional problems of these patients. The importance of this skill should be recognized, and the doctor who develops it must be considered as a very special kind of specialist.

Dr. Tarachow has mentioned reaction formation in doctors and attendants who deal with dying patients. Without disagreeing with him, I should like nevertheless to emphasize sublimation, usually of sadism, as a factor in the situation which is quite different from reaction formation and is far more healthy.

The many references to denial suggest a further hypothesis; namely, that there may be something age-specific in the use of denial. Defects of recent memory are commonly observed in the aged, and the textbooks classically have assumed that these defects are pathognomonic of organic brain disorder and therefore irreversible. I have a suspicion, however, that they may represent or include a form of denial, a notion that is supported by my clinical experience with several cases where defects of recent memory were reversible. In such instances the recent memory defect was in the service of denial of present and sad circumstances. The fact that elderly persons characteristically show good recall for events of the remote past, events of childhood and early life, in their meditations and reflections would fit this hypothesis, although typically such reminiscences are often romanticized and glamorized. Kurt Eissler (1964) once suggested in a panel discussion that when patients with senile dementia lose the ability to maintain any representation of the future, their own death becomes meaningless, and they lose their fear of death. One might wonder whether a reverse relationship would also occur, in which a strong need to deny the threat of death might lead to a decathexis of the future and result in a state of pseudo senility.

There is something more than denial involved in managing the anticipation of death. When a member of a family is dying or is in a terminal stage of old age, the family knows he will die, expects him to die, and yet under the circumstances, there must be a postponement of grief. It is a difficult situation, a waiting in a kind of no man's land, and the family may need the professional help of a psychiatrist or a social service agency in going through this phase. When the death finally occurs, members of the family often say that it came as a shock, even though they had known so well that it was going to happen. The whole slow-motion crisis of waiting is over; now they are released and can show overt grief. But what about the patient in the condition of expected death? Is there not a postponement for the patient also? It has been mentioned that many patients show equanimity up to the final phase and then break down. The factor of postponement, whether psychologically or biologically determined, could also be operating here. In any case, the pattern suggests that more than denial is involved in the anticipation concerning death—both within the patient and in the object milieu surrounding the patient.

DR. CATH: In discussing the terminal phase of life, we have focused upon the response of the patient's ego when he is confronted by irreversible body changes or by death. We have said little, however, about the depressive or aggressive reactions of the family to their impending loss. How do the "others" respond to the imminent family disruption? How do they go about healing the wound and filling the gap?

The threats of loss are not always as acute as they might appear. Serious changes in oneself or in a family member may have been perceived consciously or unconsciously for many years. We all know that we are going to die, but tolerance for this fact varies tremendously from one person to another and from time to time. Beginning in the middle years of life, gradually and progressively we lose our substance and our external world in increasing increments, a process that I have called *depletion*. Messages of normal aging or of pathological processes may reach consciousness, but the capacity of the ego to integrate these signals is determined partly by our individual tolerance for anxiety and loss. When loss is threatened, age-specific mechanisms of defense, based upon the need for denial, are called into play in each member of the family. For example, the observing and experiencing parts of the ego may undergo an adaptive splitting process. Under extreme stress, family members, like the patient, appear to react to the threat of disease or death in a disinterested manner, as though this event were happening to someone else—a form of depersonalization. Furthermore, they may clearly acknowledge what is happening at one moment, but completely deny it subsequently. The use of denial, to a significant extent, depends on the tolerance manifested by others. On rare occasions complete awareness of the painful reality suddenly occurs, and shocklike reactions, associated with despair and apathy, may arise.

Recently I had an opportunity to observe a case of terminal illness which will illustrate some of the effects of family inter-action. An intelligent, successful mother of four (in her mid-dle forties) developed a malignant breast lesion. She came to her family physician when she no longer could deny the ex-istence of pathology; the involved breast protruded so mark-edly that her doctor described it as "virginal." In contrast, the other breast was found to lie flat, as one might well expect in a woman with four children. Over a month before her first visit to the doctor, she had attended a cancer society meeting and listened to a speaker as he outlined the cardinal danger signs of malignancy. She had betrayed no emotion and in ret-rospect had seemed noticeably unconcerned in the interval before her physician's diagnosis. Unable to understand how such a glaring discrepancy in the size and shape of her breasts could have been missed for several months, the physician, a personal friend, could not refrain from asking, "Didn't your husband notice anything either?" He later told me it seemed evident the husband must have also denied the change. What may we call such an unconscious interaction between hus-band and wife? Isolated and by itself, it was remarkable. But the impression it reflected of deep personal and marital con-flict was later reinforced by a reaction of the husband which indicated his unconscious hostility. He refused his wife's last request for a trip overseas, using the rationalization that med-ical care would not be readily available.

On one occasion, after acknowledging her terminal state to me, the wife suddenly asked, "Why couldn't I have gone to Europe?" She knew I had backed up her request by telling the family that there were no contraindications. Many patients who know they are going to die experience traveling to some new part of the world as a symbolic rebirth. I had told the

[215]

family that in my experience these patients not only live through the trip quite well, but seem to catch a "second wind."

As her illness progressed, this patient sadly told me several times that she knew she was going to die, but that it seemed to be happening to someone else. Her family remained committed to the thesis that one does not acknowledge cancer and death, adhering to this policy to the end except when talking to me. This patient proceeded, apparently cheerfully, and, as far as her family or friends knew, unknowingly, to her death.

This case illustrates several points: first, the use of denial by more than one member of a family; second, how a special relationship to a doctor may permit the patient and the family to acknowledge an impending death even when they cannot discuss it with each other; and, third, how considerable aggression in the form of deprivation may be mobilized toward a terminal patient who, as it became apparent in this case, unconsciously is felt to be deserting the survivors.

In the terminal phase of a patient's life many realignments and changes in attitude within the family may be observed. One oversolicitous man, after turning to his dying wife's unmarried sister for help with the children, began to depend on her openly for his primary emotional support. Undisguised anxiety over loss, admixed with not too subtle aggression directed toward the ailing member, may also be seen. Thoughts that are usually unacceptable, such as "I wish my spouse were dead for her own sake," may be tolerated. This statement conceals a still deeper longing: "I wish death would release me from the pain of watching someone die." It also imperfectly conceals aggression mobilized by feeling deserted. These reactions may manifest themselves in predisposed egos by suspiciousness or delusions of persecution (the paranoid defense against loss). So it is that hostility may be expressed by withholding, as in the first case cited, or by oversolicitousness, as in the second. In still other instances, concern about loss and future *depletion* may lead to premature withdrawal of libido from a "deserting" object. The ailing patient may then respond by pulling away from real objects and regressing physiologically and psychologically. In some marriages, both the dying patient and the surviving partner find it necessary to deny any change in each other's health or in their relationship in order to "hold onto what is left."

The capacity of the ego to face the reality of death and to neutralize or hold in check one's "rage against the night" may be significantly influenced, then, by the capacity of the family to tolerate loss. We may be justified in wondering whether the mother who was dying of cancer, cited above, had maintained an overt denial of cancer signals as a masochistic response to her husband's unconscious wish to be rid of her. He had felt that she threatened his equilibrium by opposing his obsessive needs for orderliness, overcleanliness, and rigid self-control. She had bitterly resented the isolation imposed upon her by his pattern of immersing himself in his work. Her death both gratified his hostile wish and freed her from the burdens of this marriage. Is it not possible that the use of denial and therefore the timing of death may be influenced by such unconscious factors?

There is much to suggest that, with aging, shifts in psychic energy take place in the direction of an "inward turning." This change leads to a condition of psychic economy in which there is an increased awareness of physiological functioning. There is considerable scientific evidence that the ego can register signals of distress arising from physical disease long

[217]

before clinical symptoms become apparent. Still, as we have seen, many people refuse to acknowledge the significance of pain or distress signals even when symptoms are far advanced. The mechanisms involved are those of denial, ego splitting, and depersonalization. Within predisposed family constellations aggression, guilt, masochism, depression, and "evil" introjects may all conspire to promote denial. This mechanism may represent a suicidal equivalent, and the patient's family unwittingly may reinforce his motivation for such a pathological solution.

PART III:
AGING—A SURVEY OF THE
PSYCHIATRIC LITERATURE
1961-1964

Foreword

ROBERT E. MOSS, M.D.

THE LAST VOLUME of the Proceedings of the Boston Society for Gerontologic Psychiatry (*Geriatric Psychiatry: Grief, Loss, and Emotional Disorders in the Aging Process,* edited by Berezin and Cath, 1965) included my abstracts of informative articles from the psychiatric literature on aging for the period 1950-1960. When the question arose of continuing this review of the literature for the present volume, it was decided that a group of members of the Society would carry out the project.

As in the preceding volume, the abstracts are grouped into seven categories: General Articles on Aging and the Problems of the Aged; Personality Characteristics and Disorders; Individual Therapy; Hospital and Clinic Programs; Psychological Tests; Research Studies and Surveys; and Community Programs. The coverage is not intended to be all-inclusive and is confined primarily to articles of psychiatric interest published in the English language.

Aging—A Survey of the
Psychiatric Literature
1961 - 1964

ACCORDING TO BUSSE AND RECKLESS (1961), who write on THE PSYCHIATRIC MANAGEMENT OF THE AGED, two symptoms frequently observed as part of illness in aging persons are depressive episodes and hypochondriasis.

Recurrent depressive episodes cannot always be attributed to a process of long standing; they often represent a response to new and unfamiliar stress resulting from altered life situations peculiar to older persons, such as a decline in the speed of psychomotor reaction or reduction in the ability to learn new information and to retain knowledge previously acquired. Insecurity and fear may be aroused by reduced efficiency of hearing and vision.

The change in the social role, due to loss of responsibility in the social circle or professional organizations and loss of authority in the family structure, may result in dependency upon the children with consequent loss of status and self-esteem.

Compulsory retirement at an arbitrary age and the loss of the opportunity to engage in satisfying activity make more difficult the maintenance of self-respect. Guilt is a relatively unimportant factor. Depressive episodes most often arise from inability to deal with altered life situations and with physiologic and anatomic changes associated with the aging process. Ill health or bereavement may trigger a reactive depression, especially when there has been a reduction in financial security, social status, satisfying activity, and physical health.

The physician always should be alert to the possibility of depression, which may be recognized by loss of energy, appetite, or weight, inability to sleep, and loss of sex drive. There may be a tendency toward self-depreciation, indicated by expressions indicating lowered self-esteem, verbalization of worries, and manifest anxiety.

Both depression and senility may present a picture of apathy, inertness, retardation, gloom, and a decline in personal standards suggesting advancing senile decay, an impression which may be strengthened by the presence of agitated behavior and rudeness. If the condition is due to depression, treatment will alleviate or cure it. If the depression deepens or is prolonged, the patient should be referred to a psychiatrist.

Old age seems to emphasize the problem of living with the hypochondriacal patient. Energy which the aged person formerly directed toward subordinates now must be invested in the functioning of his bowels, or may be shifted from some specific psychic area to a less threatening preoccupation with bodily disease and function. Another patient may see discomfort as punishment and partial atonement for guilt, resulting from hostility toward the people who are close to him.

The author suggests that the physician avoid explaining to the patient the nature of the disease affecting him because the knowledge that he has no organic ailment will deprive him of the necessary psychologic defenses and of his only means of self-esteem. Trying to maintain his defenses at all costs, the patient attempts desperately to convince the physician and others that his symptoms have a physical basis, often becoming extremely "hostile and difficult to manage." The doctor should listen attentively to the full "organ recital" and should not challenge the facts. The patient gradually will develop a feeling of security with the physician when he finds he may express himself without being contradicted. Then the physician may guide the patient into investigating areas of emotional conflict.

Skill is needed in handling the patient's relatives. The physician should avoid telling them or the patient that the symptoms are of psychogenic origin in order to save the patient from loss of face and to enlist the relatives in the supportive program.

Finally, more attention should be allotted to persons in the middle years when the foundations for mental health in later years are laid in order to prevent psychiatric problems in later years. This is the time to develop activities fostering mental health, such as social investment and the development of interests outside one's occupation.

The older person should be helped to live in his own home as long as possible while maintaining some direct contact with the community. Loneliness may decrease mental vigor and emotional stability in old age. It may be relieved by visiting services of the church or of civic and old-age groups.

Norvell L. Peterson, M.D.

Lenzer (1961), in SOCIOCULTURAL INFLUENCES ON ADJUST-MENT TO AGING, is concerned with the relationship between sociocultural phenomena and the way in which aging is perceived and experienced.

Many of the serious difficulties people undergo in adjusting to becoming older are a result of negative social attitudes toward the elderly, the absence of status and role for the aged in our society, and the failure of our society to provide social mechanisms to enable people to move from middle age into old age. To age in the United States it is necessary to change one's attitudes and behavior, and because this change is viewed in our culture as moving from a desirable to an undesirable stage in life and is accompanied by a minimum of social support, the elderly person is usually dissatisfied.

The place of the elderly person in our culture is vague. Little is expected of him except in work and in family council. The individual family is less likely to take responsibility for the welfare of its older members; society-at-large assumes this responsibility at the present time. Many elderly persons, however, see social programs for the aged as a last resort to which they dislike to turn. Older persons may react to their environment by rejecting the fact that they have become older, and sometimes this resistance is a positive factor causing them to remain active in life. In other situations, they may show a desperate and unsuccessful attempt to return to an earlier age, or they may decline to associate with peers or to take advantage of what society provides for the elderly.

The aged may lose their sense of identity and feelings of importance as they become less important to others. Typically, in old age, props which have maintained the individual are lost, and many of the elderly are unable to re-establish their sense of self-importance after they have undergone such losses.

When the elderly lose financial security, sense of importance, and affection, they may try to regain these satisfactions by aberrant behavior, or they may become apathetic and resigned. Our society, however, does provide the elderly with opportunities for self-satisfaction and further maturation. Free from major responsibility and the restrictions of thought and behavior that obligations impose, they have the free time which is afforded to no other group. Many elderly persons are financially secure, and the prognosis is that there will be increasing economic security for the elderly.

In old age, as in the other stages of life, there is neither inherent goodness nor inherent badness, but potentialities for both. Separation and loss take place and problems develop, but although some of these stresses are inevitable, others may react to different kinds of help.

The advantages of growing old are recognized and utilized by a few of the aged. These people are able to make the most of this stage of their life, even though society neither recognizes nor encourages such opportunities. It remains to be seen whether or not society will allow the elderly to make full use of their lives.

Donald Wexler, M.D.

Contrary to the thesis postulated by Cumming and Henry (1961) that aging is characterized by an inevitable withdrawal or disengagement, research by Tobin and Neugarten (1961), on LIFE SATISFACTION AND SOCIAL INTERACTION IN THE AGING, indicates that with advancing age, engagement rather than disengagement is more closely associated with with well-being.

The 187 cases that constituted the present study were divided into two age groups: 50-69 and 70 and over. All the measures are based on data from lengthy interviews conducted at approximately six-month intervals and covering many aspects of the respondent's life pattern, his attitudes, and his values.

In summary, social interaction was positively associated with life satisfaction for all ages included in this study, and in advanced age this association is increased rather than decreased.

Joel Ordaz, M.D.

In EXPLORATION IN PERSONAL ADJUSTMENT AFTER AGE 65, Taves and Hansen (1962) find that to meet the needs of the elderly it is necessary to correlate the changes in the social structure and attitudes with factors such as good personal adjustment, happiness, and satisfaction. Agencies dealing with the elderly should direct their work toward the preservation of healthy self-concepts and rewarding social roles.

In an effort to determine the correlates of adjustment among those over 65, 500 "well-adjusted" and 400 "poorly adjusted" individuals were compared on a series of sociopsychological variables. The study of an individual's overt behavior ignores his evaluation of the situation, although it sheds light on his life style and on his capacity for experience. This paper considers both "objective and subjective evaluations of life's situations" and tries to distinguish the well-adjusted from the poorly adjusted senior citizen. A modification of Calvin's adjustment scale was used. Areas covered were health, family, work, friendship, religion, and morale. The elderly person was considered to have good personal adjustment if he was satisfied with his health, had close friendships, was satisfied with work, gained security or comfort from religion, felt useful, thought there was something valuable about being elderly, was happy in relation to his early

[227]

life, and had satisfactory relations with his family. This definition of good personal adjustment rests on certain socio-psychological assumptions: (1) that the elderly place emphasis on the areas mentioned above; (2) that these values produce goals for which the adjustment score indicates success or failure in achieving; (3) that the individual's responses are greatly influenced by how his peers' "reference group" and by how other important people feel about him.

The authors feel that an important future study could be made of the effect of others on an individual who may be satisfied with his own achievements and situation, but who feels criticized by his group members who do not share his values. The study should include the possibility of a different kind of group's applauding his achievements and enabling the elderly person to receive reinforcement of his satisfactions.

Selecting 65 as the age above which to define a population as elderly has its limitations. Sixty-five, however, is the age at which our society arbitrarily has determined that people should retire.

The methodology of this study involved the interviewing of 6,700 people in five Midwestern states. Comparable adjustment data were obtained for 4,130 of these people from Missouri, South Dakota, and Minnesota. From this group the 510 scoring highest and the 428 scoring lowest on the adjustment scale were chosen for comparison. In the findings, 13 percent were classified as very well adjusted and 11 percent as very poorly adjusted. Six out of every ten women and five out of every ten men achieved a good adjustment score. Urban or rural residence seemed to have no effect on the adjustment of the elderly. Seventy percent of the married, but only 55 percent of the widowed were well adjusted, and a greater proportion of married persons were well adjusted than of those who were single or divorced or separated. Homeowners seemed to be better adjusted than those who lived in apartments.

Two-thirds of the high school or college graduates were considered well adjusted, whereas those who had completed only grade school or less were equally divided into well adjusted and poorly adjusted. There is strong evidence that the elderly who were members of organizations, especially those who played leadership roles, were well adjusted: 93 percent of the leaders and 57 percent of the nonleaders were considered to be getting along satisfactorily. Seventy-nine percent of members of civic, social, or professional organizations were well adjusted people. The characteristics mentioned above were considered to involve a social role or a higher socioeconomic status and are seen as positively associated with adjustment. The findings make it very clear that partial or full employment helped the elderly to be highly well adjusted, whereas those who were in full retirement were poorly adjusted.

More objective criteria and self-perceptions of age, income, and health revealed the following findings. When the persons studied were divided into five-year age groupings, the older the group, the smaller the proportion of persons who were well adjusted. This difference is considered to be based upon social and physical changes in aging, combined with the changing self-concept of being middle-aged to that of being elderly or old. Those who saw themselves as middle-aged were better adjusted than those who felt they were elderly, and these in turn were better adjusted than those who saw themselves as old. With the change in self-concept, there was a reduction in expectations and an acceptance of this reduction. It is not surprising that those who felt that they had a high income or had more than they needed to live on and those who felt that they were in good health were well adjusted. Home ownership, employment, and social participation are considered strong elements in assessing social class, and those who scored well on these factors had a good adjustment.

To summarize this study, the more social role activity and the higher the socioeconomic status, the more likely is good adjustment. Active role-playing in marriage, social, organizational, leadership, and work areas contributes to good adjustment. A favorable self-image on the part of the elderly person—seeing himself as in good health, middle-aged, and having sufficient funds—also indicated good adjustment. Whether the individual lives in the city or in the country or is male or female does not affect the score; chronological age and actual living arrangements also seem to be relatively unimportant.

Donald Wexler, M.D.

Kemp (1963), in his paper OLD AGE, A REGRET, describes first the "lonely lady complex." The elderly woman is the isolate, the woman living on her own with fewer and fewer friends and visitors. Increasingly, there becomes less point in going out, eating properly, keeping the house clean, or indeed keeping herself clean. The diagnosis can be made at the front door: the neglected garden, the peeling paintwork, the uncleaned windows and dirty curtains, and the complete silence; finally, the shuffling footsteps and the smell of inactivity. No wonder the old lady begins to keep cats, talk to herself, and wander about at night. Technically, the diagnosis is late paraphrenia, and in Park Hospital, Liverpool, there are 300 such foolish and confused old ladies who have reached the wards by this route. They are destined to spend many years there in a futility which probably could have been avoided if they had not been allowed to live on their own meagre resources for so long.

The other major clinical picture is that of "retirement rot" in men. Nearly all of Kemp's patients meet his inevitable question, "What do you do with your time now that you are retired?" with the inevitable reply: "Nothing, Doctor—nothing." The man who fails to manage retirement successfully in his 70's often enters into a fearful contest as to whether his mind will give out before his body gives up. There is the danger that all such cases, whether the psychiatric trouble is emotional, toxic, organic, or psychotic, will reach the stage where they can be seen as senile dementia and be admitted to an institution.

In the author's opinion, the hospital is a dangerous place for old people. There is the physical danger of the hospital staphylococcus; the moral danger of overdiagnosis, overinvestigation, and overtreatment; the emotional danger of dependence; and the strong possibility that the patient's outside world will disintegrate. In short, admission is the most likely way of producing a permanent patient.

To avoid the last part of Disraeli's observation that "youth is a blunder, manhood a struggle, old age a regret," Kemp recommends the following measures: The geriatrician should extend his interest to the years before he is called in as a clinical undertaker. The community should set up geriatric and pregeriatric outpatient clinics in every general hospital. Efficient discharge and placement should be arranged so that patients can remain in the mainstream of life. All old people should be registered so that they can be supervised if necessary. There should be local-authority geriatric clinics and prophylactic clinics for the elderly. Lastly, there should

[231]

be increased education for growing old. Those who know what is to be done prove in everyday life to be those who need neither immediate nor preventive help.

Earl M. Wedrow, M.D.

Leveen and Priver (1963), in SIGNIFICANCE OF ROLE PLAYING IN THE AGED PERSON, investigate what happens to persons who, as a result of aging, find their whole lives changing and have to adjust to new and ill-defined roles. Individuals with psychopathology are shown to have maintained themselves and to function with some comfort as a result of playing particular kinds of roles. These roles act as ego boundaries, and without them the individuals would encounter serious trouble.

The aging person is less adaptable to change, and yet is expected to adjust to major alterations in his life. In the past, the elderly could rely on their homes, possessions, friends, and organization memberships to be with them until death. Today, with mechanization, urbanization, and the destruction of the family, a social vacuum exists in which the elderly become emotionally insecure and re-experience the anxieties of childhood and early adolescence. The well-integrated individual will probably make a satisfactory adjustment to old age, but those who have been maladjusted are likely to develop emotional disorders, often similar to those previously experienced.

Good adjustments stem from social development and personal attainment. These goals are often difficult to achieve for the elderly in our society. There are four areas in which people have roles: economic, familial, physical, and social. In each category there is a specific role which becomes strengthened as it is played, and the more the individual is attuned

[232]

to the expectations of the role, the better he is able to anticipate the responses of others. By the time a person has aged, he is familiar with his role, has accepted it, and is usually comfortable with the stresses involved. But with the abrupt changes of aging and loss of status, uncertainty and confusion develop. The role is less clearly defined, and the patient's self-esteem is threatened. Anxieties develop, with a resulting sense of worthlessness. The abrupt changes in one or more of the categories mentioned can produce psychological decompensation.

In the economic sphere, forced retirement may release repressed emotional difficulties. Employment has promoted ego strength, escape from tensions in the home, and acceptance by one's peers, whereas retirement can cause dwelling on one's self, loss of income and status, and being forced into a dependent situation.

The well-adjusted person is emotionally flexible, able to involve himself with first one person and then another and to shift from one activity to another. Those who are unable to make these changes suffer an increasingly impoverished emotional life, become more rigid, and are unable to deal with the loss of a spouse or children. In considering the area of the family role in marriage, it is often observed that couples have become dependent in a symbiotic way. The loss of the partner often leaves the survivor unable to find a substitute for the parental or filial role.

The physical role is mainly dependent on physical health during adult life. A person who has been physically well often feels very much threatened by signs of the climacteric, and the resulting anxiety may lead to hypochondriasis and compulsive behavior designed to prove that one is still young. Sudden limitation of activity, such as that caused by the loss

[233]

of a limb or by heart disease, may produce emotional disorders of varying severity.

The social role often can hold a fragmented ego together. The loss of friends or relatives may give the elderly person a feeling of isolation and insecurity. Social isolation can result in cultural isolation; loss of friends may mean lessening of emotional and intellectual experiences.

The patient who has been in a public psychiatric institution for a long time depends upon it for a way of life and plays the appropriate role. He is often comfortable, and his dependency needs are now satisfied. A sense of security replaces a desire to strive or compete in a regressive way, and discharge from such a setting can be highly threatening. The aged person also becomes institutionalized to the role he has played for the time under 65; his style has been developed. Patients who have undergone prolonged institutionalization have narrow interests, narrow flexibility; they cannot tolerate social change, think in stereotypes, have fixed views, and exaggerated fears. The aged have similar attitudes and feelings and, just as the institutionalized person may break down when faced with the possibility of discharge from hospital care, the aged may decompensate when the roles that have satisfied them begin to deteriorate. It is difficult for the aged to transfer energies to new ways of functioning. They become less adaptable to change, but are expected to make radical changes in their way of life. "They are in an ambiguous situation which is the root of intense anxiety, dependency, and regression leading to emotional breakdown. The role, which can be likened to a container which keeps the individual intact, has been shattered."

Donald Wexler, M.D.

Linden (1963a), in THE AGING AND THE COMMUNITY, discusses Pennsylvania's program for the care of the aged, where a governor's council on aging reports to the governor's advisory committee on aging. To the question: "Do you feel we reject our aged?" Dr. Linden replies, "I feel that our community and culture reject the aged less than they did, although we do over-emphasize the values of youth." Dr. Linden describes the case of a woman of 83 who, although advanced in physical deterioration, was still alert, interested in life and love, and unwilling to remain in a home for the elderly because there she felt isolated from the younger generations.

A wish for independence is common in the aged. Surveys made in St. Petersburg, Tucson, and other areas where many elderly retired people live indicate that the overwhelming majority prefer independnce from their children; 95 to 98 percent prefer to live by themselves. The elderly who return to live with their children usually are in a "state of reverse responsibility," with the parent depending upon the child. This relationship is bad for both parent and child.

Careless mental diagnosis of the aged is frequent; the diagnoses made of aged persons in mental hospitals are often of the wastebasket variety. Such a diagnosis as "psychosis with cerebral arteriosclerosis" is meaningless in many instances. Medical misdiagnosis is likewise common: many of the aged who are not institutionalized are misdiagnosed and badly treated, receiving little more than medication. Even the case of the patient who has been followed by the same physician over a long period of years may be misdiagnosed because the physician fails to recognize the changes that are taking place, and that new diseases may be developing in the elderly patient.

In Philadelphia, as in most cities, general hospitals do not like to admit elderly patients because they may become chronic patients, run out of money, and then have to be transferred to another hospital or given continued treatment without reimbursement to the hospital. In the Philadelphia psychiatric program, psychiatric treatment and facilities for the elderly have been difficult to obtain. In 1963, $105,000 was allocated by the Division of Mental Health for mental health clinics to pay for treatment of the elderly on a fee-for-service basis. Seventeen percent of the patients in these clinics were elderly, twice their proportion in the general population.

The adult health and recreation center is described in detail. It provides many facilities for recreation and occupational therapy as well as psychiatric services and social work services. The most impressive statistic involving the use of this center is that of the 650 "oldsters" who have used the facility in over three years, not one has had to be institutionalized. The author concludes, therefore, that although there was a self-selection factor in that those who came to the center volunteered for the activities it afforded, nevertheless the center tended to prevent psychological and physical breakdown in average elderly persons. Another type of facility, the retirement hotel, enables the elderly to live normal lives which are responsibility-free in their own communities, and the cost is so low that those on social security or old age assistance may have some funds left over at the end of each month.

Psychotherapy for the aged should be intensive and compassionate. The older patient develops a strong positive transference to the psychiatrist, perhaps because the psychiatrist is often the first person who has taken a real interest in him and his needs for many years. It appears that eight or nine office visits will often end the depression of the elderly patient without the need for either medication or electroshock treatment. Over 50 percent of the elderly show prompt and long-lasting response to therapy, and another 20 percent show a positive reaction. The remainder are close to death and can respond only in a superficial way.

The article suggests that the psychiatrist should not treat only the elderly, because his view of what families in the community do to the elderly may become distorted and unrealistic. Frequently when an elderly patient is in trouble, his children are having their own emotional problems. What happens to the old person may have a great effect on the well-being of his children, and it is not uncommon for adult children to develop neurotic or psychotic conditions concurrently with the admission of a parent to a hospital or his release from it.

Donald Wexler, M.D.

Scott and Devereaux (1963a), in HABILITATION POTENTIAL OF ELDERLY STATE HOSPITAL PATIENTS, define "habilitation" as "the movement of a patient from a state psychiatric hospital to a community-centered resource which could meet the patient's needs at least as satisfactorily as a state psychiatric hospital." A project team at DeWitt State Hospital (Oroville, California) studied a population of 1,047 geriatric patients.

The major conclusion is that "the majority of the patients studied do not belong in a psychiatric treatment center." Overcrowded and understaffed mental hospitals are regarded by the authors as undesirable facilities for most elderly patients. Carefully selected protective settings in the community seem to be more appropriate. Few patients could afford these settings, however, and relatives seldom could be located or prevailed upon to assist. Also, tax-supported public institutions are resistant to accepting elderly persons. Because of the absence of practical alternatives, not because of positive indications for treatment, so many elderly persons remain in state hospitals for general psychiatry.

Robert J. Kastenbaum, Ph.D.

In a study by Lowenthal (1964) on SOCIAL ISOLATION AND MENTAL ILLNESS IN OLD AGE, four subgroups of institutionalized and noninstitutionalized elderly people were drawn from a larger sample of 1,200 persons who are being studied in a long-range investigation. In these subgroups, a pattern of lifelong isolation or alienation was "not necessarily conducive to the development of the kinds of mental disorder that bring persons to the psychiatric ward in their old age." On the other hand, the social isolation that begins in the later years of life does seem to be linked with mental disorder, and the study suggests that this isolation may be more of a consequence than a cause of mental illness among the elderly. Physical illness often seems to be the critical antecedent to both the social isolation and the mental illness.

This study includes a discussion of the concept of social isolation and presents a method for categorizing elderly persons with respect to isolation. The long-range program of which this study is a part is being conducted at Langley Porter Neuropsychiatric Institute, San Francisco.

Robert J. Kastenbaum, Ph.D.

Wolff (1964), in THE CONFUSED GERIATRIC PATIENT, finds that acute schizophrenic patients who show confusion may also be out of contact, have delusions and hallucinations, and

[238]

show bizarre behavior. Prompt recovery from confusion is the rule, although chronic schizophrenic patients may remain confused for months or years. Patients with brain syndrome show confusion usually combined with disorientation, memory loss, decreased intelligence, emotional lability, and loss of judgment. Confused patients talk incoherently, wander aimlessly, lose their direction, and make mistakes in identification.

The author reviews his own and others' experience in treating the confused geriatric patient. Pentylenetetrazol given in doses of .400 to .800 gm. daily over a period of four months produced significant improvement in 30 percent of elderly patients with chronic brain syndrome.

Glutamic acid treatment was given in four groups of patients. In three out of the four groups, clinical improvement was noted in 44 to 78 percent of patients. In the fourth group it was felt that improvement could not be expected because brain damage was so severe. Dosage ranged between 10 gms. and 30 gms. daily.

Procaine injection is reported to have produced improvement in "memory attention and various aspects of vitality" in a large group of geriatric patients (1,400) in Rumania. Attempts to repeat these findings in two smaller groups failed to show encouraging results.

Hormonal therapy, especially estrogens and androgens, appears to be of value in aiding circulation, increasing physical and mental activities, and reducing fatigue. Disorientation, impairment of memory, and confusion do not appear to be improved.

Ribonucleic acid given over a period of seven months is reported to produce improvement in mental functioning, alertness, and state of confusion.

Psychotherapy, individually or in groups, is cited by the author as important, especially when confusion is the result of emotional factors. Elderly patients may become confused as a reaction to loss of a loved person, change of environment, loss of social status, or loss of occupation or physical capability. Weekly psychotherapy for a minimum of three months is beneficial.

Edward L. Zarsky, M.D.

In a study of PHYSICAL ILLNESS AND DEPRESSIVE SYMPTOM-ATOLOGY, aged patients with cardiac disease were compared by Dovenmuehle and Verwoerdt (1963), with a younger group of patients in order to elucidate the reasons for depressive symptoms, which had been found in 64 per cent of cardiacs in a previous study. Part II is concerned with "Factors of Length and Severity of Illness and Frequency of Hospitalization." No direct relationship between severity of cardiac disease and severity of depressive symptoms could be shown. Mild and severe disease are apt to be accompanied by equally severe depressive symptoms, early in the disease. Mild cardiac illness that has persisted more than three years is not apt to be accompanied by severe depressive symptoms. Severe cardiac illness produces severe depressive symptoms both early and late in the illness.

Frequent hospitalization is associated with moderate and severe depressive symptoms in both mild and severe cardiac disease. It is possible that depressive symptoms contribute to frequent hospitalization, especially in mild cardiac disease; or hospitalization itself may be an important factor in producing a depressive response.

In Part III of this study, "Aspects of Awareness," the authors (1964) find that, in mild cases, depressive symptoms are rather

[240]

severe during the first several years, but only mild later. In severe illness, severe depressive symptoms continue throughout the illness. Regardless of severity, the more frequently a person is hospitalized, the more apt he is to have severe depressive symptoms.

In the present report the authors examined the influence of cardiac illness and depressive symptoms on the level of awareness of precipitating factors, which may appear as conscious morbid preoccupations about physical health, loss of love objects, prestige, income, and similar factors. A high level of awareness was consistently related to greater severity of the underlying cardiac disease and to no other factor. In mild cardiac illness, the depressive affect and the awareness of factors precipitating it are determined more by the individual's psychological make-up than in severe cardiac disease, where situational factors may have so overwhelming an effect that patients with different psychological backgrounds tend to react in a more uniform pattern.

Robert E. Moss, M.D.

Gardner, Bahn, and Mack (1964) report on SUICIDE AND PSYCHIATRIC CARE IN THE AGING. To cover Monroe County, New York, a cumulative psychiatric case registry was set up on January 1, 1960, to which all psychiatric cases are reported from all psychiatric facilities in the county. This registry has been used to study the epidemiology of suicide. Data have accumulated that may assist psychiatrists in predicting the probability of suicide in various types of individuals. The average annual rate of suicide for the entire county was 9.7 per 100,000; for those in the case registry, the suicide rate was 15 times as great. For those diagnosed as depressed, the rate was 230; and for those who had previously attempted suicide, the average annual rate was 905 during the two-and-a-half year follow-up period. For each group the rate was about twice as high for persons over 55 as for those under 55 years of age. The rate of attempted suicide was relatively small in the older as compared with the younger age group; but an attempt portended successful suicide, usually within the first year after the attempt. There is a high risk of suicide for the older male living in the lowest socioeconomic areas of a city, often alone and isolated, having some physical illness and a disturbed work history. In addition to noting depression in older patients, the physician must be alert to such factors as a downward and unstable work rate, social and psychological isolation, physical illness, and a low-status living area.

Robert E. Moss, M.D.

According to Spieth (1964), who writes on CARDIOVAS-CULAR HEALTH STATUS, AGE, AND PSYCHOLOGICAL PERFORM-ANCE, an important problem in the psychology of aging is the extent to which poor or slow performance is associated with age-correlated, controllable disease rather than with aging per se. Psychological performance tests were given to more than 600 men aged 23-59, who were in nominally normal health. Mild to moderate degrees of cardiovascular disease, with apparent cerebral involvement, were reliably associated with slow and, to a lesser extent, poor performance. Because cardiovascular disease is common in old persons and its incidence increases very rapidly after age 35, this study suggests that much of the typical downward trend of performance with age is a reflection of cardiovascular diseases rather than of aging per se.

Robert E. Moss, M.D.

[242]

As an anthropologist, Anderson (1964) is concerned with the culture of the aged person and its influence upon his response to stress. In STRESS AND PSYCHOPATHOLOGY AMONG AGED AMERICANS, she studies the perception, affective response, and coping mechanisms of such individuals.

One hundred and twenty-seven men and women were selected from a sample of 543 patients 60 years old or over who had been admitted to the psychiatric ward of the San Francisco General Hospital in 1959. The median income of these persons was $1,500 per year, and none had been hospitalized on a psychiatric ward before the age of 60. They had been classified as suffering from psychogenic or organic psychiatric difficulties.

Each patient was asked: What condition or event was most stressful in your lifetime? When did it occur? How long did it last? What was your reaction? What did you do, if anything? What made each condition or situation stressful or difficult? What helped to resolve it or what could have helped?

The author believes that the answers indicate two major factors as influencing the response to stress: the time of life for the particular event recalled, and the kind and degree of psychiatric disability, whether psychological or organic.

Many subjects reported death as "the hardest thing I ever had to face." They were not consciously concerned with their own death, but with those of a spouse, parents, siblings, or children. Other conscious preoccupations were those related to psychological, physical, marital-domestic, and socioeconomic matters. They were apt to regard institutionalization, rather than mental illness itself, as "the hardest thing." "Coming here. I'm 80 years old now. I just couldn't believe it. I couldn't believe it could possibly be true. It just broke me down. I'm not happy here. I don't want you to believe I'm unhappy. It's as bad as a jail."

[243]

They tend to describe their own physical difficulties as due to accidents or injuries and those of family members as caused by illness. Although 30 percent of the patients were divorced or separated, they regarded as traumatic only those events previous or subsequent to that arrangement. Socioeconomic matters were the least of their concerns. They thought about the depression of the 1930's and their job problems. "I was disappointed about the things I couldn't do. I brooded over it for 20 years."

In terms of time, the years 45-59 were perceived as the least provocative of stress, and the years 21-44 and over 60 as the most provocative.

It was possible to distinguish a self-oriented and a situation-oriented group in response to the question, "How did you feel about it?" "*I* felt so alone, nervous." "*It* was overwhelming." Reactions were more self-oriented for the experiences of old age and less self-oriented for the events of childhood and youth.

In trying to cope with stress, the elderly patients more often attempted to assuage the strain by accepting help, or by doing nothing, than by doing something about the stressful circumstance itself. This response indicates, the author states, that the old person is interested in immediate relief rather than in long-range remedies.

It was further possible to delineate different patterns of reaction among those patients suffering from psychogenic difficulties and among those suffering from organic psychiatric difficulties.

Patients with purely psychogenic disorders verbalized their recalled stress in a diffuse, rambling, amplifying way, whereas those with organic disorders were more brief and did not elaborate. The psychogenics were more stress-oriented. They were doers, were active and self-propelled, and tried to change things. The organics were more strain-oriented in their coping mechanisms. They talked about resolution and sometimes managed to reinterpret their stress to their satisfaction. In the end the stressful event became for them a closed chapter. For the better-oriented men and women, hospitalization was more traumatic than for those less aware of their circumstances. Even so, the patients with chronic brain syndrome reported events of briefest duration with the greatest frequency. Eight of ten recalls were 24 hours or less in duration. And for them, the alternative to active engagement was no activity at all.

Earl M. Wedrow, M.D.

Lerner (1963) investigates MENTAL HEALTH OF THE AGING POPULATION IN RELATION TO SOCIAL SECURITY BENEFITS. Social security benefits aid in the reduction of anxiety that might otherwise be present because of concern about meeting financial responsibilities. Freedom from this problem enables the aged to maintain dignity and security. This article gives several examples of aged persons who were better able to exercise their creative and artistic abilities because of a secure retirement income. The factors of adequate conditioning are as follows: "Good family relationships, healthy religious attitudes and neighbor-centered interests, including the capacity to enter willingly into, initiate and participate in socially meaningful activities." Change of residence for the aged, with separation from the familiar environment of family and friends, is inadvisable.

Eliot Landsman, M.D.

As stated by Bortz (1963) in his paper, A LOOK AT AGING AND GROWTH POTENTIALS, aging is "the changes which occur in tissues and performance with passing time." It is a dynamic phenomenon beginning with conception and ending with death, and it includes more than deterioration. It is the biological, human, and sociological maturation of the individual during his lifetime. There are three kinds of aging: biologic, psychologic, and social. Psychologic aging is most important in trying to understand the elderly.

Clinical experiments at the Lankenau Hospital show how easy it is to improve the health and the mental attitudes of individuals of all ages by giving them physical exercise. The elderly need continuing stimulation in order to maintain their interests and alertness; otherwise they become isolated and inactive. Responsibility to community and family helps to maintain their biological and cultural well-being. No segment of our society is immune from the problems caused by the existence of millions of elderly for whom no provision has been made.

Work of some kind is essential to the well-being of the elderly. Work involves action, and in Western civilization action is an important means of self-expression and fulfillment. Contemplation is not a part of our civilization. It is difficult to step out of a society where the emphasis is placed on production and on the acquiring of material things. Therefore, it is difficult for the elderly person suddenly to find himself with leisure and to transfer the leisure into a creative force for himself and society. Our youth-oriented culture must learn to appreciate the contributions which the elderly can make to our society. Deeper understanding of the psychological phases of aging is helping us to gain a better understanding of the drives that control behavior. The physician who treats older patients must have a great interest in them in order to give the patients a sense of satisfaction in themselves. The older physician, by working with older patients, can gain fresh knowledge of their growth potentials.

Donald Wexler, M.D.

In SOME REGRESSIVE PHENOMENA IN OLD AGE, Gillespie (1963) finds that fear of death is the basic factor in the development of a senile psychosis. When he first began working with patients over the age of 70, in 1934, psychiatric opinion held that such individuals suffered from either senile or arteriosclerotic dementia. Actually, he found, these patients did not show as much intellectual deterioration as he had expected. Instead, they demonstrated a wide variety of psychological problems. Most of these, however, could be classified as feelings of persecution, depression, and hypochondriasis. These patients are basically concerned not with intellectual deterioration, but with total bodily deterioration; and not with bodily deterioration as such, but with the death of the body.

In attempting to deal with his approaching death, the patient summons up an intensification of his usual personality traits. If this measure does not control his anxiety, he tries to deny the reality of his situation by using the process of projection: it is not that he may die because of internal causes, but that someone outside is going to kill him. In order to lend emphasis to this kind of thinking, the patient must suspend his sense of reality and regress into fantasy. By giving up his interest in both the real external world and his real internal world, he is able to escape the recognition of what he cannot accept—the fact of his own bodily disintegration. All the other conscious concerns, from fear of castration to preoccupation

[247]

with bodily functions, simply are attempts to avoid confrontation with the reality of his own death.

Earl M. Wedrow, M.D.

PERSONALITY CHARACTERISTICS AND DISORDERS

While attempting to devise a "symptoms/sign inventory" which would apply to all types of mental patients, Foulds (1960) observed what he considers to be an indication that some individuals over 60 who are diagnosed by psychiatrists as suffering from a psychotic depression in reality may be neurotically depressed. He describes his finding in a paper on PSYCHOTIC DEPRESSION and AGE.

The author bases his hypothesis on the contrast between the responses of three groups of patients to the inventory: the neurotically depressed, the psychotically depressed who are under 60, and the psychotically depressed who are over 60 years of age.

A female psychotic depressive under 60, for example, typically would reveal the following feelings in replying to the inventory:

1. She is an unworthy person in her own eyes.
2. She is a condemned person because of her sins.
3. People are talking about her and criticizing her because of things she has done wrong.
4. She is afraid to go out alone.
5. She has said things that have injured others.

Essentially, then, the psychotic depressive under 60 is primarily aware of feelings of guilt.

In contrast, the responses of a woman patient over 60 who has been diagnosed as suffering from psychotic depression differ from those of the neurotic depressive. She feels the following:

[248]

1. The future is pointless.
2. When she goes to bed, she doesn't care if she never wakes up again.
3. She is troubled by waking in the early hours and being unable to get to sleep again.
4. She is unable to understand what she reads or what people say as well as she used to do.
5. Her hand shakes when she tries to do something.
6. She has difficulty in getting to sleep.

Patients over 60, then, are primarily aware of difficulties associated with getting to sleep and remaining asleep. The problem of sleep, of course, is not the concern of those patients under the age of 60 who are obsessed with feelings of guilt.

This difference in emphasis indicated to the author that there may be many in the over-60 group who in fact are suffering from a neurotic and not a psychotic depression. He suggests that the psychiatrist may be influenced by the factor of the patients' increased age and may diagnose such individuals as psychotic when the same pathology observed in a younger person would be regarded as neurotic. He believes that this bias should be taken into account and that many of the older patients who are currently diagnosed as psychotic would then be classified as neurotic.

Earl M. Wedrow, M.D.

Zuckerman (1962) attempts to simplify what he regards as the extreme complexity of the aging process by constructing two congruent quadrangles, as described in his paper on THE PSYCHOLOGY OF AGING.

The sides of the first quadrangle are as follows: (1) The calendar or chronological age. (2) The physiologic or organic age, which includes the cosmetic morphology as well as the mechanical, chemical, and neurological functions of the body. (3) The intellectual factor of age as evidenced in psychosexual behavior and maturity. (4) The varied emotional components of an individual's life. In turn, the above factors influence the quadrangle composed of: (a) individuality, (b) vocation, (c) marriage, (d) organization.

It is the element of time, however, which alters the first quadrangle in such a way that it brings a varied influence to bear upon the second. As a consequence of physical deterioration incident to the aging process, the individual over 60 may develop feelings of insecurity and lose a sense of organization. Although these difficulties may have their beginnings in the problems of early childhood relationships, relatively modest measures may lead to considerable improvement in the patient's condition.

For example, an older person who has lost his self-critical faculties and whose discriminative and reflective judgment is on the wane may be in a difficult situation in a particular household. But moving him from the rejecting environment to an accepting one may benefit him greatly. Resocialization in group living and productive and recreational activities, with psychotherapy where possible, may produce some return of self-sufficiency, independence, tranquility, and a potential for happiness.

Because comparatively minor physical upsets may cause confusion in older persons, a complete physical evaluation with supportive medication and measures often leads to general improvement. Bowel and bladder obstruction, incontinence, dehydration, bedsores, bronchopneumonia, and urinary infections develop rapidly in elderly persons confined to

[250]

bed, and relief from these conditions may restore mental equilibrium in a relatively brief time. In contrast, stopping all medication when the patient has been under the care of more than one doctor or on medicines for long periods of time will sometimes alleviate a severe semistuporous state.

Thus, it is observed that the older patient benefits in a gratifying way from even the most rudimentary physical and psychological treatment.

Earl M. Wedrow, M.D.

Davidson, in discussing PSYCHIATRIC SYNDROMES IN THE ELDERLY, finds that although there is a general opinion that more people are living into old age today, the fact is that since 1900 the life expectancy of those who actually reach the age of 65 has increased only by 11 months. It is the large number of young people surviving into their 60's that has made the psychiatric syndromes associated with the elderly of more contemporary importance. For example, Aubrey Lewis observes that the mental illnesses of old age may replace schizophrenia in the future as the largest category in the records of admission to mental hospitals.

The author divides the psychiatric syndromes of the elderly into two groups: those involving impairment of the understanding (defects of the intellectual functions) and those involving emotional or behavioral difficulties (the affective disorders).

When the intellectual impairment is primary and permanent, the author calls the condition dementia; when it is primary and temporary, he calls it delirium or a confusional state. If a mood disorder is the main problem, he regards any intellectual malfunctioning as a complication and not as a

[251]

criterion for diagnosis. Further, he divides dementia into two types, senile and arteriosclerotic. The senile process is mild and slowly progressive, whereas the arteriosclerotic is dramatic and fluctuating in its step-like deterioration. He classifies as confusional states those cases where the impairment of understanding is temporary and is alleviated by treatment. In his opinion they are caused by a variety of organic disturbances. He stresses the importance of recognizing that an individual with some degree of dementia who is in a confusional state may appear to be extremely ill, but that even so he will respond to proper treatment.

The other large category of psychiatric illness among the elderly is the group of affective disorders. Here, depression is the most important problem, and the hypochondriasis and apathy deriving from it must not be confused with actual physical disorder and dementia. Depression, he thinks, is also a major factor in paranoid conditions in the elderly.

The prognosis is dramatically different in the dementias and the affective disorders. Seventy to 80 percent of patients with dementia are dead within two years after admission, whereas 75-90 percent of those with affective disorders are still alive, many of them out of the hospital though most of the elderly paranoids still in.

A careful, considerate, simple, psychological approach, he believes, is the best treatment for these patients. Drugs often confuse the picture. Sedatives, for example, frequently produce an effect opposite to that intended. For this reason, the cooperation of the nurses and doctors on the wards is essential. When they work well together, in his experience, the patients improve; when there is disharmony, the patients suffer.

Earl M. Wedrow, M.D.

"The purpose of this paper is to describe, identify and explore some of the behavior dynamics of geriatric delinquents." In THE GERIATRIC DELINQUENT, Wolk, Rustin, and Scott, (1963) include three case reports, a section on dynamics, and a section on treatment. The paper is an outgrowth of discussion and review of an Activities-of-Daily-Living Committee to which residents of a home for the aged who were not making a good adjustment were referred.

The delinquent is one who tends to act out his conflicts when placed in a social milieu with which he cannot cope. He may have functioned well when younger, but regression is toward more primitive defenses of projection, toward simple denial, and away from higher-level defense mechanisms such as repression, isolation, sublimation, and intellectualization. Delinquency may be better tolerated in the community than in an institution; caching food in drawers will conflict with sanitary regulations in an institution, but can be done by an aged person in his own apartment in the community. Acceptable channels of aggression are available to younger people, but an older person in an institution may be provoked to physical violence as a result of the unusual, to him, dependent close living. Reactive failures in adjustment which manifest themselves as communal asocial behavior may also be called delinquency. Reasons for referral to a geriatric guidance clinic include "minor stealing, inappropriate arguments with children, grandchildren and peers, or inappropriate sexual behavior which had never reached the point of legal recognition." The authors note the similarity of geriatric and adolescent delinquents: frustration tolerances are low; preoccupation is with body changes; focus is on daily and immediate survival; dress may be sloppy and at times inappropriate. Similar, too, are feelings of inadequacy and insecurity

[253]

with problems in development and with maintenance of masculinity, femininity, or sexuality.

Treatment may be divided into two aspects. Psychotherapy can strengthen internal controls and aid the aged to gain insight and at times morality. Activities may be oriented so as to increase self-esteem and status and thus sublimate some of the more overt antisocial behavior. Environmental manipulation of the social milieu can satisfy unconscious needs (for example, by giving some responsibility) and establish external controls (for example, discipline may include moving a resident to an area of senile patients for several days with the resident's knowledge of the intention).

Eliot Landsman, M.D.

INDIVIDUAL THERAPY

In INDIVIDUAL PSYCHOTHERAPY WITH GERIATRIC PATIENTS, Wolff (1963) reports a study of individual psychoanalytically oriented psychotherapy with 18 geriatric patients 60 years of age and older. Three of the patients suffered from chronic schizophrenia and 15 were diagnosed as psychoneurotic. All showed slight to moderate symptoms of chronic brain syndrome.

All patients received psychological testing and were given no psychopharmacological drugs. Individual psychotherapeutic sessions were given once weekly, lasting 50 minutes each for a minimum duration of three months and a maximum duration of nine months. The average duration of hospitalization was nine years, and all patients were considered chronic and hopeless.

The majority of the patients were able to gain some insight into their condition. They discussed their feelings of depression due to physical sickness and disability and increasing dependency. Impairment of mental functioning and the idea of competing with younger people made them anxious and agitated. Fourteen patients who gained partial insight were found to have a profound fear of death, and attempts to explore the psychodynamic background for this fear produced greater restlessness and agitation. The goal of full insight, therefore, had to be abandoned in favor of ego-supportive techniques. Discussions about religion appeared to help some patients to overcome their fear of dying.

Geriatric patients' sense of inferiority was found to be related to physical impairments associated with the aging process. They felt unable to compete with younger people because of a decrease in attention span, in memory, and in ability to concentrate. Female patients felt old, ugly, and unwanted. Ego-supportive techniques pointed out the advantages of emotional maturity associated with age and the importance of greater experience.

Patients were encouraged to verbalize hostility. After some resistance, resentment was expressed freely toward children, toward authorities, and about neglect and lack of understanding. They felt ambivalent about not having responsibilities and about being left without goals in life.

The author stresses the importance of a positive transference and of avoidance of countertransference phenomena. Too much or too little involvement of the therapist may be an obstacle to treatment. The therapist must be able and willing to identify with the geriatric patient. He should convey empathy and hope to his patients and convince them that he can help them. He should remind them of the possibility of remaining effective and creative in spite of age.

The patients' resistance to improvement was manifested particularly in chronic schizophrenics of the older age group.

Some showed symptoms of physical disease as soon as discharge from the hospital was discussed.

Of 18 patients treated, four were slightly improved, five moderately improved, and one was considered recovered. Of three chronic schizophrenic patients, only one showed slight improvement after 24 treatment hours. Four of the 18 patients treated have been discharged from the hospital and remain in the community after one year. In two control groups, improvements were of slight degree and only temporary. The author concludes that individual psychotherapy with geriatric patients can be of considerable value.

Edward L. Zarsky, M.D.

Goldfarb (1964) examines the PATIENT-DOCTOR RELATIONSHIPS IN THE TREATMENT OF AGED PERSONS. In treating any patient, the physician must consider the importance of the patient as a person in relation to others and in reaction to himself and his situation. Many ill and troubled people see the doctor as having power to help or to harm. The search for aid by aged patients is a continuation of the original child-parent relationship. The physician is elevated to parental status and given the tasks formerly assumed by the parents. The doctor needs to realize that the patient develops illusions about his capacities and relies on these for his own improvement. Thus, the doctor may use these illusions for the patient's benefit.

Robert E. Moss, M.D.

HOSPITAL AND CLINIC PROGRAMS

In CURRENT CONCEPTS IN THERAPY: MEDICAL MANAGEMENT OF MENTAL PROBLEMS IN THE AGED, Dale (1961) divides mental disorders of the aged into four groups:

1. Chronic brain syndrome, due to loss of brain cells from ischemia, senile changes, and metabolic disorders or toxic substances. When cell destruction significantly involves sensitive areas, mental changes appear.

2. Acute brain syndrome, due to impaired cerebral metabolism. These reactions are more acute, but are usually reversible if the underlying metabolic disorders are reversible. They include changes seen with congestive heart failure, uremia, anemia, malnutrition, liver disease, etc. Behavioral symptoms due to the changes associated with these disorders may require immediate management.

3. Psychological disorders independent of the loss of brain cells.

4. Endogenous depression, a distinct clinic entity with varied symptomatic manifestations. Most characteristically, the patient presents a depressed mood with feelings of futility and hopelessness, ideas of self-destruction and suicide, early morning awakening, and commonly loss of appetite and weight.

Depression may be confused with chronic brain syndrome. Recent evidence suggests that an intrinsic neurochemical disturbance exists which requires somatic therapy—either specific drug treatment or electric shock.

The author limits his discussion to medical agents, but he adds: "None of these will be greatly valuable without good psychotherapy, whether the well considered work of the specialist in psychiatry or the off-the-cuff, out-of-the-heart brand of the knowing physician of any specialty."

The second major problem in the area of psychologic disorders is the problem of anxiety, which is akin to fear. The anxious patient, however, seldom knows completely what he fears because the basis is usually unconscious.

Norvell L. Peterson, M.D.

REHABILITATION OF THE AGED IN A MENTAL HOSPITAL by Handford and Papathomopoulos (1962) deals with four years of work in developing a program of activities for aging patients in a large mental hospital. The program of rehabilitation was made up of three stages emphasizing increased activity and responsibility. It resulted in improving the physical, psychologic, and socioeconomic status of the patients, and more of them were able to leave the hospital than under the former conditions.

The patient's day is divided into three parts: periods of work, play, and recreation (relaxation).

The first stage begins on the ward. The level of social and work rehabilitation is similar to educating children in kindergarten. Self-care and basic needs are investigated. The program is run on a strict timetable, the achievement of the goals is rewarded, and the patient is encouraged to expand his area of operations.

The first stage is divided into four steps of increasing complexity. In step one, activities take place for an hour, and the therapist's approach is firm and persuasive, but not physically forceful. Physical exercises are introduced to improve physical state, and simple creative activities of the kindergarten level are organized. The special purpose of step one is to develop group feeling and to help the patient become aware of himself and of others.

Step two begins one or two weeks later. There is an hour of daily activities with an hour a week for recreation as a reward. Creative activity at this level involves assessing the individuals in the group and encouraging group activities.

Step three provides two recreation periods a week which take place off the ward and involve such things as movies, group singing, and parties. The purpose of this step is to

[258]

develop the patient's abilities to tolerate activity and to widen his interests. Competitive games are introduced, and there may be an effort to develop leaders within the group.

Step four increases creative activity. Daily recreation off the ward, with emphasis on social rehabilitation and creative activity, now merges into the work-like situation, with emphasis on time spent on the project and attention to the amount and quality of the work.

Stage two may begin from two weeks to two years after the patient's first participation in the activities program. Part one is an assessment in the occupational therapy workshop, lasting two to three weeks, in which vision, hearing, hand-and-eye coordination, appearance, self-care, initiative, relationship with others, and if possible degree of insight into the patient's own problems are evaluated. Simultaneously, recreation is directed toward developing the patient's participation in evening activities off and on the ward.

The second part of stage two is work training in industrial workshops, which the patient attends from two to six hours a day. If the patient is unable to improve his level of functioning, he remains in a geriatric workshop; if he is able to develop greater skills, however, he may move into areas where he is faced with younger patients and greater competition. The goal of the workshop is to help the patient to use his skills and to aid him in becoming aware of life outside the hospital.

When the patient is ready for discharge, outside organizations and agencies are contacted to help him become part of the community beyond the hospital. Alcoholics Anonymous, golden age clubs, and church and hospital volunteers play an important role here. Some patients must enter a day-care program—living outside the hospital and returning to it for work before they are discharged or obtain employment.

Upon discharge they return to the hospital for periodic check-ups in the aftercare clinic.

The results showed that the physical state of the patients was improved. They became stronger, more active, and more supple as a result of their exercise, although their gait did not change. Eating habits and table manners improved. The patients were able to sleep better, needed less sedation, decreased their hypochondriacal complaints, and participated better in activities. Certain of the activities revealed impaired vision and hearing; remedy of these conditions increased some patients' ability to adjust to work and social functions. Incontinence decreased markedly. The psychological status of the patients improved even more than their physical state. They became cooperative, improved in appearance, and looked more interested and alert. Initiative, concentration, and attention span improved, depression diminished, and those who were schizophrenic showed more appropriate behavior. In general, patients were more stable and better able to tolerate pressures, frustration, and unfamiliar situations. They became better oriented and less confused. There was least improvement in insight and judgment.

The ability to learn varied and seemed to depend on previous education or level of skills. When a patient feels that he can still rely on his memory to learn, his capacity for pleasure and his self-esteem increase and motivate him to achieve.

The third criterion, socioeconomic status, reveals that the patients improved their interpersonal relationships, becoming more cooperative and polite with fellow workers and hospital personnel. Relations with relatives improved, partly as a result of relatives' finding out that the patients still retained abilities.

The authors conclude that this four-year program of activities resulted in improvement in the physical, psychological, and socioeconomic status of the patients. The ward atmosphere became more cheerful and stimulating, but here it is more difficult to tell how much of the results derived from the activity program and how much from the use of the new drugs. It is likely that a combination of the two is most helpful.

Donald Wexler, M.D.

Very few patients admitted to the Ohio Public Mental Hospital with diagnoses of diseases of the senium are discharged, according to Locke (1962). In HOSPITALIZATION HISTORY OF PATIENTS WITH MENTAL DISEASES OF THE SENIUM, the author states that many patients die shortly after admission. He advises a review of the current admission practices and treatment for these patients and an attempt to provide alternative arrangements.

The study included 5,552 first admissions from June 1948 to June 1952 with a diagnosis of cerebral arteriosclerosis and senile psychosis. The variables considered were age, sex, race, residence, marital status, education, occupation, and religion. The primary focus of the study was to determine which of these patients would be discharged, which would die, and which would remain on the books during specified periods of time after admission.

Most discharges occurred among patients in the 50-74 age group and during the first six months following admission. Thirty-three percent were discharged as unimproved. The percentage of patients discharged in metropolitan areas was nearly twice that in nonmetropolitan areas. After the first year, the discharge rate was very low and erratic. By the end

[261]

of one year, one-third had died. One-half had died by the third year. The percentage dying was much higher for those age 75 years or over in comparison with those 55-74 years of age.

The mortality for men was higher than for women, regardless of age, race, or residence. For both sexes in both metropolitan and nonmetropolitan areas, the married group had the highest probability of being discharged. The discharge rate was higher for those with at least some high school education and poorer for those with less than eighth grade education. The lowest mortality occurred in the group with the least education, namely, those that had not completed an elementary education.

The craftsman, clerical, and sales groups had the lowest percentage of patients on the books of the hospital; craftsman mainly because of death, the clerical and sales groups mainly because of discharge. The laborers had the largest percentage of patients on the books by the end of the fifth year.

These findings provide additional data of value in program planning, especially because there will be increasing numbers of aged persons, more urbanization, proportionately fewer married, proportionately more with higher levels of education, and fewer engaged as laborers or farmers.

Joel Ordaz, M.D.

Liddel, Herbert, and Crotty (1962) investigate the PROBLEM OF THE GERIATRIC PATIENT IN THE MENTAL HOSPITAL. Their study was conducted at St. Francis Hospital, in England. The authors found that the number of patients over 65 in residence at the St. Francis Hospital increased from 30 men and 75 women in 1948 to 69 men and 163 women in 1958. They conducted a survey of the diagnosis and treatment

[262]

of these elderly patients, the problems encountered, and the prognosis for them.

The admissions came from the observation ward, the outpatient department, and the home. Diagnostically, 48 percent were classified as depression, 6 percent as mania, 12 percent as paranoid, 29 percent as organic, and 5 percent as reactive. All of the patients apparently received the usual hospital treatment.

At the end of the year only 17 of the men and 46 of the women remained in the hospital. Forty-one men and 87 women had been discharged, and 11 men and 28 women had died.

A more favorable outcome appeared related to the following considerations:

1. Type of admission. Those patients admitted from the outpatient department or from the home showed the best outcome; 67 percent were discharged. Of those admitted from the observation ward, only 50 percent left the hospital.

2. Marital status. More patients who were married left the hospital than did those who were not.

3. Time of onset of treatment. The earlier treatment was begun, the better the result.

In general, then, the person who had been cared for by a spouse, a relative, or some other actively interested person did better in the hospital than the person who had been isolated, had only himself to rely on, and had little communication with others. For this reason the authors have instituted recently a vigorous follow-up clinic where all older patients are seen on a regular basis. This contact enables the patient to discuss details which cause him anxiety before it accumulates and becomes overwhelming. Such a clinical approach in time should significantly decrease the numbers of readmissions to the hospital.

Earl M. Wedrow, M.D.

Wolff (1962) gives a brief history of efforts at group therapy with geriatric patients in a paper entitled GROUP PSYCHOTHERAPY WITH GERIATRIC PATIENTS IN A PSYCHIATRIC HOSPITAL: SIX-YEAR STUDY. The author's experience dates from September 1954. He contrasts his technique with that of Linden (1953), whose treatment of a group of 51 women included didactic talks. individual questioning, and good-natured sarcasm. Wolff's technique differed in that he included groups composed of three or four men and three or four women. The patients were treated as a group for 50 minutes, once weekly for a period of at least six months. He excluded from the groups those with too many complaints, those who were confused and disoriented, and those who had delusions and hallucinations which preoccupied them. Other requirements were that the patients show no signs of progressive decrease of intellectual faculties or memory and that they be in contact with reality. Patients were not ruled out on the basis of psychosis, neurosis, or some senile or arteriosclerotic changes. In his experience of six years, Wolff treated 110 geriatric patients in group therapy. The average age was 63 years; 70 percent were schizophrenic and had been hospitalized for an average of 20 years.

The author describes the patients' thought content. The most frequent topics chosen by them were religion, marriage and love life, historical events, and food. There was eager discussion of life after death as paradise. They frequently expressed hostility toward their children, with resentment, disappointment, and feelings of being rejected. Awareness

of similar feelings on the part of others improved interpersonal relationships remarkably.

Of the 110 old people treated by group psychotherapy,
40 percent improved sufficiently to be released from the hospital after about six months of treatment; 10 percent were
discharged after a year's treatment. "Control groups with
only male patients and control groups receiving milieu therapy showed much slower and less significant improvement";
only 18 percent of these groups were discharged after one year
of milieu therapy.

The author considers group psychotherapy more valuable
than individual psychotherapy for the aged because it is less
alarming. Acceptance by the group is more important than
by the individual, and the group offers more choice for
transference to others and with less resistance. The individual
meets with group attitudes and thereby faces reality and the
approval and disapproval of the group. He becomes involved
in increased socialization and group identity.

Eliot Landsman, M.D.

Galbraith (1963) studies INTENSIVE TREATMENT FOR GERI-
ATRIC PATIENTS. Eight hundred of the 2,300 beds at the
Mendocino State Hospital in California are reserved for patients over the age of 65. By 1960 all of these places
were taken, and there was no room for new admissions of the
elderly. In an attempt to cope with the problem, the hospital
opened a 16-bed Geriatric Intensive Treatment Unit in
April 1960.

It was staffed with a full-time resident in psychiatry, a psychiatric social worker available 80 percent of the time, a head
nurse, and three aides. The results after two years were encouraging.

Comparison of patients admitted to the hospital one year before the new program began (Group A) with those admitted one year after the intensive care unit opened (Group B) showed that although there was little difference in the number of patients who left the hospital—61 percent of Group A, 59 percent of Group B—there was a significant difference in the number of readmissions—42 percent of Group A, but only 8 percent of Group B had to return to the hospital. The hospital staff was impressed by the fact that Group A patients stayed out of the hospital only an average of 40 days, whereas Group B patients were able to stay out an average of 121 days before they had to return.

The author believes that there are two main reasons for the good results. One is the actual management of the patients on the ward. They are encouraged to care for themselves, to help with ward housekeeping in various ways, to attend group meetings three times a week, and to discuss matters of general ward interest. There is an active recreational program consisting of parlor games, group singing, parties given by community groups, picnics, and auto rides with staff members.

The other main reason is the special attention given to the eventual placement of the patient. While the doctor is talking to the newly admitted patient, the social worker interviews the relatives to evaluate the factors which led to hospitalization, to reassure them about the patient's care, and to involve them in planning for his aftercare following discharge. Throughout the patient's stay the social worker maintains contact with him and with his relatives. Patients without families or those who should not return to their families are placed, with the cooperation of the County Welfare Department which licenses them, in boardinghomes and other supervised settings.

The author believes that there is significant value in making careful and appropriate placements instead of simply returning patients to the prehospital environment, especially because many who would not have been considered well enough to return to their families were able to live in supervised boardinghomes. Since the program began, boardinghome caretakers who have worked closely with the social worker have expressed much satisfaction with their experience and increasingly have requested additional patients.

Earl M. Wedrow, M.D.

Scott and Devereaux (1963b) are concerned about PERPETUATION OF GERIATRIC PROBLEMS IN CALIFORNIA STATE MENTAL HOSPITALS. Because of the steadily increasing proportion of elderly patients in California's mental hospitals, an appraisal of the "potential social habilitation of elderly patients" was made that could be applied to a total hospital population. *Habilitation* is defined as "the movement of a patient from a state psychiatric hospital to a community-centered resource which could meet the patient's needs at least as satisfactorily as a state psychiatric hospital." Justification for a patient's continued stay in a state hospital was to be in terms of benefit to both the patient and society. Of the total sample, 53.6 percent could have been habilitated and 46.4 percent needed psychiatric services, but not necessarily those of a state mental hospital. The study found that 88.9 percent of the chronic patients, those who had been hospitalized for more than two years, had been admitted prior to age 65. Most of these elderly chronic patients could be cared for adequately somewhere other than a state hospital for general psychiatry, provided that sufficient time, manpower, and money were available. Otherwise, state hospitals will cease to be psychiatric treatment centers for acute mental illness because

[267]

they will have to devote an increasing proportion of their space and facilities to the care of chronic patients.

Robert E. Moss, M.D.

Savitsky (1963) writes on PSYCHIATRY IN INSTITUTIONAL WORK WITH THE AGED. Disordered behavior in the later years reflects organic deficits of the nervous system and inadequacies in meeting stresses; it is most evident in institutionalized older persons. The author directs this article toward the orientation of staff physicians, resident psychiatrists, and ancillary personnel. He mentions a number of psychodynamic concepts: (1) the individual's adaptive techniques in search of gratification, well-being, procurement of basic needs, or the avoidance of damage or its threat; (2) the part that emotions play in alerting, mobilizing, and communicating—the unpleasant emotions of fear and rage and the pleasant ones of love and pride; (3) developmental stages, including themes of early helplessness and dependence, later independence and mastery, and earlier patterns of dependence as returned to in later life; (4) the fact that a search into the background of the individual will reveal that the disordered behavior pattern is not irrational.

Alterations in physical capacities may have as their effects overreactive syndromes of agitation, paranoid states, or anxiety. Alterations in social relationships involving children and status may cause underreactive syndromes of anorexia, apathy, and depression. Normal changes that occur in old age include diminished energy levels, narrowing of interests, altered sleep patterns, diminished sexual interests, increased emotional lability, and difficulties in thinking, concentration, and memory. The above pattern is similar to the posttraumatic syndrome often seen following a head injury and suggests that it may be an organismic response to altered capacity which has mobilized anxiety.

The author surveys psychiatric syndromes in the aged.

1. Acute brain syndrome. Important here is the management of anxiety.

2. Chronic brain syndrome due to vascular and metabolic changes in the brain, with specific intellectual and sensory deficits. Management may be focused on preservation of interests, object relationships, mobility, and useful activity.

3. Psychoneurotic disorders. Cancerophobia is frequently a precursor of serious depression with suicidal attempt. Hypochondriacal anxieties are also common.

4. Depressions. Symptomatology is usually related to the gastrointestinal tract.

5. Functional psychoses. These include schizophrenia, rarely manic-depressive, and the involutional psychoses.

6. Personality disturbances. These include excessive or inadequate aggression, withdrawal, submission, or detachment.

7. Paranoid reactions. They are extremely common, with frequent accusations of stealing, and are a symbolic dramatization of the individual's losses in his capacities.

8. Psychosomatic disorders.

The author advocates the "total" approach, which includes the assessment of the meaning of the illness to the patient as well as therapeutic measures. Under the heading "Psychologic Aspects of Organic Disorders," he notes that the most common complaints refer to the gastrointestinal tract. In moderately advanced chronic brain disorder, one finds deviant patterns of overeating, regressive interest in "childish" foods (candy), and diminished food intake with poor nutrition and with resulting gross confusion. Other complaints of unpleasant taste sensations, dry mouth, or burning tongue often relate to depression. He suggests "correlations between difficult life situations and the precipitation of acute vascular accidents." Cardiovascular system symptoms (e.g., angina) will remit with relief of emotional pressure, and one sees in the elderly the use of "cardiac anxiety" for secondary gain.

The author then discusses the contribution of psychiatry to institutional practice and considers the following admissions problems that may cause difficulties in adaptation to a Home: (1) paranoid personalities, who are aggressive, yet have led detached lives; (2) those with moderate to advanced chronic brain syndrome showing evidence of gross neurologic damage; (3) those who have difficulty in identification with the residents of the Home, those poorly motivated and those who, brought under false pretenses, are able physically and temperamentally to fight back. The psychiatrist can help in the education and orientation of staff members; the common sources of annoyance to attendants and nurses are the lack of discipline of residents, their unreasonable demands, and their aggressive behavior. The threat of suicide is of concern particularly in the person with manic-depressive attacks and in the aggressive and detached persons. Helpful, along with drugs, are additional supervision by the attendant staff and increased visits by the family.

The author has found group therapy of limited value. Individual psychotherapy is designed to explore sources of anxiety and to buttress those mechanisms of the resident that can successfully deal with his anxieties. Management of the elderly resident involves assessment of the basic pathologic picture, his daily regimen, and his personal and social relationships. Treatment includes rehabilitation, recreation, and modification of living arrangements, and often involves the family.

Eliot Landsman, M.D.

[270]

In a paper on the MANAGEMENT OF THE GERIATRIC PA-
TIENT IN A MENTAL HOSPITAL, Haas (1963) states that the
aged population in mental hospitals in the United States is 32
percent, compared with 10-13 percent in England, Scandinavia, and Switzerland, even though these European countries have 25 percent more aged in the total population than
there are in the United States. One of many reasons is the
youth-oriented culture of the United States, which makes for
a nihilistic, fearful approach to the later years. The geriatric
psychiatric patient is defined as one who is 60 years of age or
over and who is unable to "adjust to the specific stresses associated with progressive and irreversible losses in physiologic,
psychologic and social functioning."

Management should include a separate unit for such patients, with its own chief of service and with personnel specially skilled in helping "to minimize and counteract the specific feeling of isolation and loss." An early and careful survey
of the total situation is imperative. A lifelong neurotic passive
pattern indicates poor prognosis. Rehabilitation will be more
effective in persons with good capacity for planning, adequate
intellect, and creative interests and activities.

Therapy includes the use of medication: small doses of
ataractic drugs, antidepressant drugs, and hormones (20:1 ratio combination of testosterone and estrogen in a prolonged
trial). Attention to physical well-being may be decisive psy-
chotherapeutically. A newly learned or regained skill should
be part of the goal of rehabilitation and physical medicine.
Outside activity making use of community resources is important; without it the gains made inside the hospital may be
lost.

For those who will have to stay in institutions, sheltered
and competitive workshops help to satisfy the need of older

patients to consume and to produce. Psychotherapy, supportive and rehabilitative, both individual and in groups, fulfills the need for warmth and interest.

The author introduces the concept of *expectant maturation* for preventive geriatrics. This term refers to the "capacity for young humans to progress from one stage to another with amazing rapidity and relative success." Acceptance of adulthood should not be the final desirable goal, and aging should be seen as another change to be explored. Early education should not inhibit the self-developing activity of one's creative play; emphasis should be on creativity rather than on production.

Eliot Landsman, M.D.

THE QUARTER-WAY HOUSE—A TRANSITIONAL PROGRAM FOR CHRONICALLY ILL GERIATRIC MENTAL PATIENTS is the subject of a paper by Mason, Cunningham, and Tarpy (1963). The quarter-way house, located on the grounds of a mental hospital, is a prototype of a community foster home. Its value is that, with help, the patient can release himself from deep institutional dependency, acquire new identifications, and gradually reacquire social skills and techniques needed to live in a community home. This quarter-way house at a Veterans Administration Hospital in Wisconsin is a one-story building with ten bedrooms, a living- and dining-room area, a kitchen, a hobby room, and a bathroom with a combination tub and shower. The entire furnishings contribute to a homelike atmosphere. Administration of the house is by social-work service. Social workers are surrogate parents. Patients share responsibility in caring for their rooms and participate in housekeeping and meal preparation. They center their activities around the house and may make use of hospital occupational therapy. Altered role expectations permit easier transition to social competence and to modes of behavior expected by the community. Advent into the community is gradual. The social worker meets with the patients in group discussions and in informal daily contacts. He encourages them to talk about the advantages of the hospital; later he is in a position to offer identical advantages in a community situation.

This quarter-way house operated for five years with 60 male patients. The age range was from 40 to 71, with a mean age of 57; 80 percent of the patients had a diagnosis of schizophrenic reaction. The average continuous hospitalization was 13 years; the average length of stay in the cottage was 7.5 months. In eight cases, relatives provided a place in their own homes after the patients had demonstrated successful adjustment in foster homes. Nine patients went to live in soldiers' homes. Six went directly to homes of relatives, four to wives, two to siblings, and three to a YMCA or a boarding-house. At the end of five years, 75 percent of the group still showed a satisfactory adjustment to the community. Fifteen percent (nine patients) had been rehospitalized, but seven of these returned to the community after several months. Another five who returned remained in a hospital ward.

Eliot Landsman, M.D.

Fish and Williamson (1964) present a preliminary report of their investigations in A DELIRIUM UNIT IN AN ACUTE GERIATRIC HOSPITAL. The 12-bed unit was opened in 1960 specifically to deal with acute confusional states in the aged.

Criteria for admission were established. Patients in terminal stages of illness, patients with chronic degenerative diseases of the nervous system, and patients with chronic psychosis were considered unsuitable for admission.

Of the first 93 patients, most were in the age group 75-84, and there were more males than females. Over four-fifths of the patients were admitted within one week of application, and more than half were admitted on the same day. The commonest length of stay was five to nine weeks. Of the 93 patients, 20 died and 28 remained permanent hospital patients, whereas the remaining 45 were discharged in varying degrees of fitness.

Diagnoses included cerebral arteriosclerotic and senile psychosis, cerebral infarction, cardiac failure, infection, and depressive psychosis. Barbiturates were judged to have been an important factor in producing the confusional state in six patients.

Arteriosclerotic dementia is differentiated from senile dementia by its acute onset of confusion, often associated with delirium, its episodic course, focal neurological signs, and late preservation of the personality. On the whole, depression, paranoid psychosis, and senile schizophrenia cause little difficulty in diagnosis.

The phenothiazine group of drugs was found to be extremely useful in the treatment of restlessness associated with acute confusional state. The authors feel that barbiturates have no place in the sedation of the elderly.

The authors conclude that there are significant advantages to setting up specially designed and equipped units for dealing with problems of mental disease in the elderly, units where adequate diagnostic work-up can be carried out and treatment applied in a rational manner. They believe that the clinicosocial approach of the geriatrician in a geriatric hospital is most effective for the management of mental illness in the elderly, especially when it is complicated by acute confusional states. They comment on the satisfactory treatment of the acute episode of confusion in arteriosclerotic or senile dementia, which was the condition most common in their group of patients. Patients with depressive psychosis reacted well to antidepressive treatment.

The successful functioning of the unit depends upon maintaining a patient turnover so that beds can be found promptly for suitable patients. The cases in this series are considered true emergencies, and the results of treatment depend to a large extent on the promptness with which treatment is started.

Edward L. Zarsky, M.D.

Friedman and Bressler (1964) report on their first two years' experience with A GERIATRIC MENTAL HYGIENE CLINIC IN A GENERAL HOSPITAL. Their program is designed for treatment of patients 60 years of age and over with symptoms of emotional disturbance, and includes psychotherapy for individual and group, chemotherapy, electroshock therapy, psychologic testing, social casework, and social groupwork. The program excludes persons who (1) are nonambulatory; (2) have severe disabling illness; (3) are overtly psychotic (except for depression); (4) are deteriorated chronic psychotic patients; (5) have chronic brain syndrome (except for early signs of senility); or (6) are under treatment by another agency.

Sessions are held twice weekly from 9 a.m. to 12 noon. A director, a chief, five psychiatrists, a psychologist, an internist, a group worker, and a volunteer attend each of the two sessions a week. A full-time social worker and secretary are employed. The authors have found that nearly all of their patients suffer from depressive states of psychoneurotic or endogenous types, with rejection as precipitating cause. Psychotherapy is directed toward ego-strengthening processes emphasizing patients' assets. Catharsis, encouragement, reassurance, strong suggestion, and re-education are employed. The reports covers 204 patients 60 to 84, with a mean age of 67. Although the referring source had cleared them medically, seven patients were found by the treating psychiatrist to have serious organic disease. Group psychotherapy has as its goal ventilation of feelings, overcoming of the feeling of isolation, re-evaluation of previous goals in life, and adjustment to the realities of a physical slowdown and diminution of interest. The therapist is more active with the elderly group than he would be with a younger group; he makes few demands, may initiate and guide the discussion, and acts as teacher and benevolent parent. Only five patients were referred for electroshock therapy; the elderly tolerate electroshock therapy as well as do younger patients. The psychologist found that only those tests should be given that are absolutely necessary for clinical evaluation. Test interviews were short and at least two in number. Psychologic evaluation shows a predominance of depression on an intrapsychic or environmental basis or both. The social worker is used extensively for problems in the following areas: financial problems, social security problems, job placement or relocation, need for rehabilitation services, need for recreational facilities, need for referral to special clinics or hospitals or for management of physical illness, and aid in placement in a foster home or institution. She also does group counseling with relatives. The group worker instituted a golden age club to prepare patients for eventual membership in a community club.

Of the 204 patients, 139 were discharged from active therapy. For 75 of these, no further treatment was necessary.

Eliot Landsman, M.D.

PSYCHOLOGICAL TESTS

According to a paper by Chown (1961), AGE AND THE RIGIDITIES, rigidity can no longer be regarded as a unitary concept. In a three-stage analysis, at least five kinds of rigidity were shown to preserve their individuality. Sixteen tests of rigidity and two of intelligence were administered to 200 men divided into small groups which ranged in age from 20 to 82.

The first stage consisted of the analysis of the structure of the rigidities. The second stage undertook to investigate which of them were most closely related to age and the effects of age on performance of the different rigidity tasks. The third stage was designed to discover whether any reorganization of the rigidity factors occurred among older subjects.

Three age groups of 60 subjects each were drawn from within the same sample. The mean ages of the three groups were 26.4; 40.7, and 60.7.

The results indicate that the factors of nonverbal intelligence, spontaneous flexibility, and personality are closely related in all groups. The arithmetic and speed factors are closely related in the young and middle groups. Disposition rigidity and alphabet factors are related in middle and old and in young and old groups, but not in young and middle groups. Speed, as measured in the young group, is best measured by arithmetic in the old group. Inspection of the

[277]

loadings of the speed tests reveals the shift from young to old in tests where there is a distinct speed factor.

The author stresses the relationship between nonverbal intelligence and the various forms of rigidity. The subject's level of nonverbal intelligence plays a part in his performance on rigidity tests. Unless actual level of nonverbal intelligence, regardless of age, is taken into account, individual differences in rigidities often may be masked. Because nonverbal intelligence declines fairly regularly with age, its masking effect on rigidity is especially important when relationships between age and rigidity are being studied.

Where intelligence of the problem-solving variety appears to be lower among older people, they also seem to be more rigid and slower in other respects. Older people show the greatest difficulty with complex new tasks. Their problems seem to lie in holding several conditions or aspects of the tasks in mind at the same time. The most marked changes with age in the interrelationships between factors was in the role of speed. Speed tests can thus be used as a measure of intellectual capability and of the extent of the preservation of this function among old people.

Joel Ordaz, M.D.

ATTITUDES TOWARD DEATH AMONG A GROUP OF ACUTE GERIATRIC PSYCHIATRIC PATIENTS are discussed by Christ (1961).

Because the direct outcome of many diseases in the elderly is death, it is the physician's duty to acquaint these patients with this fact and to help them deal with the attendant fears.

This study included 100 patients, of whom 89 percent needed supervision because of physical illness. Sixty-two persons were able to respond to questions about their attitude toward death. The questions had to do with persons in hospitals, aging, physical health, death, plans for the future, plans following death, mercy killing, whether doctors should tell their patients they are going to die soon, and whether their friends or relatives should be notified. All of the patients were considerably upset about death and used denial, suppression, and repression as defenses.

Fifty patients received a word-association test. The average of the association times to the "death" words was longer than the average of the association times to the seven other words used. The associations to the death words were more bizarre, and there was more blocking. The findings substantiated the subjective impression that these patients were anxious about death.

To the question, "If a patient is going to die soon, should the doctor tell him?" 23 of 47 patients said "yes," and all said that they personally would want to be told. A few volunteered that they would want to know only a few hours beforehand, so that "I could get myself ready, but not too long, because I would get too upset."

Some of the psychiatric symptoms seen in acute psychiatric geriatric patients, which include fear of being poisoned or killed or being thrown out of their homes as well as frank somatic delusions, may be symptoms of marked denial of death.

Joel Ordaz, M.D.

Kahn, Goldfarb, Pollack, and Peck (1960) have developed a method for obtaining BRIEF OBJECTIVE MEASURES FOR THE DETERMINATION OF MENTAL STATUS IN THE AGED. Because mental disorder in the aged is related to organic brain damage, it is desirable to have brief, objective, quantitative measures of mental functioning related to cerebral impairment. In the method here developed, the first item is the mental status questionnaire. Ten items were selected as most discriminating for quantitative determination of mental status: (1) name of place, (2) address, (3) today's date, (4) present month, (5) year, (6) age, (7) birth month, (8) birth year, (9) current president of U.S., (10) preceding president? The number of errors in response provides a quantitative index of mental functioning.

The second item is the face-hand test, which consists of touching the patient simultaneously on one cheek and on the dorsum of the hand and asking him to indicate where he was touched. Ten trials are made: four contralateral and four ipsilateral stimuli, interspersed with two symmetric combinations of face-face and hand-hand. If the patient fails consistently to locate both stimuli correctly, he is classed as positive; if consistently correct, he is rated as negative.

The results of both tests, applied to 1,077 persons of 65 or older residing in institutions in New York City, were highly related to psychiatrists' clinical evaluations of presence and degree of chronic brain syndrome, presence or absence of associated psychosis, opinion as to certifiability, and degree of management problem. These tests appear to be valid for the determination of mental status in the aged, especially for disorders associated with cerebral damage, and are useful for purposes of rapid screening.

Robert E. Moss, M.D.

In Part I of a paper on PERCEPTION OF SELF IN INSTITUTIONALIZED AGED SUBJECTS, Pollack, Karp, Kahn, and Goldfarb (1962) discuss RESPONSE PATTERNS TO MIRROR REFLECTION. According to the authors the use of mirror reflection in the mental examination of aged persons may be a rapid means of obtaining evidence of a derogatory attitude and may serve as an index of need for general or psychiatric treatment. The authors examined 696 testable subjects age 65 or older.

Mental status was evaluated by two tests: (1) the mental status questionnaire (MSQ) and (2) the face-hand test as described by Kahn and his collaborators in 1960. The most frequent psychiatric diagnosis was chronic brain syndrome. A 9-x-11-inch mirror was placed directly in front of the subject's face, and he was asked, "What do you see?" If self-identification was not included in the subject's initial response, the question was repeated. The patterns of response of self-confrontation were divided into a recognition and a nonrecognition group. Five subjects failed to recognize their own images, indicating a severe perceptual defect in the presence of existing language patterns which indicated a high level of functioning.

The verbal responses to mirror confrontations were subdivided into two categories, elaborated and nonelaborated responses. Pleasant or complimentary remarks were rare. Self-derogatory remarks varied from openly depressed statements, such as "An old grey guy that ought to be dead long ago" to comparison of the mirrored face to an animal face, commonly called "monkey face." These negative self-attitudes do not seem to be related to the presence of altered brain function. They seem to be characteristic of the widespread depressive symptomatology found in institutions for the aged.

Joel Ordaz, M.D.

In MEASUREMENT OF AGE IDENTIFICATION: A METHODOLOGICAL NOTE, Jeffers, Eisdorfer, and Busse (1962) state that

[281]

the use of common words, such as young, middle-aged, elderly, old, and aged, lacks consistency. Individual, and perhaps regional, differences in usage make it important to examine individual definitions of terms in specific contexts. The authors tested 168 community volunteers, negro and white, male and female, 60-94 years of age, representing a wide spread of occupations, in a series of comprehensive physical, psychological, and social evaluations.

There was a marked shift from younger to older self-placement as to age category when individuals were faced with a situation requiring self age-identification. Of the total of 168 persons, 41 percent retained the same age placement as when questioned an hour earlier, whereas 59 percent rated themselves in a different category: 55 percent of the total group changed to an older age category and only 4 percent to a younger one.

Joel Ordaz, M.D.

Birren (1963) presents RESEARCH ON THE PSYCHOLOGIC ASPECTS OF AGING. The psychology of aging is divided into four subtopics: (1) moods and attitudes, both transient and persistent, toward self and toward feelings of life's satisfactions; (2) the psychological resources of the individual, both actual and potential, covering language skills, problem-solving capacity, memory, psychomotor dexterity, and other functions; (3) the nature, intensity, and extent of interpersonal relations; (4) behavior deviations and psychopathology.

The aging nervous system differs from other organs in that it modifies its functions as a result of experience, causing behavior to become organized on this basis rather than on that of heredity alone. Thus, heredity and experience develop our behavior and can have effects on other organ systems. Usually, however, in aging the nervous system seems to be passive, reacting to changes in hormone secretions, in circulation, or in nutrition. There is an increasing tendency to consider the nervous system as well as the vascular and connective tissue systems as playing a basic role in the aging of complex organisms; in particular it is believed that the vascular and nervous systems have mutual influences on each other in the aging process.

In studies of psychomotor slowing using the Wechsler Adult Intelligence Scale (WAIS), the digit symbol subtest shows a decline with increasing age, and this decline is highly correlated with measures of speed response. Studies have also indicated that speed of presentation of material has an effect on the speed of the judgments and that the difference seen in the aged is a matter of set, of ability to respond quickly. Slowing of behavior with advancing age is also seen in albino rats, and because the rat is relatively free from vascular disease, it is believed that the slowing is not a result of circulatory interference.

The psychomotor slowing seen in advancing age is believed to have the property of a general behavioral characteristic of a rather broad nature. Young people seem to be able to modulate their speed of behavior in response to the needs of the situation or the test performed, but older subjects have a characteristic behavior that tends to be less flexible than that of younger adults.

Word-association time of older adults tends to be slower than that of younger adults, to an extent beyond that which would be expected as a result of slowing speech. This effect, too, is seen as an indication of the slowing of the functioning of the central nervous system.

Certain studies indicate that there is a correlation between cardiovascular changes and psychomotor slowing. Whether these changes are only parallel or whether they have a more direct interrelationship remains to be demonstrated.

An earlier study by Birren and Spieth (1962) indicated that there is a closer correlation between chronologic age and psychomotor speed than between age and blood pressure. This study postulated that a factor of psychomotor reactivity in the central nervous system might be looked for, a factor that would have implications for psychomotor and vascular phenomena.

In conclusion, the slowing of behavior may be divided into two aspects: cortical damage and modification in "a subcortical process of alerting." This latter change may lead to "correlations of reaction time, heart rate and blood pressure." Research on psychomotor slowing with advancing age serves the important purpose of placing emphasis on the study of the central nervous system.

Donald Wexler, M.D.

In MEASUREMENT OF MENTAL IMPAIRMENT IN GERIATRIC PRACTICE, Isaacs and Walkey (1964) assert the need in geriatric hospitals for a simple test measuring mental impairment in the elderly patient, which does not require the services of a clinical psychologist. The following three tests were administered to the population of Foresthall Hospital, Glasgow, Scotland, and from them a composite score was obtained.

1. Building blocks. Five colored, toy building blocks of diminishing size are placed before the patient, who is asked to build them into a column. The patient's performance is then rated.

2. Questionnaire. The patient is asked nine questions relating to his personal circumstances and spatial temporal environment, and the answers are scored.

[284]

3. Paired associates. The patient is given word pairs and then asked to repeat: for example, "When I say knife, I want you to say fork; when I say East, you say West."

In patients over 75, the mean score indicating mental impairment is significantly greater in females. The distribution of scores in six different diagnostic groups into which the test group was divided follow expectation with the highest mean scores found in patients with dementia.

In another paper, A SIMPLIFIED PERFORMANCE TEST FOR ELDERLY HOSPITAL PATIENTS, the same authors (Isaacs and Walkey, 1963) describe the use of the building blocks. The test was given to the entire population of the Foresthall Hospital, consisting of 522 elderly patients with a variety of chronic physical and neurological diseases, many accompanied by psychotic disorders. Half of the patients tested performed the task without error. As the age of the patients increased, the proportion of patients who succeeded tended to drop. The difference was more evident in women than in men. Prognostic studies are cited which show survival to be greatest among patients with a good performance on the test and lowest among those who failed the test.

Edward L. Zarsky, M.D.

Pierce (1963), in NOTE ON TESTING CONDITIONS, presents a study investigating the possible effect of differential testing conditions on the mental test performances (selected WAIS subtests) of elderly persons. The subjects included psychiatric patients and individuals living in the community. Testing situations were rated as "good," "fair," or "poor," depending on the amount of noise and distraction in the milieu. Results failed to uncover any differences in test performance that could be attributed to the situational variables. The authors

[285]

conclude that "at the least, we have evidence that intelligence tests are more robust than test authors have thought."

Robert J. Kastenbaum, Ph.D.

RORSCHACH PERFORMANCE AND INTELLECTUAL FUNCTIONING IN THE AGED is the subject of an investigation by Eisdorfer (1963). Rorschach tests were given to 242 subjects, aged 60-94, who had received Wechsler Adult Intelligence Scale examinations. The results indicated that level of intellectual functioning, perhaps more than age, plays an important role in the Rorschach performance. Generalizations about "the aged" made on the basis of Rorschach findings from institutionalized subjects, or without regard to intellectual level, were not supported by data from the present sample of aged persons of adequate intelligence and adaptation to the community-at-large. The data obtained were presented in an effort to offer some baseline values for normal Rorschach performance in aged persons.

Robert E. Moss, M.D.

RESEARCH STUDIES AND SURVEYS

Cooper (1964) was led to study the effects of Cosaldon in the treatment of dementia because it had been fairly widely used in Europe and had been reported as useful by Meyer (1957), Leube (1959), Sperling (1960), Schmidt (1960), and Donati (1960). He presents the results of his study in a paper entitled A CONTROLLED TRIAL OF COSALDON IN ARTERIOSCLEROTIC DEMENTIA.

Cooper's results reveal no significant difference between those patients using Cosaldon and those not using the drug. These findings are in direct opposition to those of previous workers, and he believes that the earlier reports were not

[286]

valid because the experimental methods used were deficient. For example, none of the other studies, except Schmidt's, included definite statements about the neurological status of the patients. In no case was a control group used, and only Bjurwill (1963) attempted to assess his patients objectively. Cooper, on the other hand, set up the following criteria for defining arteriosclerotic dementia:

1. An illness characterized by dementia and emotional lability with a fluctuating course showing exacerbations and remissions, but with progressive mental deterioration.

2. Moderate hypertension greater than 165/110.

3. Evidence of cerebrovascular lesions either transient or permanent (hemiparesis, aphasia, field defects, epileptic convulsions).

4. Evidence of peripheral arteriosclerosis (tortuous and rigid radial arteries).

5. Retinal arteriosclerosis.

6. Absence of gross physical illness except arteriosclerosis or hypertension.

7. Absence of primary depression or schizophrenia.

He included in his study only those patients who showed unequivocal evidence that they suffered from arteriosclerotic dementia. These patients were divided into two groups of ten each. They were examined carefully both by direct clinical means and by extensive objective psychological tests. One group was placed on placebos and the other on Cosaldon. After three months the patients were again evaluated; statistical analysis revealed no significant difference between the two groups of patients.

Another factor possibly responsible for these results may be the nature of the drug and the pathology of the illness. Cosaldon consists of hexyl 3:7 dimethyl-xanthine (SK_7) 200 mg. and nicotinic acid 50 mg. per tablet. It has a vasodilator effect upon the cerebrovascular tree. Nicotinic acid has been included in the formulation because it has been shown to potentiate the action of SK_7. Florey's physiological experiments, however, indicate that the cerebral arteries are among the least reactive of the body. They are thin-walled, and their media contain little muscle. Because of this fact and the nature of the pathological changes in cerebral arteriosclerosis, namely the patchy softening and scarring, it seems unlikely that much improvement could be expected from the use of a drug such as Cosaldon.

Earl M. Wedrow, M.D.

Hamilton, Bennett, and Silver (1964), in NANDROLONE PHENPROPIONATE IN THE TREATMENT OF GERIATRIC PATIENTS WITH CHRONIC BRAIN DAMAGE, report on a study planned to determine the effects of the anabolic steroid nandrolone phenpropionate on the physical state and mental symptoms of debility in elderly patients with psychosis due to senile brain disease or cerebral arteriosclerosis, and to determine whether the anabolic effects can modify the psychiatric symptoms usually attributed to organic brain disease.

Eighteen of 26 patients were given 25 mg. of the steroid by IM injection weekly, and eight received 1 cc. of a placebo. Treatment lasted for 12 weeks. All of the patients were debilitated and showed the basic syndrome of organic brain disease.

The steroid effectively relieved many manifestations of generalized debility—94 percent (17) of the 18 treated patients gained weight; 72 percent (13) showed increased physical activity and improved general health, but only three of these 13 improved in mental attitude, slept better, had fewer somatic complaints, were less irritable, and were more alert and aware of their surroundings. The ability of the patients to care for themselves was not improved, however, nor was there any change in their over-all behavior. The steroid had little effect on the basic clinical syndrome of organic brain disease.

Eliot Landsman, M.D.

In THE CRITICAL ROLE OF DEFENSE MECHANISMS IN THE OUTCOME OF CHRONIC BRAIN SYNDROMES IN THE AGED, Gericke and Lobb (1964) speculate that what defeats some people over age 65 is that the world demands that they disengage themselves from meaningful struggles. The acknowledged goals of the project here reported were (1) to improve management of and planning for the individual patient and (2) to explore the psychodynamics of aging, normal and abnormal.

In order to obtain as complete case histories as possible, it was necessary to get help from relatives. The authors found a repetitiousness of pattern, especially in a number of women who had been extraordinarily competent and active in their lives. They give three case histories illustrative of a basic pattern. These women were competent, active women, all with elements of pioneer spirit; they were self-sustained and supportive of others, and they appeared to have established sexual relationships.

Societal forces reduce the older person's participation in a larger society's milieu, and the authors raise the following questions as to how they can reorient activities and interests: "What defenses can we offer our patients in exchange for those that have been breached? What defenses are we building against our own hours of 'disengagement'?"

Eliot Landsman, M.D.

[289]

It is the opinion of Kral, Cahn, and Mueller (1964), as stated in their paper on SENESCENT MEMORY IMPAIRMENT AND ITS RELATION TO THE GENERAL HEALTH OF THE AGING INDIVIDUAL, that an amnestic syndrome in an old person is a grave prognostic indicator of his general health. Observations in a mental hospital were made on 695 patients aged 60 years and older over a three-year period. A comparison of patients with organically based amnestic syndromes as against patients of the same age with functional psychoses and a benign type of senescent forgetfulness or with no memory deficit (schizophrenic and manic-depressive) revealed a much higher death rate in the amnestic patients.

The authors divide memory dysfunction into two types, "benign" and "malignant." Patients with the benign type can recall an experience, but not relatively unimportant data (e.g., name, place, or date). They may recall the date at another time. Disorientation or confabulation is not apparent, and the memory dysfunction grows slowly. Patients with the malignant type are characterized by inability to recall an entire experience, including data. This loss of memory leads to disorientation and retrogressive loss of remote memories. Some events with a strong emotional charge may still be evoked occasionally. These subjects are unaware of their defect and may confabulate. The malignant type is identical with the Korsakoff syndrome, which forms the axis syndrome of senile dementia and is also found in presenile dementia and arteriosclerotic heart disease.

The study included yearly assessments by a team consisting of a consulting psychiatrist, two staff psychiatrists, a social worker, an occupational therapist, and the head nurse on the ward. There were seven criteria: physical condition, memory function, other possible psychopathologic conditions, incontinence, appearance and cleanliness, activity level, and social contact.

Findings suggest that confinement to a mental hospital is not an important influence on the amnestic syndrome. Incontinence and activity variables paralleled the decline of memory ratings in the organic groups, and the triad of amnestic syndrome, incontinence, and significant diminution of activity indicates a bad prognosis.

Eliot Landsman, M.D.

Meer and Krag (1964) write on CORRELATES OF DISABILITY IN A POPULATION OF HOSPITALIZED GERIATRIC PATIENTS. Geriatric patients in Stockton (Calif.) State Hospital numbered 18 percent in 1940, 31 percent in 1959, and 38 percent in 1961. These figures prompted a disability survey of the entire geriatric population as a guide to re-evaluating the hospital's treatment program. A 14-item disability rating scale was devised on which a higher score indicated greater disability. The results indicated that (1) female patients had a higher score than male patients; (2) patients with organic mental diseases produced higher scores than those with functional disturbances; (3) a direct relationship existed between age and higher scores; (4) length of hospitalization was associated with higher scores in functional disorders, but less clearly so in organic disorders; (5) the scale predicted directly the outcome one year later.

Why do female patients show consistently greater disability than males? A basic psychological difference between males and females in their attitude toward sickness appeared. Women generally accept illness as a matter of course (whereas men do not) because of experience with menses, pregnancy, child-birth, and menopause. With men, their status in our culture depends largely on their work achievement, and physical illness is considered a nonmasculine characteristic. The male's denial of symptoms may be an advantage in later years, when taking to bed readily leads to muscular weakness and progressive deterioration, as well as to isolation and withdrawal. Hence, the yielding to symptoms by women may lead to more rapid deterioration than in men.

The conclusion is that geriatric patients are not a homogeneous group, and that data relating to male and female patients and to patients with organic and functional mental diseases should be considered separately.

Robert E. Moss, M.D.

There has been a tendency to view mentally ill, elderly patients simply as geriatric patients. A study by Scott and Devereaux (1964) on HETEROGENEITY OF AN ELDERLY STATE HOSPITAL POPULATION indicates that elderly patients are not a homogeneous group. One hundred and twelve patients over 65 were studied in detail with respect to the problems of each and the types of services needed. A judgment was then made as to each patient's potential for habilitation—his ability to get along outside the hospital environment. Considerable differences were found between certain diagnostic groups (chronic brain disorders and psychotic disorders) in terms of a patient's potential for leaving a state hospital setting and the type of alternative facility demanded by his physical condition and needs.

Robert E. Moss, M.D.

Stratton and Barton (1964) report on THE GERIATRIC PA-
TIENT IN THE PUBLIC MENTAL HOSPITAL. Although the residents of public mental hospitals are aging, the annual number
of admissions of patients over 65 to Massachusetts hospitals
has been relatively stable from 1955 to 1961. Thus, the rate of
admissions of the aged has been decreasing as the number of
aged persons in the general population has been increasing.
It appears that elderly persons with psychiatric problems seldom seek help in general hospital outpatient clinics. Such patients tend to be sent to public mental hospitals after their
families have become exhausted by their care. Many of those
admitted have a history of severe mental illness of varying
type, and only 15 percent conform to the general stereotype
of the elderly psychiatric patient who shows confusion, memory loss, or incoherence. More than 25 percent of these aged
patients exhibit moderate to severe physical disability. Patients over 65 represent 20 percent of admissions to mental
hospitals: about one-third die rather promptly, one-third
return home, and one-third receive prolonged care which
averages less than five years. Those tending to remain longer
most frequently have disorders other than senile or arteriosclerotic brain disorders.

Robert E. Moss, M.D.

According to Jeffers, Nichols, and Eisdorfer (1961), who
study ATTITUDES OF OLDER PERSONS TOWARD DEATH, fear of
death and illness plays an important part in the unconscious
life of individuals, and attitudes toward death may have a
direct effect upon adjustment and attitudes toward life.

A biracial group of 260 community volunteers, 60 years of
age and older, was asked two questions: "Are you afraid to

[293]

die?" and "Do you believe in a life after death?" Those subjects who did not fear death gave the impression that they read the Bible more often, believed in life after death, and experienced fewer feelings of rejection and depression. They made higher scores on full-scale and performance IQ, gave more responses on the Rorschach, and engaged in more leisure-time activities. Those who did not have a religious outlook manifested ambivalent attitudes in their responses, and their answers pointed to fears of death.

Clinical impressions were drawn which underline Schilder's observations of 1942: "There is no common human idea of death; it is a highly individualized concept determined by individual experiences." The authors refer to the distinction between the words "death" and "dying"—a distinction which requires clarification.

The authors agree with Shrut's observations (1958) that "older people who have less institutionalized living arrangements have less fear of or preoccupation with death." They also agree with the Duke University Geriatric Research Group concerning anxiety and old age: "Denial is a very important mechanism of defense employed by persons beyond the fifth decade of life." Denial is promoted by perceptual distortion due to concomitant changes in cortical and receptor processes and to changes in body image with aging and chronic disease.

Clinical depth interviews, preferably repeated, may be the most favorable single method to determine an individual's attitude toward death. The projective methods, such as TAT, sentence completion, and word-association tests, specifically designed to elicit responses to illness and death, should be useful, especially if interviews are designed to elicit affects and defenses which are involved with aging.

[294]

A careful review of and reference to the works of other authors is included: Faunce and Fulton (1958), Feifel (1956; 1959), Neugarten and Gutmann (1958) concerning the sorting of TAT responses to death and illness; Golde and Kogan (1959) concerning the utilization of sentence-completion data for assessing attitudes; Osgood and co-workers (1958), Nunnally and Kittross (1958), Altrocchi and Eisdorfer (1960), concerning the semantic differential procedures for the assessment of attitudes toward such concepts as illness, death, and dependency.

Joel Ordaz, M.D.

In a study of AGING AND SOCIAL PARTICIPATIONS, Zborowski and Eyde (1962) find that older people "desire to continue their contacts on the same level of intensity as in the past." Individual differences found in this study were related not to chronological age, but to an interdependent constellation of age, sex, socioeconomic status, and occupational variables.

The 204 subjects studied were drawn from the Age Center of New England, a nonprofit organization devoted to research on aging. The subjects ranged in age from 51-92, with a median age of 69 for both men and women. They were above average in education and income and had been gainfully employed for most of their lives. The subjects were asked 70 questions (Recreation II and Avocation I and II) probing the extent of their social participation at present and in the past. The information provided measured (1) differences in the kind and number of friends maintained outside the home and in frequency of contact with them; (2) changes in satisfaction with social contacts; (3) differences in home and social contacts in respondents' place of residence and with

[295]

relatives; (4) differences in the duties and social contacts involved in vocational or volunteer activities.

Eighty percent of the women were either single or widowed; 65 percent of the men were still married. A comparison between various aspects of present patterns of social participation with those of the past did not reveal significant differences. All social contacts of the respondents were classified into four groups: (1) relatives vs. nonrelatives; (2) "social" friends; (3) "intellectual" friends; (4) "close" friends.

The respondents had not experienced major changes in their contacts with other people. They believed that they were seeing fewer nonrelatives and fewer "social" friends every day, but they did not believe that they had fewer relatives whom they were close to. Age did not contribute to a decrease in the number of friends with whom they could discuss serious topics. The frequency of their contacts remained the same, but it decreased considerably with friends who were identified as "social." These findings suggest a phenomenon which might be characteristic of the aging process: whenever aging requires a curtailment of social relationships, it takes place in the less intense and less important areas in order to preserve intact those relationships which are more intense and more important for the individual—"economy of social energy." Thus, some of the subjects had been experiencing a decline in the range of their social relationships.

When it came to living arrangements, the respondents tended to express a preference for living alone. This preference is not an indication of withdrawal, but rather a preference for maintaining their privacy and independence. Only 18 percent of the men said that they would enjoy living with other persons of their own age. Eighty-two percent wanted to maintain their earlier patterns of living with persons of all ages.

SURVEY OF LITERATURE

In general, the results showed a major trend toward the maintenance of the habitual modes of living despite increase in chronological age.

Findings in the group of women in many ways were similar, with a few exceptions. The women felt that they were not seeing their relatives as much as they would like to. This finding was interesting in view of the never-married status of the majority of the sample of women. They claimed that they had made significantly more new friends than did the men during the past years. As far as income, education, and retirement status were concerned, it was clear that the older people, especially women of 70 and over, were less privileged in terms of socioeconomic criteria than the younger group. Their patterns of social participation were therefore significantly more affected.

The authors observe that the significant changes which are seen in the older group are also true of the lower income group, the less educated, and the fully retired.

Joel Ordaz, M.D.

Dean (1962), in AGING AND THE DECLINE OF AFFECT, states that the meaning of loneliness changes with age and is associated with inactivity. This study was undertaken as a partial test of one hypothesis of the disengagement theory of aging, as postulated by Cumming and Henry (1961). They attribute decline in the frequency and intensity with which people experience certain emotional states, especially such "active" ones as anger and irritation, to the old person's withdrawal from interpersonal interaction; loneliness and boredom are "passive" states which increase with age.

Two hundred men and women, aged 50-95, were asked questions which tended to elicit affect, such as states of anger, boredom, irritation, and loneliness. The responses fell into two main categories: absence of interaction, corresponding to middle age; and absence of activity, corresponding to old age.

The four most common affective states reported were irritation, boredom, anger, and loneliness. The decline of "feeling angry" from one decade to the next showed a straight-line relationship. An abrupt drop in reported anger can be noticed at about age 60, suggesting that retirement from gainful employment may be a contributing factor.

Boredom and loneliness acquire a different meaning when attention is paid to their occurrence as a consequence of invasion of one's privacy by others and interference with one's self-assertion or self-expression by others. The effects are clearly seen when 70 percent of the respondents to the question: "What is the most boring thing that happened to you?" gave answers which conveyed meanings such as "Every day I hate to hear the door bell ring" or "When I came out of the hospital and company came and stayed too long, I was not very sociable after the first hour." To the question: "When are you most likely to feel lonely?" the middle-aged reported that they felt lonely when they were literally alone; the elderly felt lonely when they had nothing to do.

Inactivity seemed unrelated to the presence or absence of others. The tentative conclusions of this study (1) support that aspect of disengagement theory which considers that there is diminished emotional energy in old age; (2) reveal boredom as an "active" rather than a "passive" state; (3) suggest that because loneliness is defined by the elderly as an absence of activity, not an absence of people, its increase with age does not refute the hard core of disengagement theory.

The author indicates that appropriate therapy for the elderly may not necessarily consist of raising the level of face-to-face interactions. They also observe that for the elderly, anger is positively associated with loneliness, and loneliness in turn is associated with inactivity.

Joel Ordaz, M.D.

An article on PREVALENCE OF PSYCHIATRIC DISORDERS IN METROPOLITAN OLD AGE AND NURSING HOMES, by Goldfarb (1962), is a plea for psychiatric services in old-age and nursing homes and for the strengthening and expansion of psychiatric and social services in state hospitals. Most of the aged admitted to old-age and nursing homes need medical and psychiatric care and supervision, but most of these institutions have insufficient financial or social resources to supply such services.

The author bases his observations on work carried out from 1957-1960 by a special office created in 1956 by the Department of Mental Hygiene to explore the need among the aged for psychiatric care. The unit surveyed old-age homes, nursing homes, and state hospitals to determine the characteristics of first admissions to these institutions of persons aged 64 and older. Information was collected about the services offered, and a bibliography was drawn up on care and treatment of mentally ill aged persons. The unit served as a link between New York metropolitan nonprofit community welfare agencies and the Department of Mental Hygiene.

The report showed that there is not unwarranted admission or retention of aged patients in psychiatric hospitals. Many aged persons with mental disorders of "organic" type were found in nursing homes with no formal medical and psychiatric supervision.

Management of persons with organic brain syndrome (disorientation, defects of memory, and deficient intellectual powers) can be made adequate through improved psychiatric understanding on the part of the staff responsible for

[299]

their care. Management of transient disturbances can be taught, and the staff needs help in understanding their own reactions to the aged.

In the survey of psychiatric care of the aged, the investigators found twice as many women as men. The median age on admission for those over 65 was 76 years in both state hospitals and old-age homes; in nursing homes, it was 79. Symptoms and signs often develop after admission that would have made patients ineligible for admission; and all homes try to retain such persons, although it increases the need for supervision, protection, and guidance. Although the disorders are usually attributed to senility, psychiatric examination revealed that "a high proportion of residents had disorders which probably needed psychiatric care, supervision or understanding." The major problem is that of disturbed behavior associated with chronic brain syndrome. State hospitals showed 94 percent of patients with chronic brain syndrome; nursing homes, 87 percent, and old-age homes, 80 percent. Chronic brain syndrome with behavioral disorders that justified the term "psychosis" amounted to 60 percent in state hospitals, 22 percent in old-age homes, and 36 percent in nursing homes.

Psychiatric examination revealed that 57 percent of the aged in state hospitals had improved, to the extent that if they had not already been in the hospital, they would not now have had to be hospitalized. The same was true of 277 of those in old-age homes and 40 percent of those in nursing homes. Also to be noted is that one can assume a qualitative difference in the behavior of patients in settings outside of the state hospital, and, if it is so, recommendations for treatment can then be specific.

It was considered that about one in ten of all institutionalized persons could profitably receive individual psychiatric attention. Group therapy was recommended for about 10 percent. Four in ten persons in each type of institution required a therapeutic milieu. Drug therapy was advised for 28 percent of persons in old-age homes, 32 percent of those in nursing homes, and 71 percent of those in state hospitals. Electroshock therapy was recommended for less than 1 percent of all persons examined.

Proportionately more aged persons functioned well in the old-age homes than in the other two types of institution. The poorest functional status was in largest proportion in the nursing homes. In old-age and nursing homes, a direct relationship was found between mental functional states and severity of physical impairment, but the same was not true of the state hospitals, where severe mental impairment combined with good physical functional status occurred in high proportion.

Eliot Landsman, M.D.

In THE LIFE REVIEW: AN INTERPRETATION OF REMINISCENCE IN THE AGED, Butler (1963) views as universal the occurrence in older persons of an inner experience of reviewing one's life, a process known as reminiscence. It contributes to late-life disorders, especially depression, but it also promotes positive attributes such as candor, serenity, and wisdom.

Reminiscence in the aged is not a psychological dysfunction or a symptom, but a progressive return to consciousness of past experiences in which the resurgence of unresolved conflicts can be surveyed and reintegrated.

The universal tendency to deny the reality of death is often inappropriately minimized by psychiatric writers or dismissed as basic castration anxiety.

Review of one's life is seen as a general response to crises in young and old, and imminent death is one such crisis. Such a review potentially proceeds toward personality reorganization. It includes reminiscence and may occur either unbidden or by the purposeful seeking of memories. A mild degree of reminiscence is reflected in mild nostalgia, mild regret; a severe degree, in anxiety, guilt, despair, and depression. Extreme cases may involve obsessive preoccupation with the past, proceeding to terror and even suicide, indicating that this normative process may eventuate in severe psychopathology.

The group especially prone to anxiety and total catastrophe consists of those who tend to avoid the present or to put great emphasis on the future. Another group prone to the more severe outcomes consists of those consciously intent on injuring others. The characterologically arrogant and prideful are especially disturbed by the threat of death to their excessive narcissism.

Intensive, detailed study of the aged is needed to obtain detailed information concerning mental functioning in the face of approaching death. The personal sense and meaning of the life cycle are more clearly unfolded by those who have nearly completed it. Awareness of the vital process of life review may help one to listen, to tolerate, and to understand the aged, and not to treat reminiscence as devitalizing and insignificant.

"The aged particularly need a participant observer, professionally or otherwise, and the alleged danger of psychotherapy should be reevaluated. . . . Probably at no other time in life is there as potent a force toward self-awareness operating as in old age."

The importance of the meaning of experience should be noted, as well as positive, affirmative changes reported by the aged.

The entire life cycle cannot be comprehended without inclusion of the psychology of the aged.

Norvell L. Peterson, M.D.

Mensh (1963) presents STUDIES OF OLDER PSYCHIATRIC PATIENTS. Demographic studies of the mentally ill elderly in both the United States and Great Britain show an increase in the number of admissions of elderly patients to mental hospitals despite the trend toward fewer beds. An increasing proportion of these beds are for the elderly. Female geriatric patients are more numerous than male, possibly because of the higher death rate for elderly males. Of the elderly admitted for the first time, those with diseases of the senium far outnumber those with schizophrenia. The low release rate for the elderly is noted, as well as the high mortality soon after admission. The author reports a study of nonhospitalized patients in which the ten health districts of Los Angeles, California, were reviewed to determine the population at risk by age and sex. The data on patients of the Psychiatric Outpatient Department of the Medical Center were tabulated, also by age and sex, for the six years of operation of the clinic, and compared with the figures for the population at risk. Using these data, ratios were computed for the OPD total sample and the best estimate of the population at risk. Very low ratios (OPD/LA) were found for the 65-84 age range, considerably lower than for the 60-65 age range. Better psychological health among the older individuals seems to the

[303]

author a less likely explanation of these trends than the observation that older patients are less acceptable to treatment centers for many and complex reasons on the part of the staff. Other data to which the author refers suggest that medical or administrative decisions may confuse psychologic and physical illness in patients in later life. One study indicated considerable "misplacement" of elderly patients both in a mental hospital and in a general hospital. These trends all point to selective biases in the training of mental health personnel, and to a need for the study of aged psychiatric patients, their care, and their rehabilitation.

David A. Browne, M.D.

In TOWARD A CONCEPTUAL MODEL OF GERIATRIC PSYCHO-PHARMACOLOGY: AN EXPERIMENT WITH THIORIDAZINE AND DEXTRO-AMPHETAMINE, Kastenbaum, Slater, and Aisenberg (1964) report on a study of 27 patients. Eleven men and 16 women with a mean age of 79.7 years, selected at random from patients at the Cushing Hospital, a state institution for the aged in Framingham, Massachusetts, served as subjects of a double-blind study of the comparative effects of dextro-amphetamine, administered at a dosage of 10 mgm., three times a day; thioridazine (Mellaril), at a dosage level of 10 mgm., three times a day; and placebo. A battery of 16 psychological tests, including the Bender-Gestalt, Porteus Maze Test, and Shipley-Hartford Scale of Verbal and Abstract Reasoning, were administered before and after the six-week phase of drug administration. These data were supplemented by a ward observation checklist determined by the nurses.

Results showed no systematic evidence for improvement in cognitive function with either of the drugs or with placebo. Certain patients receiving thioridazine showed a broadening and deepening of their framework for organizing experience, along with intensification of the content within this framework. They tended to think further into both the past and the future and to report more experiences of a personal and significant nature with an increase in a sense of conflict and anguish. A general enlivening effect was seen in the placebo group, with higher ratings on scales of contentment, interviewer rapport, and vivacity. The tranquilizer and stimulant groups generally showed opposite trends from one another, but in a paradoxical fashion contrary to the supposed action of the drugs tested. The "tranquilized" patients tended to show more affect, less contentment, more self-criticism, less rapport with the interviewer, and more liveliness. The "stimulated" patients showed reduced affectivity and vivacity, completed fewer test items, and were more likely to perceive themselves as old.

These paradoxical responses led the investigators to develop a conceptual model in which they hypothesize that certain subjects operating at a lowered developmental level interpret the drug effects as an external threat to self-organization. In the process of neutralizing the drug effect and compensating for the intrusion, these "counterreactors" overshoot the mark and react paradoxically. The social responses to these disparate maneuvers may then lead to increasing turmoil and counterreaction. The investigators report some success in prediction using this conceptual model.

David A. Browne, M.D.

The problem of drug research is also dealt with by Rosenfelt, Kastenbaum, and Kempler (1964) in a paper entitled "THE UNTESTABLES": METHODOLOGICAL PROBLEMS IN DRUG

[305]

RESEARCH WITH THE AGED. In the process of evaluating the effects of psychotropic drugs at Cushing Hospital, a state hospital for the elderly in Framingham, Massachusetts, the authors found that administering psychological tests to elderly and severely handicapped subjects was possible, although it required time and patience in obtaining cooperation and adequate response output. In selecting subjects for drug research, the authors point out, subjects may be dropped because they are thought "untestable," despite the fact that such subjects are often the very ones needing such drugs for treatment. Because of the subject's social impoverishment, the authors feel that the testing situation may make a greater impact upon elderly subjects than on those who are younger. Fear of revealing decline in mental abilities may lead to a small volume of scorable responses, and conventional scoring methods may not yield differentiating information. Because of small samples, which are due in part to a limitation of the subject's energies, the authors have found it especially productive to refine hypotheses in several stages and to test in serial replications. Also useful has been evaluation of test responses in graduated levels of precision, from the most conventional scoring to the least. Because of unevenness in the level of psychological functioning in the elderly, the authors feel it important to explore all variables more fully than would be usual for younger subjects. They also point out that termination of a research project may be seen by the subjects as a rejection, if provision is not made for such effective measures as follow-up visits.

David A. Browne, M.D.

VALUE PROBLEMS IN GERIATRIC PSYCHOPHARMACOLOGY are discussed by Aisenberg and Kastenbaum (1964). The authors describe certain ethical, moral, or value-decision aspects of drug usage which arise from their research on the effects of psychotropic agents on elderly patients at Cushing Hospital, a state hospital for the aged in Framingham, Massachusetts.

Many situations are cited, such as attempting to make the patient more aware of his life situation by using drugs, even if it means that he will probably feel miserable about it; or, conversely, the use of drugs to make the patient as comfortable as possible, even if it means that his intellectual functioning will be impaired. They point out that their research suggests that some drugs not only affect the target symptom but also help to reorganize the patient's total life perspective. If so, the patient may be able to experience more profound affects and to gain greater perspective on his situation, but he may also feel an increase in a sense of hopelessness and impotence. Another issue is raised by the wish to do something where one feels helpless in the face of old age, decrepitude, and death or where one is faced with social pressure to be active in intervening and in controlling an elderly person's behavior.

The authors close with the hope that drug usage will be seen as a form of behavior embedded in a context of strong conscious and unconscious social attitudes and that we will increase our ability to "behave with drugs" in such a manner as to implement effectively society's most positive and mature sentiments toward the aged.

David A. Browne, M.D.

PERSONALITY FACTORS AND MORTALITY IN THE RELOCATION OF THE AGED is the subject of Aldrich's (1964) investigation. The author continues in this article to analyze data

[307]

collected and reported in an earlier paper in which he and a colleague described the effects of relocation on 182 residents of a home for the chronically disabled. Psychotics or near-psychotics had the highest death rate; neurotic, depressed, and compulsive residents and residents who denied their physical disabilities had death rates three times as high as those with a satisfactory adjustment and twice as high as those with hostile and demanding behavior. The death rate was higher than expected and greatest in the first three months following relocation.

In the present study, the author attempts to further his case for the contribution of psychological factors to death by comparing the 26 elderly patients who died in the crucial three months following transfer with a control group of patients, matched for sex, age, and primary (physical) diagnosis who survived the first 12 months of relocation. The results support the hypothesis that psychological factors play a significant role in determining the survival of elderly persons following relocation. Four times as many psychotics died as survived; the same number of neurotics or depressed residents died as survived; and almost three times as many residents with satisfactory, angry, or demanding adaptation survived as died. Twenty residents with philosophical, angry, or anxious reactions to the news of relocation survived, as contrasted with one who died; six residents who reacted with regression, depression, or denial, or who were psychotic, survived as contrasted with 24 who died.

The author concludes that the nature of the psychological response to the stress of institutionalization or relocation seems to be more significant as a determinant of survival than physical condition.

David A. Browne, M.D.

In A GENETIC STUDY OF AFFECTIVE ILLNESS IN PATIENTS OVER 50, Hopkinson (1964) hoped to clarify some of the findings regarded as evidence for genetic factors in the affective illness of patients over 50. He selected 100 cases of patients over 50 who were diagnosed as suffering from affective disorders.

These patients had been admitted to a university clinic between 1955 and 1962. Because only 15 were diagnosed as suffering from endogenous or cyclothymic depression from 1955 to 1958, but because 62 were so classified from 1959 to 1962 and the rest as involutional melancholiac, he concluded that the term *involutional melancholia* had fallen out of fashion. He further divided the group into those who had suffered from attacks before the age of 50 and those who had not. He compared his findings, including the incidence of emotional illness among first-degree relatives of his patients, with those of Kallman and of Kay and Stenstedt.

Kallman believed that there is a genetic relationship between involutional melancholia and schizophrenia, which is greater than that between involutional melancholia and the manic-depressive psychoses, and that there is no inherited tendency to suicide among relatives of involutional melancholiacs. The author reasons that if Kallman's hypotheses are correct, it would be reasonable to expect an increased incidence of schizophrenia among the relatives of late-onset or involutional cases in the current study. Only one case of schizophrenia was present, however, and that case was among the relatives of the early-onset cases. No cases were present in relatives of involutional melancholia or late-onset patients.

Kay and Stenstedt also reported that they did *not* observe an increased risk of schizophrenia among the relatives of their involutional-type patients. Therefore, Hopkinson maintains,

[309]

no support was obtained for Kallman's findings in respect to a genetic relationship between schizophrenia and involutional melancholia.

The author found that his results corresponded more closely to those of Stenstedt (1952). In the current study, the over-all morbidity risk for first-degree relatives of involutional melancholiac patients of having an affective disorder was 11.3 ± 2.8 percent. This figure agrees with those of Stenstedt, who considered the morbidity risk for manic-depressive psychosis in parents, siblings, and children of manic-depressive patients to be 15 percent. In the Hopkinson series, therefore, the risk of affective disorders for first-degree relatives of involutional cases is almost the same as that for the relatives of manic-depressives.

Stenstedt (1959) also found a lower risk for manic-depressive psychosis in relatives of those cases over 55 years of age suffering from involutional melancholia. This finding also agrees with the author's study, and he considers it likely that the view that genetic factors are of less importance in affective illness of late onset is correct.

In general, then, it would appear that there is a greater relationship between involutional melancholia and the manic-depressive psychoses than there is between involutional melancholia and schizophrenia.

Earl M. Wedrow, M.D.

Kay, Beamish, and Roth (1964) set out to study OLD AGE MENTAL DISORDERS IN NEWCASTLE UPON TYNE. PART I of this work is A STUDY OF PREVALENCE. They selected cases over age 65 at random from the total population by referring to the electoral register of the town and by taking a census of patients and residents in mental hospitals, geriatric wards, and welfare homes whose home addresses lay within the community.

They found that the prevalence of organic brain syndrome in this population was 10.3 percent. Senile and arteriosclerotic syndromes were about equally common, but the latter was more frequently diagnosed in men. Brain syndromes due to other causes occurred in 1.9 percent. In about half the cases the mental deterioration was severe and was similar in degree to that usually found in demented mental hospital patients. Fewer than one-fifth were actually being cared for in a hospital or special home.

The most impressive statistics revealed that the total prevalence of all forms of functional disorder was 31 percent, with a somewhat higher rate among women than among men. The majority of these cases—24 percent—fell into the category of minor functional disorders. The illness consisted of an admixture of depression and anxiety, usually in response to environmental or physical stress, but sometimes of uncertain causation.

Neither of the major functional psychoses, schizophrenia or endogenous affective disorders, could be identified with confidence among the subjects seen at home. Chronic or mild incipient forms (including paranoid states) were judged present in about 3 percent.

During the study the following considerations became important.

There were difficulties in making demarcations (1) when there were mild organic syndromes and the normal changes of aging, (2) when anxiety and depression had to be evaluated in a chronically anxious and worrying person, or (3) when mild and transient symptoms arose in response to some environmental change.

[311]

Because the role of the aged person in the community is not well defined, several of the ordinary criteria of mental illness are not appropriate. Old people have usually retired, so that regular employment cannot be regarded as indicative of health; in the social sphere no definite role seems to be expected. In the authors' opinion, the patterns of sexual adjustment do not provide useful information.

The authors agree with Post (1962) that the outcome in endogenous cases of major functional psychoses is best when the family history is positive, when previous attacks with recovery occurred earlier in life, when the personality is extraverted, and when the illness is severe.

Their findings also parallel those of Kessel (1960) and Kessel and Shepherd (1962), which showed that while the rate of referral of neurotics to hospitals falls steeply after the age of 60, the prevalence of neurosis in general practice remains surprisingly constant throughout adult life at about 10 percent of the population at risk among men and 15 percent among women. Phillips (1962) found that about a third of his sample of old people were suffering from "emotional maladjustment," according to reports from their own doctors.

The authors conclude that their findings demonstrate again that only a very small fraction of old people with psychiatric disorders, which are usually of a neurotic-like nature, are being cared for either as hospital inpatients or as residents of special homes. There is clearly an urgent need, therefore, to extend the facilities for community care for the aged portion of the population.

Earl M. Wedrow, M.D.

COMMUNITY PROGRAMS

Boek, Harris and Shoro (1962) report on a project of COMMUNITY RESEARCH FOR SOLVING PROBLEMS OF SENIOR

[312]

CITIZENS. A group of professional men interested in the problems of the older person organized a Center for the Study of Aging, in Albany, New York. The Center decided that it would be important to have accurate information about the actual lives of the senior citizens in the community if a useful program of aid were to be planned. A survey was therefore made of 1,200 households in the Albany area. They were selected after an assessment of various records which included the U.S. Census block statistics, census tract data, recent population estimates of various departments of the state government, geologic survey maps, city hall records of buildings, and accounts from real estate offices.

The questionnaire asked the name, age, and sex of each member of the selected household, as well as the employment situation, social security status, and health of each person over the age of 50. The 1,177 replies revealed the following information.

There was an average of 3.2 persons per household, with somewhat more women than men. In the 75 to 89 age category, there were three women to every two men. Twenty-six percent of the population was over 50 years of age, and 10 percent was over 65.

The week before the contacts were made, 10 percent of the men and 12 percent of the women over 50 were ill. Men over the age of 60 became ill at an increasing rate, whereas the trend was somewhat reduced for women.

Fifty percent of the men and 15 percent of the women over 60 were employed. Only one person out of 100 over 50 years of age was looking for a full-time job, and three out of 100 were looking for part-time work.

Those over 50 lived more frequently in the city than in the country, and the men over 60 lived in smaller and poorer households than did the women.

Because so much information was obtained from a relatively limited questionnaire, the authors believe that even more useful material could be gathered by interviewing the same persons more thoroughly. It might be possible then to find out what people do who are born and live out their lives in the slums. What do they die from and at what age? Is the pattern of illness alike for the rich and the poor in the same and in different localities?

The authors suggest that a statistically significant sample of families be kept up to date, with changes in addresses, deaths, and births listed as they occur. Such accurate information could provide a basis on which program specialists, boards of agencies, and medical and social scientists could make active and helpful plans for older persons.

Earl M. Wedrow, M.D.

Cath (1963a) provides A SURVEY OF SELECTED GERIATRIC-PSYCHIATRIC FACILITIES IN NORTHERN EUROPE. This survey attempts to determine current status and foreseeable progress in caring for the aged in Northern Europe. Part I concerns England. As elsewhere, the number of aged has increased tremendously in England since World War II. Ninety-five percent of the elderly live in their own homes and reluctantly enter residential homes as a last resort. Little social casework is available in England, but, when needed, domestic help is usually obtainable. When the National Health Service was instituted, the facilities were nearly swamped by the elderly, whose care fell to the general practitioner, to whom patients are returned from a hospital as soon as possible. The system provides bed care, day hospitals, and outpatient services, which are based in the nearest general hospital. Hospital, general practitioner, and local authority are linked by an integrated service, and much effort is devoted to keeping the elderly in their homes to obviate feelings of loneliness and rejection. Problems with patients may be evaluated in general hospitals, and a geriatric psychiatrist is available for consultation.

The mental hospital population includes about 30 percent over 65. Effort is directed to activating as many as possible, and patients come and go readily. Inpatients are divided into "short-stay" patients, discharged within three months, and the remainder, the majority, who leave within two years. As yet, there is little specialization in geriatrics in English medical training. Psychiatrists are part of the medical team and engage practically in direct medical care. Every effort is made by home visiting teams and hospital staffs to "maintain painless physical independence," thereby keeping the patient in the community. The assumption is that the patient can manage by himself and perhaps can avoid regressive changes and dependency encouraged by prolonged hospitalization.

However respectable the British effort to care for the elderly, it is admittedly inadequate. Evidence exists of the need of the elderly to be stimulated continually by interaction with others to avoid regression and withdrawal.

Part II of the Survey (Cath, 1963b) deals with the Scandinavian countries. Scandinavia, despite shortages, has made great strides in caring for an increasing number of aged persons. As elsewhere, shifts from rural to urban-industrial living have tended to dissolve family solidarity and identity and to contribute to the isolation of the aged as a separate group. Since World War II, governments increasingly have provided acceptable living for the aged through social security systems. Such responsibility is constantly increasing. Every effort is made to keep the elderly at home and to provide district buildings in which activities for the elderly are concentrated. Three-generation homes are no longer preferred by the young and persist chiefly in rural areas. Older workers in all categories are encouraged to remain at work as long as possible, because there is a shortage of labor, a situation that has a salutary effect upon them. Costs of medical care are minimal in Scandinavia, as in Great Britain. Housing shortages are acute, however; apartments are small and expensive and not suited to three-generation living.

Housing for the elderly was initially segregated in ghetto-like "silent streets," which led to unfortunate isolation and exile. The recent trend has been toward intermingling age groups by placing specially designated apartments for the aged on the lower floors of apartment buildings. The tendency in psychiatric care is toward occupational, physiologic, and somatic approaches, with little attention to dynamically oriented therapy.

Many retired Swedes are isolated and rejected by their families, and three-generation homes are disappearing. Every effort is made to return a patient to his home as soon as possible. Geriatrics is not considered a specialty, and there is no move toward preventive measures.

Part III (Cath, 1963b) is an examination of facilities in Holland and France. Holland presents features in geriatrics that could serve as a model. Lack of housing has made "togetherness" mandatory. In Amsterdam free psychiatric care is available 24 hours a day. The aim is to maintain family and patient as a unit, and only the most desperate cases are admitted to the hospital. The Dutch want additional community services to keep the aged out of institutions, even though there are sufficent beds. If a patient requires hospitalization, he goes to an observation center; then, if necessary, to a halfway house or foster home; if this is insufficient, he goes to a long-stay annex in the country. Only if this treatment fails is the patient sent to a mental hospital. The Dutch use a doctor-nurse-social-worker team to manage a family crisis from beginning to end. There is little confidence in psychotherapy for the aged; physical, occupational, recreational, and vocational support are the mainstays, as is general in Europe.

France has a limited recognition of geriatric-psychiatric problems, and training in psychiatry in medical schools is inadequate.

The Scandinavians and the Dutch seem furthest along toward meeting the problem of the aged and recognizing the potential in preventive measures and the role of dynamic psychiatry. The English have made a moderately successful pragmatic approach. France seems least advanced and least concerned.

In general, European efforts at rehabilitation are based on programs designed to: (1) keep older people at home, (2) provide emergency consultation services, (3) provide care for the chronically ill.

Three-generation homes are declining in Europe for essentially the same reasons as in the United States.

The author ends this informative paper with an extensive summary of recommendations for improving the lot of the aged.

Robert E. Moss, M.D.

The GERIATRIC GOAL: HELP PATIENT ENJOY LIFE ON HIS TERMS is discussed by Linden (1936b). To the question: "What do you believe to be the goals of the geriatrician?" Dr. Linden replies that more emphasis should be given to the fundamentals; the geriatrician should treat the individual instead of the disease. The effort should be to help the patient

[317]

to enjoy life on his own terms as much as possible, rather than to prolong life; for example, prescribing a Spartan diet for an obese gourmet might raise great emotional hazards.

Many physicians as well as their patients are so concerned with postponing death that they neglect to live. Does this preoccupation with death or its postponement often cause the elderly patients themselves to ignore basic needs? Some of the aged seek out a physician because their needs have not been met either by themselves, their doctors, or society. The elderly often neglect themselves for others in their families. Some of the apparent dementia and behavioral changes seen in the elderly may be due to avitaminosis (of B complex) or to pellagra. Some elderly persons become malnourished as a result of depression and loss of interest in food. Difficulties may result from the doctor's not being alert to the possibility that the elderly are medicating themselves out of habit. Self-medication, especially "fads and funny notions," can interfere with sleep or can cause paranoid attitudes and cantankerousness. It is important to check in great detail what regimen the elderly patient is following. Dr. Linden utilizes a questionnaire of 300 items which helps him to learn about the patient's drug usage, habits, hobbies, living arrangements, and medical history.

Many important needs of elderly patients are ignored by society. Everyone needs a chance to express himself, and society denies to older people some of these opportunities because of such social factors as compulsory retirement and lack of community interests and services. Some persons can overcome such obstacles; others need assistance. The young may despise the weakness of the aged, but the aged also reject themselves, and this attitude can result in depression and decline.

Donald Wexler, M.D.

REFERENCES

References

Parts I and II

Allport, G. W. (1942), The Use of Personal Documents in Psychological Science. *Soc. Sci. Res. Coun. Bull.,* No. 49.

Anthony, S. (1940), *The Child's Discovery of Death.* New York: Harcourt, Brace.

Arlow, J. A. (1959), The Structure of the *Déjà Vu* Experience. *J. Am. Psa. Assn.,* 7:611-631.

Barnes, M. (1964), Reactions to the Death of a Mother. In *The Psychoanalytic Study of the Child,* 19:334-357. New York: International Universities Press.

Benedek, T. (1950), Climacterium: A Developmental Phase. *Psa. Quart.,* 19:1-27.

——— (1952), Personality Development. In *Dynamic Psychiatry,* ed. Franz Alexander & Helen Ross. Chicago: University of Chicago Press, pp. 63-113.

Berdyaev, N. A. (1950), *Dream and Reality: An Essay in Autobiography,* trans. Katharine Lampert. New York: Collier Books, 1962.

Berelson, B. & Steiner, G. A. (1964), *Human Behavior: An Inventory of Scientific Findings.* New York: Harcourt, Brace & World.

Bibring, E. (1953), The Mechanism of Depression. In *Affective Disorders,* ed. Phyllis Greenacre. New York: International Universities Press, pp. 13-48.

Bibring, G. L., Dwyer, T. F., Huntington, D. S., & Valenstein, A. F. (1961), A Study of the Psychological Processes in Pregnancy and of the Earliest Mother-Child Relationship. In *The Psychoanalytic Study of the Child,* 16:9-72. New York: International Universities Press.

Birren, J. E., Butler, R. N., Greenhouse, S. W., Sokoloff, L., & Yarrow, M. R., eds (1963), *Human Aging: A Biological and Behavioral*

Study. Washington, D. C.: U. S. Public Health Service Publication No. 986.

Bjorksten, J. (1946), The Limitation of Creative Years. *Scient. Monthly,* 62:94.

Bluestone, H. & McGahee, C. L. (1962), Reaction to Extreme Stress: Impending Death by Execution. *Am. J. Psychiat.,* 119:393-396.

Brozek, J. (1951), The Age Problem in Research Workers: Psychological Viewpoint. *Scient. Monthly,* 72:355-359.

Bunker, H. A. (1951), Psychoanalysis and the Study of Religion. In *Psychoanalysis and the Social Sciences,* Vol. 3, ed. Géza Róheim. New York: International Universities Press, pp. 7-34.

Burr, A. R. (1909), *The Autobiography: A Critical and Comparative Study.* Boston: Houghton Mifflin.

Busse, E. W. (1959), Psychopathology. In *Handbook of Aging and the Individual,* ed. James E. Birren. Chicago: University of Chicago Press, pp. 364-399.

Butler, R. N. (1960), Intensive Psychotherapy for the Hospitalized Aged. *Geriatrics,* 15:644-653.

—— (1961a), Fiction concerning Later Life, Memory, Time, Aging, Disease and Death. Mimeographed.

—— (1961b), Re-Awakening Interests. *Nursing Homes: J. Am. Nursing Home Assn.,* 10:8-19.

—— (1961c), Usefulness in Old Age: Some Considerations towards Prevention of Emotional Problems in the Old. Mimeographed.

—— (1963a), The Facade of Chronological Age: An Interpretive Summary. *Am. J. Psychiat.,* 119:721-728.

—— (1963b), The Life Review: An Interpretation of Reminiscence in the Aged. *Psychiatry,* 26:65-75.

—— (1963c), Privileged Communication and Confidentiality in Research. *Arch. Gen. Psychiat.,* 8:139-141.

—— (1963d), Psychiatric Evaluation of the Aged. *Geriatrics,* 18:220-232.

—— (1963e), Recall in Retrospection. *J. Am. Geriat. Soc.,* 11:523-529.

Clague, E. (1951), The Age Problem in Research Workers: Sociological Viewpoint. *Scient. Monthly,* 72:359-363.

Columbia University, Oral History Research Office (1960), *The Oral History Collection of Columbia University.* New York: Columbia University.

REFERENCES

——— (1962), *The Oral History Collection of Columbia University: Supplement.* New York: Columbia University.

Commager, H. S. (1947), Memoirs: The Personal Touch. *New York Times Book Review,* 3 August.

——— (1963), A Reluctance to Reflect. *Book Week, New York Herald Tribune,* 10 November.

Cumming, E. & Henry, W. E. (1961), *Growing Old.* New York: Basic Books.

Darwin, C. (1876), Recollections of the Development of My Mind and Character. In *The Autobiography of Charles Darwin and Selected Letters,* ed. Francis Darwin. New York: Dover Publications, 1958.

Dennis, W. (1956), Age and Achievement: A Critique. *J. Gerontol.,* 11:331-333.

Denny-Brown, D. (1958), The Nature of Apraxia. *J. Nerv. Ment. Dis.,* 126:9-32.

Deutsch, F. (1936), Euthanasia: A Clinical Study. *Psa. Quart.,* 5:347-368.

Dibner, A. S. & Cummins, J. F. (1961), Intellectual Functioning in a Group of Normal Octogenarians. *J. Consult. Psychol.,* 25:137-141.

Eissler, K. R. (1955), *The Psychiatrist and the Dying Patient.* New York: International Universities Press.

——— (1964), Psychoanalytic Consideration of Aging. Panel Discussion held at the Annual Meeting of the American Psychoanalytic Association, St. Louis, May 1963, reported by Norman E. Zinberg. *J. Am. Psa. Assn.,* 12:151-159.

Erikson, E. H. (1954), The Dream Specimen of Psychoanalysis. *J. Am. Psa. Assn.,* 2:5-56.

——— (1956), The Problem of Ego Identity, *J. Am. Psa. Assn.,* 4:56-121.

——— (1959), Identity and the Life Cycle. *Psychological Issues,* 1 (1). New York: International Universities Press.

Fenichel, O. (1945), *The Psychoanalytic Theory of Neurosis.* New York: W. W. Norton.

——— (1953), *Collected Papers,* 1st Series. New York: W. W. Norton.

——— (1954), *Collected Papers,* 2nd Series. New York: W. W. Norton.

Ferenczi, S. (1913), Stages in the Development of the Sense of Reality. In *Sex in Psychoanalysis,* trans. Ernest Jones. New York: Basic Books, 1950, pp. 213-239.

[323]

―――― (1926), The Problem of Acceptance of Unpleasant Ideas—Advances in Knowledge of the Sense of Reality. In *Further Contributions to the Theory and Technique of Psycho-Analysis*, ed. John Rickman. London: Hogarth Press and Institute of Psycho-Analysis, 1950, pp. 366-379.

Foerster, O. & Gagel, O. (1934), Ein Fall von Ependymcyste des III. Ventrikels. Ein Beitrag zur Frage der Beziehungen psychischer Störungen zum Hirnstamm. *Ztschr. f. d. g. Neurol. u. Psychiat.*, 149:312-344.

Frankfurter, F. (1960), *Felix Frankfurter Reminisces*, ed. Harlan B. Phillips. New York: Reynal & Co.

Freud, A. (1936), *The Ego and the Mechanisms of Defense*. New York: International Universities Press, 1946.

―――― (1958), Adolescence. In *The Psychoanalytic Study of the Child*, 13:255-278. New York: International Universities Press.

Freud, S. (1900), The Interpretation of Dreams. *Standard Edition*, Vols. 4 and 5. London: Hogarth Press, 1953.

―――― (1904), On Psychotherapy. *Standard Edition*, 7:257-268. London: Hogarth Press, 1953.

―――― (1905), Wit and its Relation to the Unconscious. In *The Basic Writings of Sigmund Freud*, ed. A. A. Brill. New York: Random House, 1938, pp. 633-803.

―――― (1911), Psycho-Analytical Notes on an Autobiographical Account of a Case of Paranoia. *Standard Edition*, 12:9-82. London: Hogarth Press, 1958.

―――― (1917), Mourning and Melancholia. *Standard Edition*, 14:243-258. London: Hogarth Press, 1957.

―――― (1923a), The Ego and the Id. *Standard Edition*, 19:12-66. London: Hogarth Press, 1961.

―――― (1923b), Two Encyclopaedia Articles. *Standard Edition*, 18:235-259. London: Hogarth Press, 1955.

―――― (1926), Inhibitions, Symptoms and Anxiety. *Standard Edition*, 20:87-174. London: Hogarth Press, 1959.

Furman, R. A. (1964a), Death and the Young Child: Some Preliminary Considerations. In *The Psychoanalytic Study of the Child*, 19:321-333. New York: International Universities Press.

―――― (1964b), Death of a Six-Year-Old's Mother during His Analysis.

In *The Psychoanalytic Study of the Child,* 19:377-397. New York: International Universities Press.

Gitelson, M. (1948), The Emotional Problems of Elderly People. *Geriatrics,* 3:135-150.

Hackett, T. P. & Weisman, A. D. (1962), The Treatment of the Dying. In *Current Psychiatric Therapies,* Vol. 2, ed. Jules Masserman. New York: Grune & Stratton, pp. 121-126.

Haley, J. (1963), *Strategies of Psychotherapy.* New York: Grune & Stratton.

Harley, M. (1951), Analysis of a Severely Disturbed Three-and-One-Half-Year-Old Boy. In *The Psychoanalytic Study of the Child,* 6:206-234. New York: International Universities Press.

Hartmann, H. (1958), *Ego Psychology and the Problem of Adaptation,* trans. David Rapaport. New York: International Universities Press.

Heckscher, A. (1963), *The Arts and the National Government: Report to the President.* Washington, D. C.: U. S. Government Printing Office.

Himmelfarb, G. (1959), *Darwin and the Darwinian Revolution.* Garden City, N. Y.: Doubleday.

Hunter, I. M. L. (1957), *Memory: Facts and Fallacies.* Baltimore, Md.: Penguin Books.

Inglis, J., Shapiro, M. B., & Post, F. (1956), "Memory Function" in Psychiatric Patients over Sixty: The Role of Memory in Tests Discriminating between "Functional" and "Organic" Groups. *J. Ment. Sci.,* 102:589-598.

Jacobson, E. (1957), Denial and Repression. *J. Am. Psa. Assn.,* 5:61-92.

——— (1964), *Self and the Object World.* New York: International Universities Press.

Jones, E. (1957), *The Life and Work of Sigmund Freud.* Vol. 3: *The Last Phase, 1919-1939.* New York: Basic Books.

Kiell, N. (1963), *Universal Experience through Adolescence.* New York: International Universities Press.

Kral, V. A. (1958), Neuro-Psychiatric Observations in an Old Peoples Home: Studies of Memory Dysfunction in Senescence. *J. Gerontol.,* 13:169-176.

Kris, E. (1952), *Psychoanalytic Explorations in Art.* New York: International Universities Press.

REFERENCES

Lasswell, H. D. (1930), *Psychopathology and Politics*. Chicago: University of Chicago Press.

Laurendeau, M. & Pinard, A. (1962), *Causal Thinking in the Child*. New York: International Universities Press.

Lehman, H. C. (1953), *Age and Achievement*. Princeton, N. J.; Princeton University Press.

———— (1956), Reply to Dennis' Critique of *Age and Achievement*. *J. Gerontol.*, 11:333-337.

Lewin, B. D. (1946), Counter-Transference in the Technique of Medical Practice. *Psychosom. Med.*, 8:195-199.

———— (1950), *The Psychoanalysis of Elation*. New York: W. W. Norton.

Lichtenstein, H. (1963), The Dilemma of Human Identity. *J. Am. Psa. Assn.*, 11:173-223.

Lillard, R. G. (1956), *American Life in Autobiography: A Descriptive Guide*. Stanford, Calif.: Stanford University Press.

Lomax, A. (1950), *Mister Jelly Roll: The Fortunes of Jelly Roll Morton, New Orleans Creole and "Inventor of Jazz."* New York: Duell, Sloan & Pearce.

McDonald, M. (1964), A Study of the Reactions of Nursery School Children to the Death of a Child's Mother. In *The Psychoanalytic Study of the Child*, 19:358-376. New York: International Universities Press.

McMahon, A. W. & Rhudick, P. J. (1964), Reminiscing: Adaptational Significance in the Aged. *Arch. Gen. Psychiat.*, 10:292-298.

Meyerhoff, H. (1962), On Psychoanalysis as History. *Psa. & Psa. Rev.*, 49 (2):3-20.

Misch, G. (1951), *History of Autobiography in Antiquity*, 2 vols., trans. E. W. Dickes. Cambridge, Mass.: Harvard University Press.

Nagy, M. H. (1959), The Child's View of Death. In *The Meaning of Death*, ed. Herman Feifel. New York: McGraw-Hill, pp. 79-98.

Nevins, A. (1938), *The Gateway to History*. Boston: D. C. Heath.

Olin, H. S. & Hackett, T. P. (1964), The Denial of Chest Pain in 32 Patients with Acute Myocardial Infarction. *J. Am. Med. Assn.*, 190: 977-981.

Pear, T. H. (1922), *Remembering and Forgetting*. New York: E. P. Dutton.

Pelikan, J. (1961), *The Shape of Death: Life, Death, and Immortality in the Early Fathers.* New York and Nashville, Tenn.: Abingdon Press.

Phillips, W., ed. (1963), *Art and Psychoanalysis: Studies in the Application of Psychoanalytic Theory to the Creative Process.* Cleveland and New York: World Publishing Co.

Piaget, J. (1929), *The Child's Conception of the World.* Paterson, N. J.: Littlefield, Adams, 1963.

Plank, E. N. (1953), Memories of Early Childhood in Autobiographies. In *The Psychoanalytic Study of the Child,* 8:381-393. New York: International Universities Press.

Pogue, F. (1963), *George C. Marshall: Education of a General.* New York: Viking Press.

Rapaport, D. (1958), The Theory of Ego Autonomy. *Bull. Menninger Clin.,* 22:13-35.

―――― (1959), Introduction: A Historical Survey of Psychoanalytic Ego Psychology. In E. H. Erikson, Identity and the Life Cycle. *Psychological Issues,* 1 (1). New York: International Universities Press.

―――― (1961), *Emotions and Memory.* New York: Science Editions.

Rickman, J. (1940), On the Nature of Ugliness and the Creative Impulse. *Int. J. Psa.,* 21:294-313.

Rochlin, G. (1963), The Thought of Dying: Some Origins of Religious Belief. Paper presented at a scientific meeting of the Boston Psychoanalytic Society, January 1963.

Rogow, A. A. (1963), *James Forrestal: A Study of Personality, Politics, and Policy.* New York: Macmillan.

Sachs, H. (1942), *The Creative Unconscious.* Cambridge, Mass.: Sci-Art.

Saunders, C. (1959), *Care of the Dying.* (*Nursing Times* reprint) London: Macmillan, 1960.

Schreber, D. P. (1903), *Memoirs of My Nervous Illness,* trans. Ida Macalpine & Richard A. Hunter. London: William Dawson, 1955.

Shapiro, M. B., Post, F., Löfving, B., & Inglis, J. (1956), "Memory Function" in Psychiatric Patients over Sixty: Some Methodological and Diagnostic Implications. *J. Ment. Sci.,* 102:233-246.

Shaw, G. B. (1921), Preface to *Immaturity.* In *Selected Prose,* ed. Diarmuid Russell. New York: Dodd, Mead, 1952, pp. 25-66.

Sherrington, C. (1951), *Man on His Nature.* New York: Doubleday Anchor Books, 1953.

Shumaker, W. (1954), *English Autobiography: Its Emergence, Materials, and Form.* Berkeley: University of California Press.

Simmons, L. W. (1946), Attitudes toward Aging and the Aged: Primitive Societies. *J. Gerontol.,* 1:72-95.

Smith, G. (1964), *When the Cheering Stopped: The Last Years of Woodrow Wilson.* New York: William Morrow.

Spark, M. (1958), *Memento Mori.* Philadelphia: J. B. Lippincott.

Spiegel, L. A. (1951), A Review of Contributions to a Psychoanalytic Theory of Adolescence: Individual Aspects. In *The Psychoanalytic Study of the Child,* 6:375-393. New York: International Universities Press.

Stein, M. I. & Heinze, S. J. (1960), *Creativity and the Individual: Summaries of Selected Literature in Psychology and Psychiatry.* Glencoe, Ill.: Free Press.

Stern, W. (1930), Personalistic der Erinnerung. *Z. Psychol.,* 118:350-381.

Sternberg, R. S., Chapman, J., & Shakow, D. (1958), Psychotherapy Research and the Problem of Intrusion on Privacy. *Psychiatry,* 21:195-203.

Stone, A. A. (1964), Consciousness: Altered Levels in Blind Retarded Children. *Psychosom. Med.,* 26:14-19.

Tolstoy, L. (1886), The Death of Ivan Ilyich. In *The Cossacks, etc.,* trans. Rosemary Edmonds. Baltimore, Md.: Penguin Books, 1960, pp. 99-161.

——— (1910), *Last Diaries,* ed. Leon Stilman. New York: Capricorn Books, G. P. Putnam, 1960.

Van Zooneveld, R. J. (1958), An Orientation Study of the Memory of Old People. *Geriatrics,* 13:532-534.

Von Vischer, A. L. (1958), Die Lebensbilanz. *Vita Humana, Basel:* 1:129-141.

Wechsler, D. (1944), *Measurement of Adult Intelligence,* 3rd ed. Baltimore, Md.: Williams & Wilkins.

Weinstein, E. A. & Kahn, R. L. (1955), *Denial of Illness: Symbolic and Physiological Aspects.* Springfield, Ill.: Charles C Thomas.

Weisman, A. D. (1959), The Psychodynamic Formulation of Conflict. *Arch. Gen. Psychiat.,* 1:288-309.

——— (1965), *The Existential Core of Psychoanalysis: Reality Sense and Responsibility.* Boston: Little, Brown.

—— & Hackett, T. P. (1962), The Dying Patient. *Special Treatment Situations* (Forest Hospital Publications, Des Plaines, Ill.), 1:16-21.

Whitehead, A. (1925), *Science and the Modern World.* New York: Macmillan.

Winnicott, D. W. (1958), The Capacity to Be Alone. *Int. J. Psa.,* 39:416-420.

Worcester, A. (1940), *The Care of the Aged, the Dying, and the Dead,* 2nd ed. Springfield, Ill.: Charles C Thomas.

Zeman, F. D. (1957), Recent Contributions to the Medical Problems of Old Age. *New Eng. J. Med.,* 257:317-322, 369-374, 411-416.

PART III

Aisenberg, R. & Kastenbaum, R. (1964), Value Problems in Geriatric Psychopharmacology. *The Gerontologist,* 4:75-77.

Aldrich, C. K. (1964), Personality Factors and Mortality in the Relocation of the Aged. *The Gerontologist,* 4:92-93.

Altrocchi, J. & Eisdorfer, C. (1960), A Comparison of Attitudes toward Old Age, Mental Illness, and Other Concepts. Paper presented at the Fifth Congress of the International Association of Gerontology, San Francisco, August 1960.

Anderson, B. G. (1964), Stress and Psychopathology among Aged Americans: An Inquiry into the Perception of Stress. *Southwestern J. Anthropol.,* 20:190-217.

Birren, J. E. (1963), Research on the Psychologic Aspects of Aging. *Geriatrics,* 18:393-403.

—— & Spieth, W. (1962), Age, Response Speed, and Cardiovascular Functions. *J. Gerontol.,* 17:390-391.

Bjurwill, B. (1963), [The Effect of Cosaldon in Elderly Patients with Cerebral Sclerosis on the Ability to Orientate, Memorize and Think.] *Svensk Lakartidn., Stockholm,* 60:192-199.

Boek, W. E., Harris, R., & Shoro, C. (1962), Community Research for Solving Problems of Senior Citizens. *N.Y. State J. Med.,* 62:3940-3943.

Bortz, E. L. (1963), A Look at Aging and Growth Potentials. *Geriatrics.* 18:233-237.

REFERENCES

Busse, E. W. & Reckless, J. B. (1961), Psychiatric Management of the Aged. *J. Am. Med. Assn.*, 175:645-648.

Butler, R. N. (1963), The Life Review: An Interpretation of Reminiscence in the Aged. *Psychiatry*, 26:65-76.

Cath, S. H. (1963a), A Survey of Selected Geriatric-Psychiatric Facilities in Northern Europe. Part I: England. *Am. J. Psychiat.*, 119:739-742.

———— (1963b), A Survey of Geriatric-Psychiatric Facilities in Northern Europe. II: Scandinavia; III: Holland and France; IV: Summary. *J. Am. Geriat. Soc.*, 11:679-698.

Chown, S. M. (1961), Age and the Rigidities. *J. Gerontol.*, 16:353-362.

Christ, A. E. (1961), Attitudes toward Death among a Group of Acute Geriatric Psychiatric Patients. *J. Gerontol.*, 16:56-59.

Cooper, A. J. (1964), A Controlled Trial of Cosaldon in Arteriosclerotic Dementia. *Brit. J. Psychiat.*, 110:415-418.

Cumming, E. & Henry, W. E. (1961), *Growing Old*. New York: Basic Books.

Dale, P. W. (1961), Current Concepts in Therapy: Medical Management of Mental Problems in the Aged. *New Eng. J. Med.*, 265:84-86, 185-187.

Davidson, R. (1963), Psychiatric Syndromes in the Elderly. *Medical World, London*, 99:206-209.

Dean, L. R. (1962), Aging and the Decline of Affect. *J. Gerontol.*, 17:440-446.

Donati, A. (1960), [The Treatment of Cerebral Sclerosis.] *Praxis*, 49:37-39.

Dovenmuehle, R. H. & Verwoerdt, A. (1963), Physical Illness and Depressive Symptomatology. II: Factors of Length and Severity of Illness and Frequency of Hospitalization. *J. Gerontol.*, 18:260-266.

Eisdorfer, C. (1963), Rorschach Performance and Intellectual Functioning in the Aged. *J. Gerontol.*, 18:358-363.

Faunce, W. A. & Fulton, R. L. (1958), The Sociology of Death. *Soc. Forces*, 3:205-209.

Feifel, H. (1956), Older Persons Look at Death. *Geriatrics*, 11:127-130.

————, ed. (1959), *The Meaning of Death*. New York: McGraw-Hill.

Fish, F. & Williamson, J. (1964), A Delirium Unit in an Acute Geriatric Hospital. *Gerontologia Clinica*, 6:71-80.

Foulds, G. A. (1960), Psychotic Depression and Age. *J. Ment. Sci.*, 106:1394-1397.

Friedman, J. H. & Bressler, D. M. (1964), A Geriatric Mental Hygiene Clinic in a General Hospital: First Two Years of Operation. *J. Am. Geriat. Soc.*, 12:71-78.

Galbraith, B. S. (1963), Intensive Treatment for Geriatric Patients. *Ment. Hosp.*, 14:205-206.

Gardner, E. A., Bahn, A. K., & Mack, M. (1964), Suicide and Psychiatric Care in the Aging. *Arch. Gen. Psychiat.*, 10:547-553.

Gericke, O. L. & Lobb, L. G. (1964), The Critical Role of Defense Mechanisms in the Outcome of Chronic Brain Syndromes in the Aged. *J. Am. Geriat. Soc.*, 12:646-651.

Gillespie, W. H. (1963), Some Regressive Phenomena in Old Age. *Brit. J. Med. Psychol.*, 36:203-209.

Golde, P. & Kogan, N. (1959), A Sentence Completion Procedure for Assessing Attitudes toward Old People. *J. Gerontol.*, 14:355-363.

Goldfarb, A. I. (1962), Prevalence of Psychiatric Disorders in Metropolitan Old Age and Nursing Homes. *J. Am. Geriat. Soc.*, 10:77-84.

———— (1964), Patient-Doctor Relationships in the Treatment of Aged Persons. *Geriatrics*, 19:18-23.

Haas, A. (1963), Management of the Geriatric Psychiatric Patient in a Mental Hospital. *J. Am. Geriat. Soc.*, 11:259-265.

Hamilton, L. D., Bennett, J. L., & Silver, J. (1964), Nandrolone Phenpropionate in the Treatment of Geriatric Patients with Chronic Brain Damage. *J. Am. Geriat. Soc.*, 12:373-378.

Handford, J. M. & Papathomopoulos, E. (1962), Rehabilitation of the Aged in a Mental Hospital. *Geriatrics*, 17:809-814.

Hopkinson, G. (1964), A Genetic Study of Affective Illness in Patients over 50. *Brit. J. Psychiat.*, 110:244-254.

Isaacs, B. & Walkey, F. A. (1963), A Simplified Performance Test for Elderly Hospital Patients. *J. Am. Geriat. Soc.*, 11:1089-1094.

———— & ———— (1964), Measurement of Mental Impairment in Geriatric Practice. *Gerontologia Clinica*, 6:114-123.

Jeffers, F. C., Eisdorfer, C., & Busse, E. W. (1962), Measurement of Age Identification: A Methodological Note. *J. Gerontol.*, 17:437-439.

————, Nichols, C. R., & Eisdorfer, C. (1961), Attitudes of Older Persons toward Death: A Preliminary Study. *J. Gerontol.*, 16:53-56.

Kahn, R. L., Goldfarb, A. I., Pollack, M., & Peck, A. (1960), Brief Objective Measures for the Determination of Mental Status in the Aged. *Am. J. Psychiat.*, 117:326-328.

[331]

Kastenbaum, R. J., Slater, P. E., & Aisenberg, R. (1964), Toward a Conceptual Model of Geriatric Psychopharmacology: An Experiment with Thioridazine and Dextro-Amphetamine. *The Gerontologist*, 4:68-71.

Kay, D. W., Beamish, P., & Roth, M. (1964), Old Age Mental Disorders in Newcastle upon Tyne. I: A Study of Prevalence. *Brit. J. Psychia.*, 110:146-158.

Kemp, R. (1963), Old Age, a Regret. *Lancet*, 2:897-900.

Kessel, W. I. N. (1960), Psychiatric Morbidity in a London General Practice. *Brit. J. Prev. Soc. Med.*, 14:16-22.

—— & Shepherd, M. (1962), Neurosis in Hospital and General Practice. *J. Ment. Sci.*, 108:159-166.

Kral, V. A., Cahn, C., & Mueller, H. (1964), Senescent Memory Impairment and its Relation to the General Health of the Aging Individual. *J. Am. Geriat. Soc.*, 12:101-113.

Lenzer, A. (1961), Sociocultural Influences on Adjustment to Aging. *Geriatrics*, 16:631-640.

Lerner, J. (1963), Mental Health of the Aging Population in Relation to Social Security Benefits. *J. Am. Geriat. Soc.*, 11:551-557.

Leube, H. (1959), [Contribution to the Therapy of Cerebral Sclerosis.] *Arzt. Praxis*, 12:388-390.

Leveen, L. & Priver, D. (1963), Significance of Role Playing in the Aged Person. *Geriatrics*, 18:57-63.

Liddell, D. W., Herbert, E., & Crotty, I. (1962), Problem of the Geriatric Patient in the Mental Hospital. *Int. J. Soc. Psychiat.*, 8:250-255.

Linden, M. E. (1953), Group Psychotherapy with Institutionalized Senile Women. *Int. J. Group Psychother.*, 3:150-170.

—— (1963a) The Aging and the Community. *Geriatrics*, 18:404-410.

—— (1963b), Geriatric Goal: Help Patient Enjoy Life on His Terms. *Geriatrics*, 18 (6):60A-62A.

Locke, B. Z. (1962), Hospitalization History of Patients with Mental Diseases of the Senium. *J. Gerontol.*, 17:381-384.

Lowenthal, M. F. (1964), Social Isolation and Mental Illness in Old Age. *Am. Sociol. Rev.*, 29:54-70.

Mason, A. S., Cunningham, M. K., & Tarpy, E. K. (1963), The Quarter-Way House—A Transitional Program for Chronically Ill Geriatric Mental Patients. *J. Am. Geriat. Soc.*, 11:574-579.

[332]

Meer, B. & Krag, C. L. (1964), Correlates of Disability in a Population of Hospitalized Geriatric Patients. *J. Gerontol.*, 19:440-446.

Mensh, I. N. (1963), Studies of Older Psychiatric Patients. *The Gerontologist*, 3:100-104.

Meyer, J. (1957), Die Cerebralsklerose und ihre Behandlung mit Cosaldon. *Med. Klin., Berlin*, 52:1073-1074.

Neugarten, B. L. & Gutmann, D. L. (1958), Age-Sex Roles and Personality in Middle Age: A Thematic Apperception Study. *Psychol. Monogr.*, 72, No. 17 (Whole No. 470).

Nunnally, J. & Kittross, J. M. (1958), Public Attitudes toward Mental Health Professions. *Am. Psychologist*, 13:589-594.

Osgood, C. E., Suci, G. J., & Tannenbaum, P. H. (1958), *The Measurement of Meaning*. Urbana: University of Illinois Press.

Phillips, B. S. (1962), *The Aging in a Central Illinois Community*. Urbana: University of Illinois Press.

Pierce, R. C. (1963), Note on Testing Conditions. *J Consult. Psychol.*, 27:536-537.

Pollack, M., Karp, E., Kahn, R. L., & Goldfarb, A. I. (1962), Perception of Self in Institutionalized Aged Subjects. I: Response Patterns to Mirror Reflection. *J. Gerontol.*, 17:405-408.

Post, F. (1962), The Significance of Affective Symptoms in Old Age. *Maudsley Monogr.*, No. 10.

Rosenfelt, R. H., Kastenbaum, R., & Kempler, B. (1964), "The Untestables": Methodological Problems in Drug Research with the Aged. *The Gerontologist*, 4:72-74.

Savitsky, E. (1963), Psychiatry in Institutional Work with the Aged. *J. Am. Geriat. Soc.*, 11:44-57.

Schilder, P. (1942), *Goals and Desires of Men*. New York: Columbia University Press.

Schmidt, B. (1960), [The Treatment of Cerebral Sclerosis.] *Med. Welt*, 22:1222-1224.

Schwartz, E. D. & Goodman, J. I. (1952), Group Therapy of Obesity in Elderly Diabetics. *Geriatrics*, 7:280-283.

Scott, T. & Devereaux, C. P. (1963a), Habilitation Potential of Elderly State Hospital Patients. *Comprehen. Psychiat.*, 4:351-357.

———— & ———— (1963b), Perpetuation of Geriatric Problems in California State Mental Hospitals. *Am. J. Psychiat.*, 120:155-159.

[333]

———— & ———— (1964), Heterogeneity of an Elderly State Hospital Population. *J. Gerontol.,* 19:27-30.

Shrut, S. D. (1958), Attitudes toward Old Age and Death. *Ment. Hyg.,* 42:259-266

Silver, A. (1950), Group Psychotherapy with Senile Psychotic Patients. *Geriatrics,* 5:147-150.

Sperling, R. (1960), [Treatment of Cerebral Arteriosclerosis with Cosaldon.] *Med. Klin., Berlin,* 55:845-847.

Spieth, W. (1964), Cardiovascular Health Status, Age, and Psychological Performance. *J. Gerontol.,* 19:277-284.

Stenstedt, A. (1952), A Study in Manic-Depressive Psychosis. *Acta Psychiat. Neurol. Scand., Copenhagen,* Supplement 79.

———— (1959), Involutional Melancholia. *Acta Psychiat. Neurol. Scand., Copenhagen,* Supplement No. 127.

Stratton, D. & Barton, W. E. (1964), The Geriatric Patient in the Public Mental Hospital. *Geriatrics,* 19:55-60.

Taves, M. J. & Hansen, G. D. (1962), Exploration in Personal Adjustment after Age 65. *Geriatrics,* 17:309-316.

Tobin, S. S. & Neugarten, B. L. (1961), Life Satisfaction and Social Interaction in the Aging. *J. Gerontol.,* 16:344-346.

Verwoerdt, A. & Dovenmuehle, R. H. (1964), Physical Illness and Depressive Symptomatology. III: Aspects of Awareness. *J. Gerontol.,* 19:330-335.

Wolff, K. (1962), Group Psychotherapy with Geriatric Patients in a Psychiatric Hospital: Six-Year Study. *J. Am. Geriat. Soc.,* 10:1077-1080.

———— (1963), Individual Psychotherapy with Geriatric Patients. *Dis. Nerv. Sys.,* 24:688-691.

———— (1964), The Confused Geriatric Patient. *J. Am. Geriat. Soc.,* 12:266-270.

Wolk, R. L., Rustin, S. L., & Scotti, J. (1963), The Geriatric Delinquent. *J. Am. Geriat. Soc.,* 11:653-659.

Zborowski, M. & Eyde, L. D. (1962), Aging and Social Participations. *J. Gerontol.,* 17:424-430.

Zuckerman, S. (1962), The Psychology of Aging. *J. Am. Coll. Neuropsychiat.,* 1:74-76.

INDEX

Index

Acheson, D., 30
Adams, H. B., 47
Adams, J., 58, 60, 61
Adams, J. Q., 60, 61
Adams, S., 58
Adaptation, 65
  through denial, 82
  in old age, 32
  regressive, 72
  See also Reminiscence
Adjustment, personal, 227-230
Adolescence, creativity in, 40
Affect, 85
  decline of with aging, 297-299
  reversal of, 88
Affective illness, 309-310
Age Center of New England, 295
Age identification, measurement of,
  281-282
Age and Achievement, 26
Aggression, 19
  in dying patient, 211
  toward dying patient, 216
  and fear of dying, 126-128
Aging
  and community, 235-237
  and decline of affect, 297-299
  factors affecting, 26-27
  and growth potentials, 245-247
  psychology of, 249, 282-284
  and social participation, 295-297
Aisenberg, R,, 306, 329, 332
Albany, N. Y., Center for the Study of
  Aging, 313

Alcoholics Anonymous, 259
Aldrich, C. K., 307, 329
Aldrovandi, Ulisse, 35
Alexander, Franz, 321
Allport, G. W., 46, 48, 321
Altrocchi, J., 295, 329
Ambivalence, 187-188
  toward dying patient, 185-186
American Psychiatric Association, 59
Anderson, B. G., 243, 329
Anosognosia, 97
Anthony, S., 114, 117, 118, 119, 321
Anticathexis, 113
Anxiety, 13, 302
Archimedes, 42
Aristotle, 56
Arlow, J. A,, 183, 321
"As if" personality, 170
Atkin, S., 3, 167, 206-211
Autobiography, 45-49
Autodidacticism, 50-57
Austen, J., 41
Austin, M., 48

Bahn, A. K., 241, 331
Bancroft, G., 36
Bancroft, H. H., 30
Barnes, M., 82, 321
Bartok, B., 130
Barton, W. E., 293, 334
Beamish, R., 332
Beauty, and death, 179
Benedek, T., 32, 71
Bennett, A., 41

Bennett, J. L., 288, 331
Benton, T. H., 41
Berdyaev, N. A., 48, 51, 55, 321
Berelson, B., 20, 321
Berezin, M. A., 3, 8, 13, 167, *211-213*, 221
Berenson, B., 48, 49
Bergson, H., 41
Berlioz, H., 41
Berkeley, G., 53
Bibring, E., 113, 321
Bibring, G. L., 131, 321
Birren, J. E., 26, 42, 199, 200, 282, 284, 321, 322, 329
Bismarck, O. von, 47
Bjorksten, J., 20, 31, 322
Bjurwill, B., 286, 287, 329
Blindisms, 198
Bluestone, H., 186, 322
Boek, W. E., 312, 329
Bortz, 245, 329
Boston Society for Gerontologic Psychiatry, 8, 13, 221
Boston Veterans Administration Hospital, 64
Boswell, C., 41
Bottome, P., 48
Brain function, and denial, 86-87
Brenan, G., 48
Brentano, F., 37
Bressler, D. M., 275, 331
Breuer, J., 44
Brill, A. A., 324
Brisseau, P., 37
Britten, B., 39
Brönte family, 40
Brown-Séquard, C. E., 37
Browne, D. A., 3, 303, 308
Brozek, J., 31, 322
Bunker, H. A., 186, 187, 188, 191, 322
Burr, A. R., 46, 48, 322
Busse, E. W., 73, 222, 330, 331
Butler, R. N., 3, 13, 15, 18, *21-63*, 73, 167, 168, 172, 175, 181, 182, *198-201*, 202, 301, 321, 322, 330

Caesar, Julius, 42
Cahn, C., 332
Cajal, Ry., 49
Camus, A., 40
Cardano, G., 46
Cardiovascular disease, and psychological performance, 242
Carlyle, T., 47
Casals, P., 35
Cassanova, G. J., 47
Castration, fear of, 119, 121-122
Cath, S. H., 4, 8, 13, 167, *213-218*, 221, 314, 315-316, 330
Cellini, B., 46
Cervantes, M., 33
Chabrier, 56
Chapman, J., 198, 328
Characteristic mode theory, 34-39
Chateaubriand, F. R., 37, 47
Chestnut Lodge, 24, 28
Chown, S. M., 277, 330
Christ, A. E., 278, 330
Clague, E., 32, 322
Colette, 48
Columbia University, 29, 30, 322-323
Commager, H. S., 58, 59, 60, 323
Community programs, for aging, 312-318
Confabulation, 182, 290
Confusion, in geriatric patients, 238-240, 274
Colle, G., 37
Coping, 65, 74
Cosaldon, in treating dementia, 286-288
Cooper, A. J., 286, 287, 330
Countertransference, 64-65, 181, 200, 255
  with dying patient, 185
  in psychoanalytic investigation, 22, 25
Craft, R., 41, 48
Creativity, 175-181, 199
  and age, 14-15, 21-63, 35-39
  decline of, with aging, 31-34, 39
  influences on, 33

and life cycle, 40-41
and longevity, 41-42
and significance of death, 42
sources of data on, 40-41
Croce, B., 41
Crotty, I., 262, 332
Cultural attitudes, and aging, 26
Culture, transmission of, 57-58
Cumming, E., 70, 226, 297, 323, 330
Cummins, J. F., 65, 323
Cunningham, M. K., 272, 332
Cushing Hospital, 304, 306, 307

Dale, P. W., 256, 330
DaPonte, L., 47
Darwin, C., 47, 51, 55, 56, 323
Darwin, F., 323
Davidson, R., 251, 330
Dean, L. R., 297, 330
Death
    attitudes toward, 278-279, 293-295
    fear of, 16-17, 99-101, 103, 106, 108,
        112-128, 186, 206, 208, 247, 293-
        295
    and psychological factors, 308
    See also Dying
Death wishes, 119
    toward dying patient, 186
Defense, 65
    mechanisms of, 15-16, 79-80, 83-88,
        289
Déjà vu, and reminiscence, 183
Dementia
    arteriosclerotic, 274
    senile, 231, 274
    treatment of, 286-288
DeMorgan, W. F., 34
Denial, 15-16, 156, 160, 179, 182, 186,
        192-198, 200, 206, 207, 212-218,
        253, 294, 302
    and brain function, 86-87
    cognitive, 94, 105
    of death, 119, 127, 131-135, 191, 247
    dimensions of, 97-99
    in dying patient, 143-149, 151
    dynamic interpretation, 91

manic, 182
ontological, 94-95, 105-107, 197
purposes of, 88, 96, 105, 170
static interpretation, 89-90
as social act, 79-110
steps in, 91-92
Dennis, W., 20, 32, 323, 326
Denny-Brown, D., 97, 323
Depersonalization, 218
Depletion, 214, 217
Depression, 13, 222-223, 252, 257, 270
    clinical criteria, 67
    and mortality, 200
    and physical illness, 240-241
    psychotic, 248-249
    and reminiscence, 68-69, 76, 175,
        192, 205
Deterioration, and reminiscence, 67-69
Deutsch, F., 71, 142, 210
Devereaux, C. P., 237, 267, 292, 333
De Witt State Hospital, 237
Dextro-amphetamine, 304
Diaz, B., 36
Dibner, A. S., 65, 323
Dickes, E. W., 326
Di Lampedusa, 50
Disease
    and creativity, 33
    as factor in aging, 26
Disengagement, 70, 297
Disorientation, in memory dysfunc-
    tion, 290
Displacement, 88
Disraeli, B., 231
Donati, A., 286, 330
Dovenmuehle, R. H., 240, 330, 334
Drug research, 305-306
Drugs, psychotropic, 305
Dying
    adjustment to, 128-155
    defensive use of, 200-201
Dying patient, 188-189, 196, 200-201
    and creativity, 177-178
    family of, 155-162, 213-218
    management of, 103-106, 111-163,
        178-179, 185, 212-213

problems of, 190-191
Duggar, B. M., 34
Duke University Geriatric Research Group, 294
Dwyer, T. F., 131, 321

Eckermann, J. P., 47
Eddy, M. B., 47
Edmonds, R., 328
Ego psychology, 62, 66
"first phase," 80
Ego splitting, 218
Ego structure, 13
Eisdorfer, C., 286, 295, 329, 330, 331
Eisenhower, D. D., 48, 59, 60
Eissler, K. R., 45, 213, 323
Electroshock therapy, 301
Elgar, E., 35-36, 40
Ellis, H., 48
Emerson, R. W., 39, 61
Erikson, E. H., 32, 44, 50, 56, 66, 168, 323, 327
Ernst, M., 48
Euthanasia, 210
Eyde, L. D., 295, 334

Fantasy
as adaptation, 72
in senile psychosis, 247
Faraday, M., 40
Faunce, W. A., 295, 330
Feifel, H., 295, 326, 330
Fenichel, O., 81, 323
Ferenczi, S., 187, 188, 323
Fernel, J., 54
Fish, F., 273, 330
Floyer, J., 37
Foerster, O., 182, 324
Forrestal, J., 60
Forster, E. M., 39
Foulds, G. A., 248, 330
Foundations Fund for Research in Psychiatry, 79
Franck, C., 33
Frankfurter, F., 29, 41, 48, 181, 324
Franklin, B., 37, 47, 58, 61

Free association, 181
Freud, A., 66, 79, 82, 131, 193, 324
Freud, S., 23, 33, 37, 46, 47, 56, 62-63, 71, 77, 79, 119, 122, 199, 203, 204
and old age, 42-45
Friedman, J. H., 275, 331
Fugue states, 207
Fulton, R. L., 295, 330
Furman, R. A., 82, 324

Gagel, O., 182, 324
Galbraith, B. S., 265, 331
Gallilei, G., 35
Gardner, E. A., 241, 331
Geriatrics
goal of, 317-318
patient management, 271-272
Geriatric delinquent, 253-254
Geriatric patient, in mental hospital, 262-264, 293
Geriatric Psychiatry, 13
Gericke, O. L., 289, 331
Ghandi, M., 42
Gibbon, E., 56
Gillespie, W. H., 247, 331
Gitelson, M., 69, 325
Glutamic acid, 239
Goethe, 33, 41, 47, 49
Golde, P., 295, 331
Goldfarb, A. I., 211, 256, 279, 280, 299, 331, 333
Goodman, J. T., 333
Grant, U. S., 47
Greenacre, P., 321
Greenhouse, S. W., 26, 321
Group therapy, 264-265, 270, 301
Gutmann, D. L., 295, 333

Haas, A., 271, 331
Habilitation, 237, 267-268, 292
Hackett, T. P., 4, 14, 15, 73, 79-110, 179, 325, 326, 329
Haley, J., 95, 325
Halo effect, in reminiscence, 72
Hals, F., 33

Hamilton, A., 58, 61
Hamilton, L. D., 288, 331
Handford, J. M., 258, 331
Hansen, G. D., 227, 334
Harley, M., 118, 325
Harris, F., 47
Harris, R., 329
Hartmann, H., 30, 72, 74, 325
Harvey, W., 36-37
Health, and aging, 26-27
Heckscher, A., 61, 325
Heinze, S. J., 31, 328
Heiser, V. G., 47
Henry, W. E., 226, 297, 323, 330
Henry, P., 58
Herbert, E., 262, 332
Himmelfarb, G., 55, 325
Historical determination, 61
Historiography, 29-31
History, theories of, 61
Hitler, A., 60
Hoffman, F., 37
Hoover, H., 60
Hopkinson, G., 309, 310, 331
Hormonal therapy, 239
Hudson, W. H., 47
Hugo, V., 33
Humboldt, A., 33, 36
Hunter, I. M. L., 70, 325
Hunter, R. A., 327
Huntington, D. S., 131, 321
Hypochondriasis, in aged, 222-224, 233, 252

Identification, 205
Identity, 50, 66, 72, 135
  crises of, 168
  group, 74
"If only" personality, 170
Independence, 13
Inglis, J., 69, 325, 327
Institutionalization, of self, 56
Intensive treatment, for aged, 265-267
Isaacs, B., 284-285, 331
Isolation, of aged, 238

Jacobson, E., 81, 205, 325
Jeffers, F. C., 293, 331
Jefferson, T., 58, 60, 61
Jones, E., 43, 323, 325
Jung, C. G., 48

Kahana, R. J., 4, 13-19
Kahn, R. L., 86, 97, 279, 280, 281, 328, 331, 333
Kallman, F. J., 309, 310
Kant, I., 39
Kardiner, A., 30
Karp, E., 280, 333
Kastenbaum, R. J., 4, 108, 237-238, 285-286, 304, 306, 329, 332, 333
Kaufman, I., 13
Kay, D. W., 309, 310, 332
Kemp, R., 230, 231, 332
Kempler, B., 333
Kennedy, J. F., 59, 61
Kessel, W. I. N., 312, 332
Kiell, N., 49, 325
Kitross, J. M., 333
Kogan, N., 295, 331
Korsakow's psychosis, 182, 290
Krag, C. L., 291, 333
Kral, V. A., 69, 290, 325, 332
Kravitz, A. R., 8
Kris, E., 62, 325

La Farge, J., 49
Lagerlöf, S., 47
Lamarck, J. B., 35
Lampert, K., 321
Landsman, E., 4, 245, 254, 264-265, 268-273, 275-277, 288-291, 299-301
Langer, S., 41
Langley Porter Neuropsychiatric Institute, 238
Lankenau Hospital, 246
Laplace, P. S., 36
Lasswell, H., 60, 326
Laurendeau, M., 119, 326
Lehman, H. C., 20, 24, 25, 26, 27, 31, 32, 41, 45, 326

Lenzer, A., 224, 332
Lerner, J., 245, 332
Leube, H., 286, 332
Leveen, L., 232, 332
Levin, S., 5, *13-19*
Levine, J., 30
Lewin, B. D., 81, 185, 326
Libido
  in senescence, 71
  shifts in, 13
Lichtenstein, H., 205, 326
Liddell, D. W., 262, 332
Life cycle
  and creativity, 40-41
  phases of, 33
  study of, 40
  theory of, 34-39
Life review, 28-29, 168, 172, 175, 182,
  199, 200, 202, 301-303
Lillard, R. G., 46, 48, 326
Lincoln, A., 42
Linden, M. E., 235, 317-318, 332
Littre, M. P. E., 36
Live memoir, 45-49
Lobb, L. G., 289, 331
Locke, B. Z., 332
Loewenstein, R. M., 30
Löfving, B., 69, 327
Lomax, A., 31, 41, 48, 326
Loneliness, 297-299
"Lonely lady complex," 230
Longevity, and creativity, 41-42
Loss, and creativity, 33
Lowenthal, M. F., 238, 332

Macalpine, I., 327
Mack, M., 241
Madison, J., 60, 61
Magic, and respect for aged, 75
Marshall, G. C., 61
Marshall, J., 58
Mason, A. S., 272, 332
Masserman, J., 325
Masters E. L., 47
Maturation, expectant, 272
Maugham, S., 47, 49
McDonald, M., 82, 326

McGahee, C. L., 186, 322
McMahon, A. W., Jr., 5, 14, 15, 18, *64-
  78*, 107, 167, 168, 172, 175, 182,
  185, 191, 192, 200, *202-205*
Meer, B., 291, 333
Melancholia, 175, 203-204
  and mourning, 77
  involutional, 309-310
Memoirs, 58-62
  as therapy, 49-50
Memory, 82
  in aged, 69
  dysfunction of, 290
  and emotions, 70
  and general health, 290-291
  processes of, 71
  See also Reminiscence
Metapsychology, 81
Mendocino State Hospital, 265
Mensh, I. N., 303, 333
Mental disorders of old age, 238, 310-
  312
Mental health, and Social Security,
  245
Mental status, measures of, 279-281,
  284-285
Meyer, J., 286, 333
Meyerhoff, H., 25, 326
Michelangelo, 33
Mill, J. S., 47
Misch, G., 46, 326
Monsarrat, N., 190
More, T., 51
Morton, J. R., 31, 41, 48
Moses, Grandma, 34, 56
Moss, R. E., 5, *221, 240-242, 256, 267-
  268, 279-280, 286, 291-293, 314-317*
Motives, *vs.* values, 174
Mourning, 15, 200
  and reminiscence, 77-78, 184-185,
  192, 203, 205
Mueller, H., 290, 332
Multiplex theory, 32-34

Nagy, M. H., 114, 117, 119
Nandrolone phenpropionate, 288

Narcissism, 207
in senescence, 71, 183
National Archives, 58, 59, 60
National Historical Publications Committee, 61
National Institute of Mental Health (NIMH), 24, 26, 28, 32, 200
Neugarten, B. L., 226, 295, 333, 334
Nevins, A., 29, 30, 326
New York Dept. of Mental Hygiene, 299
Newman, J., Cardinal, 47
Newton, I., 56
Nichols, C. R., 331
Nietzsche F., 41
Nunnaly, J., 295, 333

Object loss, in senescence, 184
Object relations, 187-188
O'Casey, S., 48, 49
Olin, H. S., 98, 326
Ohio Public Mental Hospital, 261
Oral history, 45, 59
Oral History Collection (Columbia), 29-31
Ordaz, J., 5, *226-227, 261-262, 277-282, 292-299*
Osgood, C. E., 295, 333

Papathomopoulos, E., 258, 331
Paraphrenia, 230
Pathography, 60
Payne, E. C., Jr., 5, 14, 16-17, *111-163*, 167, 168, *191-198,* 203, 209, 210, 211
Pear, T. H., 71, 326
Peck, A., 279, 331
Pelikan, J., 109, 326
Pentylenetetrazol, 239
Perception
and denial, 133-134
of self, 280-281
Personal adjustment, in aging, 227-230
Personality
and aging, 72
characteristics and disorders, 248-249

and creativity, 33
Perversion, and denial, 87
Peterson, N. L., 6, *222-224, 256-257, 301-303*
Phillips, W., 41, 62, 327
Phillips, B. S., 312, 333
Piaget, J., 41, 119, 327
Pierce, R. C., 285, 333
Pinard, A., 119, 326
Plank, E. N., 46, 327
Pleasure ego, and denial, 81
Polk, J. K., 60
Pollack, M., 279, 280, 331, 333
Pogue, F. C., 61, 327
Post, F., 69, 312, 325, 327, 333
Priver, D., 232, 332
Procaine injection, 239
Projection
in geriatric delinquent, 253
in senile psychosis, 247
Pryce-Jones, A., 39
Psychoanalysis, 181, 198-199
with aging, 13-14, 43
as history, 25
as investigative method, 23
Psychological tests, 277-286
Psychopathology
and politics, 60
and stress, 243-245
Psychopharmacology, geriatric, 304-307
Psychiatric syndromes, in elderly, 251-252
Psychotherapy
for aged, 236, 254-256, 268-270
with confused patients, 240
of geriatric delinquent, 254
group, *see* Group therapy
See also Psychoanalysis, with aged
Psychosis, senile, 247, 261

Quarter-way house, 272-273

Rado, S., 30
Rapaport, D., 66, 70-71, 80, 204, 325, 327

Reaction formation, 88
Reality, sense of, 187
Reality testing, in pseudo reminiscence, 170
Reckless, J. B., 222, 330
Regression, 13, 210
in dying patient, 141-142
in old age, 247-248
Rehabilitation, 258-261
Relocation, of aged, 307-308
Reminiscence, 18, 169-176, 182-183, 192, 202-205, 301-303
as adaptation, 15, 64-78
and depression, 15, 175
and mourning, 77-78, 184-185
purposes of, 168-171
Renunciation, 187
Repression, 70, 73, 88
and denial, 81-82
Repudiation, in denial, 94-95, 194
Responsibility, 173
and sickness, 176, 178
"Retirement rot," 231
Rhudick, P. J., 6, 14, 15, 18, *64-78*, 107, 168, 172, 175, 192, 202, 326
Ribonucleic acid, 239
Rickman, J., 42, 324, 327
Rigidity, and aging, 277-278
Robinson, E. A., 39
Rochlin, G., 114, 117, 327
Rogow, A. A., 60, 327
Róheim, G., 322
Role-playing, in aged, 232
Roosevelt, F. D., 60
Roosevelt, T., 60
Rosenfelt, R. H., 305, 333
Ross, H., 321
Roth, M., 310, 332
Rousseau, H., 51, 56
Rousseau, J. J., 47
Ruskin, J., 47
Rouvray, L., 47
Rustin, S. L., 253, 334

Sachs, H., 179, 327
St. Augustine, 35, 46

St. Francis Hospital (England), 262
Samuel, M., 48
San Francisco General Hospital, 243
Sandburg, C., 34
Santayana, G., 34
Saunders, C., 103, 327
Savitsky, E., 268, 333
Schilder, P., 294, 333
Schizophrenia, 238-239, 310
Schlesinger, A., Jr., 60
Schmidt, B., 286, 287, 333
Schreber, D. P., 46, 47, 327
Schweitzer, A., 41
Schwartz, E. D., 333
Scott, T., 237, 267, 292, 333
Scotti, J., 253, 334
Self-esteem, maintenance of, 13
Self-object differentiation, 205
Senium, diseases of, 261
Senescence
and ego changes, 66
emotional factors in, 69-71
and memory, 69
Shapiro, M. B., 69, 325, 327
Shakow, D., 198, 328
Shaw, G. B., 33, 48, 51, 56, 57, 327
Shepherd, M., 312, 332
Sherrington, C., 34, 54
Shoro, C., 329
Shrut, S. D., 294, 334
Shumaker, W., 46, 48, 49, 328
Sibelius, J., 39
Silver, A., 288, 334
Silver, J., 331
Simmons, L. W., 74, 75, 328
Slater, P. E., 304, 332
Smith, G., 60, 328
Socrates, 42, 50, 113
Sokoloff, L., 26, 321
Sophocles, 31
Spark, M., 201, 328
Sperling, R., 286, 334
Spiegel, L. A., 40, 328
Spieth, W., 242, 284, 329, 334
Spitteler, C. F. G., 47
Starr, L. M., 30

Steffens, L., 47
Steichen, E., 48
Stenstedt, A., 309, 310, 334
Stein, M. I., 31, 328
Stern, W., 70, 328
Sternberg, R. S., 198, 328
Stilman, L., 328
Stockton (Cal.) State Hospital, 291
Stone, A. A., 198, 328
Storytelling, in aged, 73-74
    See also Reminiscence
Stratton, D., 293, 334
Strauss, L. L., 48
Stravinsky, I., 41, 48
Stress, and psychopathology, 243-245
Suci, G. J., 333
Suicide
    and aggression, 211
    and psychiatric care, 241-242
Sullivan, L., 47, 56
Survival, 173-175
Symptoms, as defenses, 84
"Symptoms/sign inventory," 248
Swerdloff, B., 30

Tannenbaum, P. H., 333
Tarachow, S., 6, 167, *180-191*, 198, 199, 203, 207, 211, 212
Tarpy, E. K., 272, 332
Taves, M. J., 227, 334
Tennyson, A., 33
Terman, L., 41
Testing, conditions of, 285-286
Therapy, of aged, 256-257
    See also Psychotherapy
Thioridazine, 304-305
Thoreau, H. D., 202
Tintoretto, 33
Titian, 33
Tobin, S. S., 226, 334
Tolstoy, L., 33, 35, 41, 47, 49, 50, 130, 160, 328
Toynbee, A., 35
Transference, in aged, 236, 255
Truman, H. S, 59, 60

Valenstein, A. F., 131, 321

Values, *vs.* motives, 174
Van Benden, P. J., 60
Van Buren, M., 60
Van Zooneveld, R. J., 69, 328
Verdi, G., 33
Vervoerdt, A., 240, 330, 334
Voltaire, 33
Von Vischer, A. L., 73, 328

Walkey, F. A., 284-285, 331
Wallace, A. R., 55
Washington, G., 58, 60
Washington School of Psychiatry, 21-22, 62
Wechsler, D., 67, 328
Wechsler Adult Intelligence Scale (WAIS), 283, 286
Wechsler-Bellevue Intelligence Test, 67-68
Wedrow, E. M., 6, *230-232, 243-245, 247-252, 262-267, 286-288, 309-314*
Weinstein, E. A., 86, 97, 328
Weisman, A. D., 6, 14, 15, 73, *79-110*, *167-180*, 186, 192-193, 195, 196, 197, 203, 205, 207, 325, 328-329
Wells, H. G., 47
Wexler, D., 7, *224-230, 234-237, 245-247, 258-261, 282-284, 317-318*
Whitehead, A. N., 83, 329
Williams, T., 186
Williamson, J., 273, 330
Wilson, W., 60
Winant, J. G., 60
Winnicott, D. W., 188, 329
Withdrawal, in aging, 226
Wolff, K., 238, 254, 264, 334
Wolk, R. L., 253, 334
Worcester, A., 142, 329

Yarrow, M. R., 26, 321

Zarsky, E. L., 7, *238-240, 254-256, 273-275, 284-285*
Zborowski, M., 295, 334
Zeman, F. D., 27, 329
Zinberg, N. E., 8, 13, 323
Zuckerman, S., 249, 334